CREATIVE HOMEOWNER® ULTIMATE

DECKS

— PLAN / DESIGN / BUILD —

T0267053

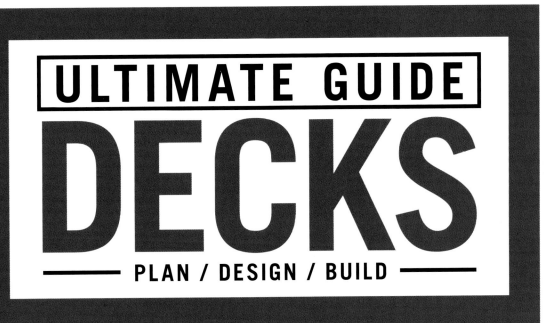

ULTIMATE GUIDE
DECKS
PLAN / DESIGN / BUILD

UPDATED 6TH EDITION

CREATIVE
HOMEOWNER®
CreativeHomeowner.com

CRE🏠TIVE
HOMEOWNER®

Ultimate Guide: Decks, Updated 6th Edition

Editors: Jeremy Hauck, Sherry Vitolo
Designer: Wendy Reynolds
Technical Consultant: Glenn Mathewson
Technical Editor: Charlie Byers
Technical Editor, Previous Edition: David Schiff
Technical Consultant, Previous Edition: Ken Kroog
Indexer: Jay Kreider
Proofreader: Nancy Arndt

Tables R507.5(1) (page 120) and R507.6 (page 122) excerpted from the 2021 International Residential Code. Copyright 2021. Washington, D.C.: International Code Council, Inc. All rights reserved. Reprinted with permission. www.ICCSAFE.org

Printed in China
Fourth printing

ISBN 978-1-58011-862-0

Library of Congress Control Number: 2022930548

We are always looking for talented authors. To submit an idea, please send a brief inquiry to acquisitions@foxchapelpublishing.com.

Creative Homeowner®, *www.creativehomeowner.com*, is an imprint of New Design Originals Corporation and distributed exclusively in North America by Fox Chapel Publishing Company, Inc., 800-457-9112, 903 Square Street, Mount Joy, PA 17552.

CONTENTS

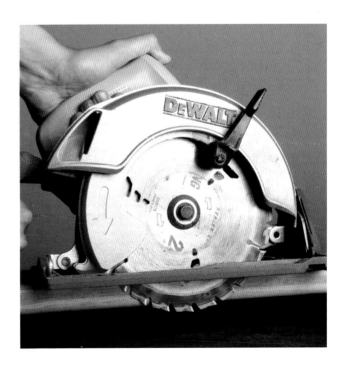

Contents

Contents

INTRODUCTION

Adding a new deck is one of the most popular ways to enhance the outdoor living area of your home. Decks make entertaining easy, providing a pleasant spot where you can enjoy the company of your family and friends. Or use your deck as a private getaway—a spot to enjoy a good book or take a nap in the warm afternoon sun.

Ultimate Guide: Decks provides both building knowledge and design inspiration. You'll learn how to build a deck, including information on framing, decking, and stairs. Use the appendices to brush up on tools, materials, and construction techniques. The second section contains 30 unique deck designs to help you envision the deck of your dreams.

GUIDE TO SKILL LEVEL

Easy. Made for beginners.

Challenging. Can be done by beginners who have the patience and willingness to learn.

Difficult. Can be handled by most experienced do-it-yourselfers who have mastered basic construction skills. Consider consulting a specialist.

Adding curves, left, to a deck makes the design more appealing and distinctive. Built-in benches add to a deck's usefulness.

"Making a Square Deck Livelier," page 254

Note: If you have a window within 5 feet of a hot tub or the bottom tread of a set of stairs or within 3 feet from any of the stair treads, it will require safety glazing (tempered glass).

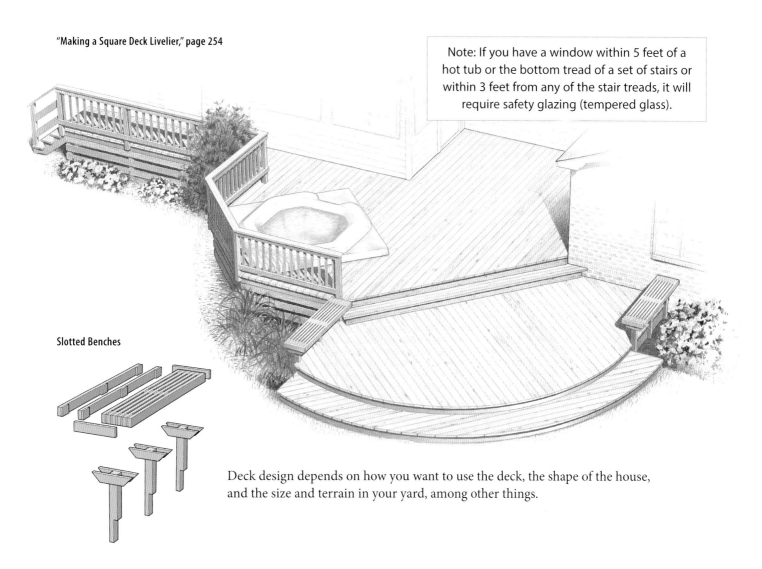

Slotted Benches

Deck design depends on how you want to use the deck, the shape of the house, and the size and terrain in your yard, among other things.

Benches, right, add seating and can provide a sense of enclosure. Entertainment features, like the wide railing cap for serving food, can be implemented as well. Note how the planters support the benches on this deck.

SAFETY

It is more than rules and guidelines it is a way of life to keep you safe.

Although the methods in this book have been reviewed for safety, it is not possible to overstate the importance of using the safest methods you can. What follows are reminders – some dos and some don'ts for working safely- to use along with your skills and using common sense.

> Always use caution, care, and good judgement when following the procedures described in this book.

PERSONAL PROTECTIVE EQUIPMENT

This category for safety can never be overlooked because this includes everything we wear and everything we need to wear to be safe which includes the following.

Safety glasses worn whenever work is to be performed to protect your eyes from dust and debris created when working with building materials. Additional care may need to be taken to include a face shield when cutting or grinding ferrous metals due to sparks and molten material slag from cutting.

Hearing protection in the form of ear plugs or earphones worn whenever you are using a circular saw, hammer drill, wet saw, gasoline powered cut-off saw or any other power equipment that creates loud or high pitch sounds.

Dust masks in the form of disposal N-95 masks or charcoal filtered respirators when sawing concrete, bricks, pavers, wood, and other exterior materials. Masonry materials contain silica and is harmful to your lungs. Other materials of older homes may contain asbestos in the siding material as well.

Work Clothes that are form fitting and not extremely loose along with sleeved shirts to protect exposed skin from the sun and other hazards on the project is very important. Long sleeve shirts are beneficial any time of the year when working around fiberglass house insulation. Work boots worn can help prevent a nail protruding from a board from going through the sole compared to wearing soft sole shoes or sneakers around the project.

Jewelry such as necklaces can be a hazard when using rotary tools such as drills and often can be a distraction when working. It is always best to remove any hanging jewelry and considered any rings on your fingers as these can get trapped on ladder rungs and cause extreme pain and or damage to your fingers.

Gloves are a good idea when handling materials, performing demolition, digging, using wheelbarrows and heavy power tools. Blisters created in the palm of your hands take time to heal or become infected and slow down the progress on the project. Use of gloves is also a good idea to prevent scratches from occurring if nail tips protrude through wood.

HAND TOOLS

Hammers are one of the most widely used tools on a project and come in many shapes, sizes, and weights. Use of a hammer requires the right one for the job and one that is comfortable for you to use and must always maintain good working condition of the steel head and the handle it is attached to. Never swing a hammer with a loose head it will create an extremely dangerous situation.

Screwdrivers come in all sorts of sizes and configurations. Always use the right one for the fastener you are trying to tighten or loosen. Using the incorrect one will damage the screw head and then require additional work and tools to complete the operation. Never use a flat blade screwdriver as a chisel.

Utility knives are very important to have to complete several tasks on the project from unpacking materials to cleaning a shoulder saw cut to sharpening our carpenter pencils. In any case make sure the knife has a retractable blade that sharp in good condition. Always store replacement blades in the knife handle if applicable.

Chisels are important to have on the project and the right size chisel for the work being performed is key, When cleaning a dado cut in a 4x4 post use the widest chisel you have, preferably 1" or wider. When cleaning out a narrow slot use the narrowest chisel you have, preferably ¼". Never use wood chisels on metal or metal chisels on wood.

Handsaws are very important on the project where a power saw may not do the job in tight spaces or if electric isn't available. Using the right hand saw for the right job is important and always keep the saw in a dry safe place when not in use.

Nail Punch can be extremely handy to have on the project. The are available in small, medium, and large point. These can be very useful in removing nails if the

> Do not leave hand tools on top of step ladders, sawhorses, or other surfaces. These tool when not in use should be placed in your special purpose tool belt for ready availability and safety on the project.

head breaks off, making a dimple for starting a screw in a tight space and other functions. Always wear safety glasses when using a nail punch because you are striking a steel punch with a steel hammer and the punch head could mushroom and pieces of metal could fly off and strike you or someone in the area.

POWER TOOLS

Electrical power tools require 120- volt ac current from the house or a stand-alone generator. In either case make sure the electrical system includes the use of a GFCI receptacle, circuit, or assured grounding cord with GFCI protection included with the cord, as shown below.

Always use power tools that are in good working condition with plastic exterior housings that are double insulated to protect the user from electrical hazards and faulty ground situations that can start a tool without an operator activating the trigger.

Older tools that are made of aluminum housing may not be double insulated. This creates a shock hazard from faulty grounds, wet areas including damp grass from the overnight dew and other hazards. These older tools can be used if they and their cords, including the third ground lug are in good condition and the extension cord and the circuit they are being connected to has a proper ground connection for the house and a 3- prong receptacle is being used. **Otherwise, do NOT use them, as hazardous conditions and sever electrical shock can occur.**

Circular saws are the most widely used and adaptable power tool available for the project. Be sure it and the cord, along with the plug are in good working order. Be sure the spring loaded retractable lower guard operates freely and the guard returns to the normal position covering the blade teeth when resting on a surface.

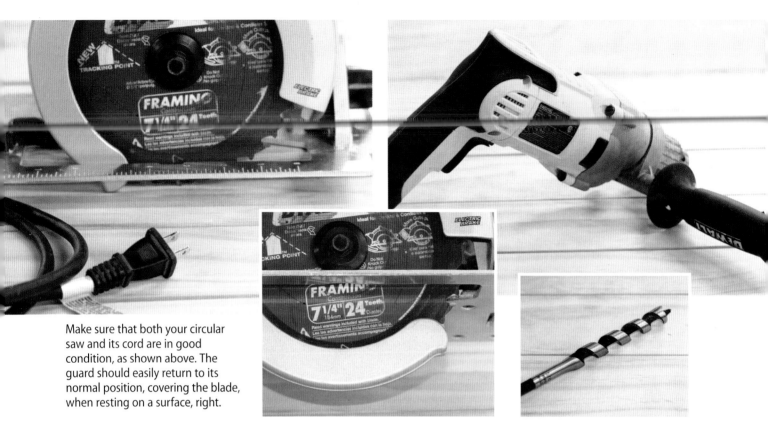

Make sure that both your circular saw and its cord are in good condition, as shown above. The guard should easily return to its normal position, covering the blade, when resting on a surface, right.

Rotary drills are available in many sizes and configurations. Using a rotary drill with a cross handle will be required when drilling any size hole with an auger style bit or anytime you are drilling overhead. Otherwise, the self- feeding design of an auger bit will severely twist your wrist if the bit becomes jammed in the wood hole. Always use the chuck key in each of the three holes to tighten the drill bit correctly and remove the chuck key before operating the drill.

Blades and bits for attaching to power tools are critical that they be in good working condition, correct size and style for the tool being used and a clear understanding of how the blade or bit is attached safely to the power tool. **Installing a blade or bit backwards can cause injury and damage to the person and the project.**

Always use the right power tool for the right job. A circular saw can be used to perform many cutting functions but should not be used in lieu of a power planer. A rotary drill with too small of a bit should not be used to elongate the smaller hole so a larger fastener will fit through the elongated hole.

Read, understand, and follow the operation instructions of all power tools. If the instruction sheet is missing, use the internet to download the instructions of any tool. It is also advisable to download a current video on how to use any power tool you are unfamiliar with before using.

Working and cutting materials with power tools you should always remember the object being cut is fixed while the blade performing the cut is moving. Therefore, certain precautions are required to be safe and not damage the material being cut or cause injury to yourself.

1. Always work with sufficient space, lighting and within proximity of your material pile, when possible, to be as efficient and safe as possible. Flat and level ground is preferred but flat and uncluttered ground provides the safest environment to perform your work.

2. Never operate power or hand tools when tired, rushed for time or under the influence of alcohol or drugs. Always understand the side effects of medication you have taken before using these tools.

3. Always keep your hands free from the cutting area and both hands should be on the handles of the tool to assure they are clear of any danger.

4. Never use your leg as a support or in lieu of a sawhorse when using a circular saw or any tool.

5. Always disconnect the power cord or remove the battery on DC powered tools before installing or replacing blades and bits.

6. Clamp or otherwise attach the material to sawhorses or other fixed surfaces to prevent the material from moving during cutting.

7. Never cut any piece of material between sawhorses as this will create a binding condition of the blade and will

result in damaging the materials or injuring the operator. Have additional supporting material under the material being cut and set the depth of the blade to the proper depth to not cut through the lower supporting material.

8. Never pin or clamp open the retractable blade guard of a circular saw or miter saw.

9. Always use hold down and push sticks when running material across a table saw to prevent kickbacks. Also **DO NOT STAND BEHIND THE BLADE**, injury will occur to you if a kick back occurs. Stand to the side of the blade.

10. Never cut any short piece of material using a circular saw as it may become lodged in the lower retractable guard causing the saw to bind, damage the material or it becomes free before the saw blade stops rotating. Cut a short piece from a longer or full piece that is clamped or attached securely before cutting.

STEP AND EXTENSION LADDERS

Falls are the leading cause of deaths in the field of all construction. The preferred height to be standing safely is always on the ground. However, the building industry requires other heights other than on the ground! Using any ladder starts with using the correct ladder for the job.

Stepladders are available in heights from 2' to 14' but most commonly are 6' and 10' high ladders. Ladders are rated for the maximum weight limit allowed and fiberglass ladders are color coded to match the weight class. Aluminum ladders are not fully color coded, but each top tray is color coded to match the weight limit as well.

Extension ladders are available in lengths from 12' to 40'. Fiberglass ladders are the most widely used styles to prevent electrical shock from power lines. The color coding by the weight class is the same as used for fiberglass step ladders. Aluminum extension ladders have the top end caps color coded to match the weight class.

Each rung is spaced 12" apart so it is easy to determine the length of an extension ladder. Count the rungs in one section and multiply times 2.

Ladder safety starts with using the ladder correctly by always facing your work as you walk up and down the ladder rungs for both step and extension ladders. It may seem odd to place the step ladder with the rungs parallel to the surface you are working on, yet this provides the best working stability when the ladder is placed level.

> Every ladder has caution labels attached. Read, understand, and follow these instructions to assure proper and safe use of the ladder assuring the safety of the operator.

> CAUTION: All ladders should be set 10' minimum in horizontal distance from any overhead power line to prevent arcing of electrical current from the overhead wire and the operator on a ladder.

Placing a ladder on unlevel ground can be challenging but remember NOT to place material under the bottom of a leg(s) above the ground surface, BUT to dig out the ground where the opposite leg(s) are touching the ground enough to have the leg(s) in the air touch solid ground. Pieces of wood as shims under leg(s) can shift and become unstable causing the operator on the ladder to fall.

Extension ladders have a label with an "L" printed on the side. The long side of the 'L' will be vertical when the ladder is not too steep or set too shallow for safe use. If the label is missing or unreadable after setting the ladder to the building, stand with the front of your legs against the bottom rung. Reach out horizontally with your hands and your fingers should easily touch the back of the ladder rails. OSHA requires the distance the bottom of the ladder is away from the building at the back is ¼ of the height of the ladder in use.

STAINS, PAINTS, AND OTHER CHEMICALS

Always read and follow the manufacturers labels for safe use, care and clean up when finished and the proper storing or disposal of any rags or brushes used to apply the material.

Never leave a rag or brush with stain on it in direct sunlight to avoid spontaneous combustion. Always use materials in well ventilated areas.

Always wear appropriate PPE items when working with these materials including, rubber gloves. Safety glasses, masks, and other pertinent safety precautions.

Remember to carefully read the labels on all your stains, paints, and chemical products.

DECK BUILDING TOOLS

A fairly modest set of tools is all you need to build basic decks. For the most part, they are the tools you would normally find in a homeowner's toolbox. However, building a deck is a big project and some power tools will make the work go faster. Consider investing in good miter and circular saws; they will prove invaluable on the job site. A good-quality drill/driver will make the drilling of holes and the driving of screws go smoothly. Beyond that, you might want to consider additional purchases carefully. If you will rarely use the tool after the deck project is completed, is it really worth the price? And if there's a tool you've just got to try, consider renting it for a day instead of buying it for a lifetime.

MEASURING AND LAYOUT

Angle Square. Often called by the brand name Speed Square, this triangular piece of aluminum is extremely versatile, yet it is tough enough to get banged around on the project and not lose its accuracy. Its triangular shape enables you to lay out a 45-degree angle as quickly as a 90-degree angle; it also enables you to find other angles quickly, though not with great precision. You will probably find it the most useful of all the squares you may own.

Carpenter's Level. An accurate carpenter's level is crucial, and its length is proportionate to its accuracy when building a deck. A 4-foot level is a good choice, but a 6-foot will provide better accuracy over longer lengths of framing materials. A level made of wood and brass is more durable than the cheaper aluminum levels but not necessarily more accurate. An aluminum model is an excellent choice for the occasional carpenter.

Take care of your level; all it takes is one good drop or a hard hit to make it inaccurate. Test the level regularly, especially before you buy it. To test, set the level on a smooth surface, and note the bubble. Flip the tool end-for-end and put it in the same spot. The bubble should read the same distance between the lines. To check for plumb accuracy, place the level on a vertical surface such as a wall. Repeat the process when checking accuracy for level.

Framing Square. This L-shaped piece of flat metal measures 16 inches along one edge and 24 inches along the other. Use it for laying out stair stringers and also for checking the squareness of your layouts and string lines and also for marking square cut lines on the face of 2x8, 2x10, and 2x12 boards.

Post Level. If your design calls for any long posts, consider getting a post level. This very specialized but inexpensive tool straps onto the post, so you don't have to keep holding up a level while you are moving heavy material. A post level usually has two bubble vials set at 90 degrees from each other so you can check for plumb in both directions at once. Some post levels use a single, round bull's-eye vial to show perfect plumb instead This type may be less accurate and less desirable.

Torpedo Level. You will find a 9-inch torpedo level handy for leveling small objects. It fits easily into your toolbox or pouch. It can be used to detect level, plumb, and 45-degree angle surfaces.

USING A LASER LEVEL

Laser levels are quickly becoming indispensable tools not only for professional contractors but also avid do-it-yourselfers, too. They project bright level lines at 50 feet or more that are easily visible indoors. Models designed for outdoor use give you level readings much farther than that. Since you'll likely be working mostly outside to build your deck, you'll want to get a laser level with a laser detector or receiver component. That's because it can be difficult to see the laser in bright daylight conditions. The detector is a separate instrument that beeps (loudly) and gives you a visual indication the closer it gets to level and sends out a solid tone when it's exactly at level. It works much like a stud finder.

Self-leveling laser levels only need to be placed upon a roughly flat surface in order to give you accurate level lines to work with—the top of a step ladder on a flat area of ground, for instance. Generally, the self-leveling operation works as long as the base is within five degrees of level. (See "Accurate Leveling" on page 68.)

Measuring Tape. Purchase a high-quality measuring tape. A 25- or 30-foot tape is preferred, and a 1-inch-wide blade is far superior to one that is ¾ inch wide, since it is more rigid and will not quickly fold when you extend it.

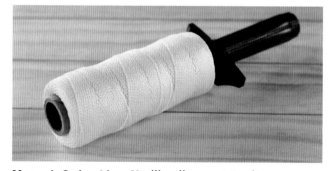

Mason's String Line. You'll pull your string line very tight and it needs to last, so it's a good idea to get the professional stuff—nylon is a good choice. They are also available on a wind-up plastic spool for ease of rewinding the string.

Reel Measuring Tape. For large decks, where you are laying out long distances, it's helpful to have a 50-foot or 100-foot reel measuring tape. This tool doesn't automatically retract, like your 25-foot measuring tape—you wind in the plastic or metal tape the way you turn a fishing reel Be sure to keep a metal measuring tape dry after use to avoid corrosion of the metal tape.

Chalk-Line Box. The tool that aligned the ancient pyramids, a chalk line will enable you to mark long, perfectly straight lines in just a few seconds. Use blue chalk because the other colors are so permanent that they often can't be washed away.

Carpenter's Pencils. Have plenty of pencils on hand—they have a tendency to disappear. Flat carpenter's pencils are better than regular pencils because they need sharpening less frequently with the use of your utility knife. A special sharpener is available for carpenter pencils too.

Plumb Bob.

To pinpoint the location of posts, you will need to drop a perfectly straight vertical line from a given spot, or an intersection of two string lines above the ground. A plumb bob hangs from a string and tapers to a sharp point. Once the bob stops swinging, gravity ensures that the top of the string and the tip of the point are in perfect plumb alignment. The tapered shape of many chalk-line boxes allows them to double as suitable plumb bobs.

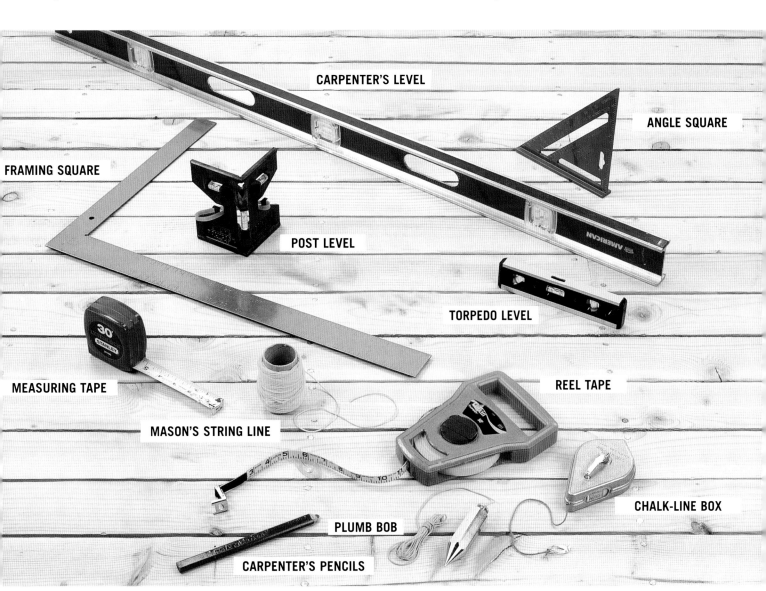

CARPENTER'S LEVEL

ANGLE SQUARE

FRAMING SQUARE

POST LEVEL

TORPEDO LEVEL

MEASURING TAPE

REEL TAPE

MASON'S STRING LINE

CHALK-LINE BOX

PLUMB BOB

CARPENTER'S PENCILS

POWER SAWS, DRILLS, AND SANDING

Power Miter Saw. If you need to make a lot of angle cuts or if you don't feel able to make consistent, precise cuts at all angles, it may be a good idea to buy or rent a power miter saw. These tools are simply circular saws mounted on a pivot assembly that allows you to make precise, repeatable cuts. Make sure you get a miter saw that will do the job: a saw with a 10-inch blade will not be able to completely cut a 2x6 at a 45-degree angle 12 inch miter saws are better for this.

Sliding Compound Miter Saw. Another version of the miter saw, called the compound miter saw, makes both miter and bevel cuts in one pass. This tool is very common, and helpful for building decks. 12" is the most common size for this tool.

A sliding compound miter saw can be very helpful for making miter and bevel cuts in one pass when building a deck.

Circular Saw. Most carpenters and do-it-yourselfers prefer circular saws that use 7¼-inch-diameter blades. This size will allow you to cut to a maximum depth of about 2⅜ inches at 90 degrees and to cut through a piece of two-by lumber even with the blade beveled at 45 degrees.

You can get a rough idea of a saw's power and overall quality from the amperage the motor draws and the type of bearings it uses. A low-cost saw will pull only 9 or 10 amps and will run its drive shaft on sleeve bearings. This will mean less power, a shorter life, a tendency to heat up during continual use, and sometimes less precise cuts because the blade might wobble a bit.

Better saws carry a 12- or 13-amp rating and use ball bearings or roller bearings on the motor's shaft. These can also include an electronic brake to slow down the brake rotation when finished cutting. This combination of extra power and smoother operation makes for long life and more precise cutting. As is often the case, a mid-priced model may well be your best choice.

Worm-drive saws have the most powerful motors and the longest-lasting bearings. They're built like tanks and weigh almost as much. These are primarily professional contractor's tools, and they take some getting used to. They last quite a long time, but do-it-yourselfers should probably avoid them.

A plastic housing is no longer the sign of an inferior tool, because many new plastic composites are actually tougher than metal and highly impact resistant.

Check out the saw's base carefully: if it is made of thin, stamped metal, one drop from sawhorse height could bend it out of shape for good. Look for a thicker base that is either extruded or cast aluminum.

Use carbide-tipped blades in your circular saw. These cost a few dollars more but last up to five times longer than comparable blades made from high-speed steel (HSS). A 24-tooth blade is usually the best choice for deck construction and general use. There is a trade-off between the number of teeth and cut rates and quality: a blade with fewer teeth will cut faster, but the cuts will tend to be ragged. More teeth will produce a finer cut. Have an extra blade on hand; wet wood and dense treated lumber can dull your saw's blade quickly.

Though you can use a file to touch up a damaged tooth on an HSS blade, send it to a sharpening shop when it needs a major tune-up. Take your carbide-tipped blades to a professional sharpening shop as well.

Router. Though by no means essential for deck-building, a router equipped with a chamfering or roundover bit can be quite handy for adding detail to your deck.

Belt Sander. Use a belt sander to clean up your decking and to round off the edge of the deck and railings as a finishing touch. Use this tool with care; it's easy to oversand, especially if you are working with soft wood such as cedar or redwood. Use 180 or 220 grit belts.

Reciprocating Saw. For demolition and for cutting off posts, a reciprocating saw works well, but don't buy one just for building a deck—a handsaw will work fine for the few cuts of this kind on your deck.

Saber Saw. This is a good choice if you need to make cutouts or if you want to make some curved cuts. If you need to do a lot of this kind of cutting, purchase a heavy-duty saber saw. Newer models have oscillating blades with an air exhaust to displace the dust from cutting. With a standard do-it-yourself model, you'll cut through two-by lumber very slowly and the saw will have a tendency to wobble, which produces a ragged-looking cut.

Pad Sander. A vibrating or oscillating pad sander is great for smoothing decking and railings, but a sanding block will often suffice for a deck project.

Sanding Block. A more common tool for rounding off sharp edges and smoothing splinters is the sanding block. There are several types, and they are all far superior to simply using a sheet of handheld sandpaper.

Handsaw. This tool comes in handy for finishing cuts that a circular cannot finish—such as when you are cutting out stringers or cutting off posts in awkward places.

Chisel. This is useful for cleaning out dado cuts, finishing notch cuts, and other trimming and wood-shaving tasks. A 1-inch-wide chisel works well for this kind of work.

Aviation Snips. For trimming metal flashing at the ledger, metal snips are the most accurate tool.

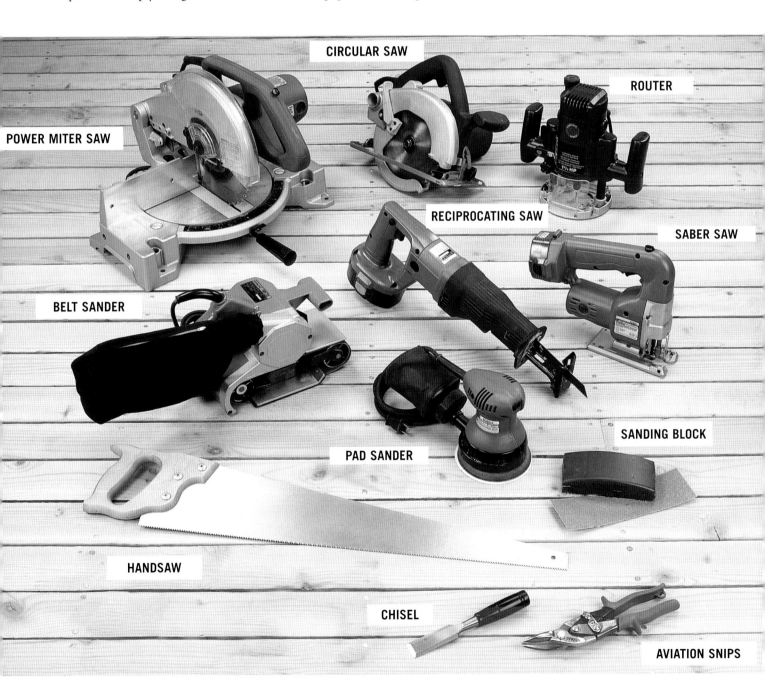

HAND TOOLS AND FASTENING

Compressor and Nail Gun. If you plan to frame or fasten your deck with a nail gun, you'll need a compressor to supply the air. Choose carefully—if the compressor is too small, you'll waste lots of time waiting for it to supply enough pressure for the next shot. A typical framing nailer shoots nails from 2 to 3½ inches long. Choose one with a restrictive or two-step trigger—this makes it much harder to fire a nail accidentally. Though safe when used properly, a nail gun can cause serious injury in a fraction of a second, so read, follow, and understand all safety precautions, especially the part about wearing safety glasses.

Cordless Drill. If it's in the budget, a cordless drill is very useful. Thanks to advances in battery technology, cordless drills have taken over most tasks you'd otherwise do with a corded drill. The most notable exception in deck building is installing decking—a corded drill still makes sense for that task since even today's batteries will soon run out of power under such concentrated use. You can now buy a powerful 20-volt drill that is quite compact, well-balanced, and easy to handle. A good cordless drill will come with a charger and an extra battery so that you'll always have a fresh battery available.

Read the owner's manual carefully, especially the part about charging batteries. Don't wait until a battery is completely dead before you charge it—pop it in the charger as soon as it starts to show signs of weakening. New cordless tools use Lithium-Ion batteries and care must be taken not to overcharge them.

Pipe Clamps. Pipe clamps are sometimes helpful for holding pieces of lumber in place temporarily—so you can check the level one last time before fastening, for example.

Bar Clamps. Bar clamps do some of the same jobs that pipe clamps do, but are usually a little easier to set up. You can adjust some models with just one hand so you have the other hand free to hold things in place.

C-Clamps. A pair of large C-clamps is useful when you need to reach past obstructions to apply pressure to the center of a board. Squeezing a pair of 2x12s on the outside of a 4x4 post prior to fastening is a good example.

Flat Bar and Wrecking Bar. The flat bar is more versatile, but the wrecking bar (sometimes called a crowbar) gives you more leverage. These are handy for demolition, such as removing siding before installing a ledger board, for prying deck boards into position, and for moving or breaking rocks you run into when digging holes.

Hammer. Your hammer is always at your side and constantly in use, so get a comfortable one. A 16-ounce hammer is a comfortable weight that will do the job, but the extra weight of a 20-ounce hammer will drive large nails more quickly. A straight-claw hammer is better for demolition work, while a curved-claw is better for pulling nails. Use of smooth-face hammers instead of waffle-face hammers will not mar the face of the finished wood surface.

Caulking Gun. Though it is used sparingly on a deck, there are places that benefit from a good bead of caulking.

Cat's Paw. This tool is for pulling framing nails back out of wood. By striking the back of its claw with a hammer, you can drive it under a nailhead, even if the head is below the surface. Then you push or strike the top of the tool to pull the nail out. A cat's paw always gets its nail but often seriously mars the face of the board in the process.

Nail Set. For places where the nails will show, you want to avoid the smiles and frowns caused by the hammer hitting the wood when you strike the nail with that last blow. Use a nail set, a small shaft of metal with one square end and one end tapered to a blunt point. With this, you can either drive nails perfectly flush with the wood or countersink them into the wood.

Utility Knife. No carpenter's apron should be without a utility knife. You'll use this inexpensive tool for all sorts of things: sharpening pencils, slicing away splinters from boards, shaving pieces of lumber, and opening bundles and packages. Get a better-quality, heavy-duty knife. Blades of cheap knives can slip out when you bear down hard. Replace a blade as soon as it gets dull. Be sure to get a retractable knife.

Zip Tool. A zip tool is used to unlock the joints between courses of vinyl siding. You'll find it handy if you are removing vinyl siding to install a ledger.

Ratchet Wrenches. If you will be installing lag screws or carriage bolts, a ratchet wrench with the right socket is much faster than a crescent wrench.

NAIL GUN AND COMPRESSOR

DRILL

PIPE CLAMPS

BAR CLAMPS

C-CLAMPS

CAULKING GUN

PRY BAR

HAMMER

UTILITY KNIFE

CAT'S PAW

NAIL SET

ZIP TOOL

RATCHET

ACCESSORIES

Tool Belt or Apron. A tool belt or apron is a definite must; without it, you will spend untold hours looking for that tool you used just a few minutes ago. It also stores your tools in a safe place, so they don't fall off surfaces like the top of a stepladder and hit someone. You can get an elaborate leather belt or a less-expensive canvas one. The belt should comfortably hold those objects you use most during a working day: your square, measuring tape, hammer, chalk-line box, nail set, chisel, pencils, and utility knife; and it should have a pocket for a good-size handful of nails. Be sure you can holster and unholster your hammer, pencil, and measuring tape with ease.

Hammer Holster. When you know you're going to do nothing but drive nails for a while, you might want to drop the full tool belt and put on a simpler tool holder with just one pocket and a hammer loop.

Extension Cord. Always check the wire-gauge number on an extension cord—the phrase heavy-duty on the package doesn't guarantee that it will supply enough current to your tools. In general, an extension cord with 14-gauge wires, designed to handle up to 15 amps, will have an orange colored outer jacket. A 12-gauge wire designed to handle up to 20 amps will have a yellow colored outer jacket. Use the correct cord for the breaker capacity you are connecting to by looking at the rating of the circuit breaker.

Stepladder. Available in wood, aluminum, or fiberglass, stepladders are a handy tool if you are working on a flat, level surface. A fold-down shelf can hold tools and finishing materials. Stepladders are available up to 15 feet high. As with other ladders, they are rated for the amount of weight the they can hold. Although they are sturdy when extended, do not stand on or above the rung labeled as such for safety purposes. See page 15 for stepladder safety precautions.

Sawhorses. Usually used to set up a temporary cutting station, sawhorses should be strong and stable.

Small Sledgehammer. For driving stakes, a standard 16- or 20-ounce hammer will usually do the job, but a small 3-pound sledgehammer is faster.

Tool Bag. A tool bag is a great way to transport and organize all those tools that don't earn a permanent place in your tool belt.

HAMMER HOLSTER AND BELT

EXTENSION CORDS WITH GFCI PROTECTION

STEPLADDER

NAIL APRONS

LEATHER TOOL BELT

SAWHORSES

EXCAVATION AND CONCRETE

Hoe. A standard garden hoe is handy for mixing concrete; a special mason's hoe, which has two holes in the blade, works even better.

Metal Rake. For spreading soil or gravel, and for sloping a site for drainage, a metal rake, or garden rake, is the best tool.

Posthole Digger. Whether you use tubular concrete forms or pour your concrete directly into the ground, you will need to dig deep, narrow holes for your footings (if you live in a region with frost) or shallow and broad (if you live in an area that does not reach freezing temperatures). Essentially two mini-shovels hinged together, a posthole digger picks up dirt in "bites" as you spread the handles. This tool allows you to work directly above the hole without creating sloping sides.

Round-Point Shovel. The most basic digging tool there is, the round-point shovel gets plenty of use on a deck site, from excavating to spreading gravel. Use a file to keep the edge of the shovel sharp—it'll cut through small roots like a hot knife through butter.

Square-Nosed Shovel. The front edge of this shovel is perfect for cutting sod when you need to remove grass from your building site. You'll also find that this is the best shovel for scooping up dirt or gravel from a driveway.

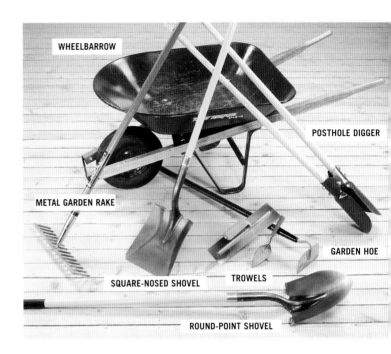

WHEELBARROW

POSTHOLE DIGGER

METAL GARDEN RAKE

GARDEN HOE

SQUARE-NOSED SHOVEL

TROWELS

ROUND-POINT SHOVEL

Trowels. For finishing and shaping concrete, a selection of trowels will be useful.
- **Steel Finish Trowel**
- **Pointing Trowel**

Wheelbarrow. This is a handy place to mix and transport small amounts of concrete. You'll also use your wheelbarrow to transport gravel, soil, sod, and sand.

RENTING TOOLS

When you need a specialized tool for just a few hours, check with your local rental yard. Chances are they have what you need and will rent it to you by the hour, day, week, or month. Some yards even rent by the half day, so if you're fast, you can save a little money. Think carefully before renting any small tools for longer than a week: after a point, it makes more sense to go out and buy the tool yourself.

A power auger makes short work of digging holes for posts, but the tools often require two people to operate safely.

CHAPTER 3
MATERIAL TYPES AND ESTIMATING FOR DECKS

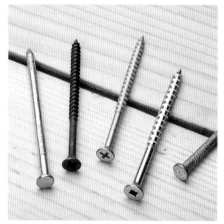

While the universe of materials used to build decks continues to expand, preservative-treated lumber is still the most popular choice. The material is relatively inexpensive; it resists insects and rot; and it is readily available. However, many homeowners and professional deck designers are turning to other materials, such as redwood, exotic hardwoods, and synthetic materials, for the decking and railing systems—the areas that are in full view. These products offer a variety of looks that cannot be matched by preservative-treated lumber. In most cases, preservative-treated lumber is still used for the structural portions of the deck, including posts, beams, and joists.

LUMBER AND AVAILABILITY

Because your deck is out in the weather all the time, you want to use wood that will resist decay and insects.

There are several choices, but the most popular are treated lumber, redwood, and cedar. Other options include cypress, synthetic decking, and Brazilian hardwood.

To get the wood that's right for your project, it's not enough to choose a certain species. Other factors that influence a wood's performance include moisture content, method of drying the wood, what part of the tree the lumber comes from, and the quality, or grade, of each piece.

Lumber Basics

Most of the lumber you buy is surfaced—smoothed, with rounded edges—on all four sides. This is called S4S, meaning surfaced on four sides. If you want a rough-sawn look (for the fascia or for posts, perhaps), you should be able to find cedar or redwood that is either rough all over or is smooth on only one side. This lumber may be a bit thicker and wider than S4S.

Lumber Sizes. The nominal size of a piece of lumber—for example, 2x4—refers to its size prior to drying and surfacing. So the 2x4 you buy will actually be 1½ inches by 3½ inches; a 2x6 is actually 1½ by 5½; a 1x8 is ¾ x 7¼, and so on. In most cases, lumberyards carry pieces in 2-foot increments beginning at 8 feet, so you can buy 8-footers, 10-footers, and up to 16' standard length and 24' maximum length.

Many people use either cedar or preservative-treated ⁵⁄₄x6 ("five quarter by six") boards for the decking and sometimes for the top cap on the railing. This material is actually 1 inch thick and 5½ inches wide. Rounded edges minimize splintering. Often only one face will be usable, so choose your boards carefully. To satisfy most codes and to build a strong deck, you will have to space joists no more than 12 inches on center to use this material.

Most people choose deck boards that are 5½ inches wide, such as 2x6 or ⁵⁄₄x6, either because they like the wider appearance or because they are less work to install. But the price for wider boards is rising fast because more lumber now comes from smaller trees, so 2x4 decking is becoming

LUMBER GRAIN

All trees have two types of wood inside: sapwood and heartwood. Sapwood is located toward the perimeter of the tree and carries sap to the branches. Heartwood comes from the center of the tree and is denser than sapwood because it is older. It is also more stable than sapwood. All parts of the tree can be used, and lumber taken from either the sapwood or heartwood region is graded accordingly. Because a lot of lumber today is cut from younger, faster-growing trees, you may find fewer distinctions between the heartwood and sapwood areas.

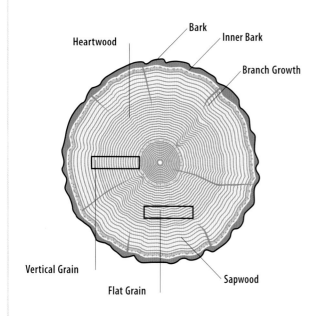

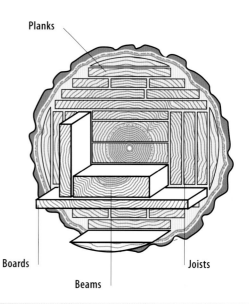

Decking products must be able to withstand the extremes of weather. A seaside deck as above must endure the abrasive effect of sand, plus the corrosive effect of salt.

a more economical choice. However, lumber prices tend to fluctuate, so it makes sense to price out both types.

Lumber Density. As a general rule, lumber of greater density will be stronger but also more prone to splitting and warping. Likewise, lower-density wood is weaker and may splinter and twist less. This is because lower-density wood can act like a sponge, absorbing moisture when the weather is wet and drying when the sun comes out. Dense wood does not have the ability to transfer moisture quickly, and the internal stresses cause warping and splinters. Treating lumber does not affect density but only adds temporary weight in the form of moisture.

So higher-density wood—Douglas fir or southern yellow pine, for instance—works well for the substructure, where strength is important and splinters and warping do not matter as much. And because you want to avoid splinters on the decking and rails, lower-density wood, such as redwood or cedar, may be a better choice.

Heartwood and Sapwood. The wood near the center of the tree, which is inactive because it has not been growing for some time, is called heartwood. Lumber milled from this portion of the tree is more resistant to rot and insects and less porous than sapwood, which is taken from the area of the tree near the bark. This is a significant difference: decking made of redwood or cedar heartwood will last far longer than will sapwood decking of the same species. (The code only recognizes redwood and cedar as decay resistant when they have 90 percent or more heartwood on each face.)

Vertical and Flat Grain. Different sawing techniques at the mill yield different grain patterns on the boards. Lumber generally either has vertical grain, with narrow grain lines running along the face of the board, or flat grain (also called plainsawn), with wider lines that often form rippling V-shapes. Most boards are a combination of the two, and in any given load of lumber, you will find boards that are both primarily flat grained and primarily vertically grained.

Vertical grain is less likely to shrink and warp, and most people think it looks better. But you don't have to go to the extra expense of specifying vertical grain when you order; when you choose boards, just pick as many of the ones with narrow lines as possible.

Moisture. Freshly cut trees delivered to a sawmill have a lot of moisture in them. And after sawing and surfacing, preservative-treated lumber gets saturated with liquid chemicals, making it even wetter. It dries out some before it gets to the lumberyard, but some lumber you buy may have a moisture content of 30 or 40 percent.

Wood that is wet—whether from natural moisture or from chemicals—will shrink as it dries out. Wood shrinks most across its width. The lengthwise shrinkage is minimal unless the board is especially long. Butt joints in a long run of decking may open up over time if the boards are installed wet. If your lumber has a moisture content (MC) of less than 20 percent, shrinkage and warping should be minimal.

The grade stamp on lumber indicates the moisture content, but don't trust this number completely; wood can pick up moisture from rain or humidity while sitting in the lumberyard. Your local yard may be willing to check some boards with a moisture meter. If not, try driving a nail into a board and see if any water squeezes out around the shank. If it does, it's too wet.

Lumber Grades. Lumber is sorted and graded on the basis of number, spacing, and size of knots, milling defects, and drying technique.

The highest-quality—and most expensive—lumber is called select structural. This lumber has the fewest knots and other imperfections.

Most often, you will be dealing with common lumber, which is graded No. 1, No. 2, or No. 3. No. 1 is the strongest, and usually the best-looking wood as well. No. 2 is the grade most commonly used in deck framing. No. 3 lumber is less structurally sound.

Another grading system uses the words Const (for construction), Stand (standard), or Util (utility). These three classifications are generally used to grade 2x4 and 4x4 lumber and No.1, 2, and 3 grade 2x6 and wider stock.

No. 2 is the most common grade and will be fine for most applications. Chances are, your building codes will require "No. 2 or better."

For the railings and other areas that are highly visible, you may want to spend the extra money to get No.1 or even select structural lumber—if you can find it. Good lumber is getting much harder to find these days. Lots of lumber is now cut from corporate forests, where fast-growing trees mature quickly but have widely spaced growth rings and yield less lumber.

LUMBER GRADES

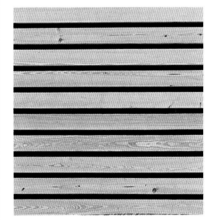

Number 1 grade of most common lumber has few, if any, knots.

Number 2 grade has more knots and defects than Number 1. It's the type specified as a minimum requirement in most building codes.

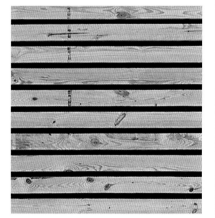

Number 3 of most common lumber has many knots and defects. It may not be approved by your local building code.

LUMBER SPECIES

Redwood

The redwood trees of northern California are legendary for their size and the quality of lumber. Redwood's beautiful straight grain, natural glowing color, and weather resistance have traditionally marked it as the Cadillac of outdoor building materials. It is a pleasure to work with, easy to cut, and sweet-smelling. Unfortunately, overlumbering has made redwood expensive and hard to get.

Because of its high price, you might want to use redwood only for the highly visible portions of your deck, such as the decking and railings. Redwood works for structural support as well, though you may have to use slightly larger joists and beams than if you were using regular preservative-treated lumber.

You can usually tell sapwood from heartwood by color: the sapwood is much lighter and hardly looks like it comes from the same tree. Redwood heartwood has the deep, rich color and is extremely weather- and insect-resistant. Sapwood may start to rot in two or three years if it has contact with the ground or if it will remain wet for long periods of time. Treat sapwood before installing it, and use it only where there will be good drainage most of the year.

If you let redwood "go gray" by not treating it with anything, it will reach a light gray color after a few years and develop a slight sheen that many people find attractive. Or you can treat it with stains and a UV blocker to keep it close to its original color.

In some parts of the country, you can find redwood that has been both treated and stained, which makes the sapwood more decay resistant and similar in color to the heartwood. This is an expensive item, but if it comes with a lifetime warranty, it's worth checking out. Inspect several pieces to make sure you like the color. The reddish-brown will fade after a few years, and the deck will turn a uniform gray unless you restain it.

The Redwood Inspection Service of the California Redwood Association establishes redwood grades. The service has two grading categories: Architectural and Garden. Architectural grades are the best-looking, most expensive grades of redwood. Garden grades are more economical and have more knots. Both categories of redwood are available kiln-dried or unseasoned and are usually surfaced on four sides.

Architectural grades include:

Clear All-Heart. All heartwood and free from knots, this wood is recommended for highly visible applications.

Clear. Similar in quality to Clear All-Heart, except that Clear contains sapwood. Clear is ideal for highly visible applications where the wood won't be subject to decay.

Heart B. Containing limited knots, but no sapwood, Heart B is a less costly alternative to Clear All-Heart.

B-Grade. Similar characteristics to Heart B but contains sapwood; same uses as Clear.

Garden grades of redwood are suitable for most deck-building applications. They include:

Construction Heart/Deck Heart. These are all-heartwood grades containing knots. Both are recommended for work on or near the ground, such as posts, girders, joists, and decking. Deck Heart is similar in appearance to Construction Heart but also carries a grade stamp for strength. Deck Heart is available in 2x4 and 2x6 only.

Many people use more than one type of wood on their deck. Visible areas receive the highest-quality lumber.

💡 SMART TIP

STACKING WOOD

When wood is delivered, some of it may be a little wet, which means it can shrink and twist on your deck. You should return any waterlogged lumber that is significantly heavier than other pieces. The rest you can store off the ground on 4x4s with strips of wood laid between layers to increase air circulation and drying. Cover the materials with a plastic tarp during rains to prevent more moisture being absorbed into the wood.

Construction Common/Deck Common. Containing knots and a combination of heartwood and sapwood, these grades are best for aboveground applications such as railings, benches, and decking. Deck Common is similar in appearance to Construction Common and has the same uses but is also graded for strength. Deck Common is available in 2x4 and 2x6 only.

Merchantable Heart. This is the most economical all-heartwood grade. The rules allow larger knots and some knotholes. It's used for garden walls or utility structures on or near the ground.

Merchantable. Having the same characteristics as Merchantable Heart but containing sapwood, this grade is suitable only for fence boards, trellises, and aboveground garden and utility applications.

Cedar

Cedar has many of the benefits of redwood and usually costs less. Like redwood, it is stable, easy to work with, and rarely splinters or checks. And like redwood, it is the heartwood of the cedar tree that is resistant to decay. Sapwood will decay relatively quickly. You can recognize cedar heartwood by its dark color and the hamster-cage smell you get when you cut it.

Cedar is fragrant and beautiful, though it tends to have a more informal feel than redwood, with its light brown color. Left untreated, cedar will turn gray.

You may want to use cedar in places where the structure will be visible—for example, for fascia. In other places, such as the outside and header joists, it is common to use preservative-treated lumber for the structure and then cover cedar with cedar fascia boards for looks.

However, unlike redwood and preservative-treated lumber, cedar is available in most any size, even up to 12x12 monster posts. So you might use it for unusually sized post-and-beam constructions.

Cedar is widely available and comes in a number of varieties. The most commonly used variety is Western red cedar. You can purchase Clear All-Heart, but this is quite expensive. Chances are, you will want to use No.1 varieties: Select Tight Knot, taken from new growth and containing some sapwood, works well for decking that will not remain wet for long periods. Architect Clear and Custom Clear come from old growth and should be used in places susceptible to rot. Stepping down from these grades you will find Architect Knotty, Custom Knotty, and No. 2. These will contain more knots, but probably have the same amount of rot-resistance. And you may like the look of the knots.

One of the most common decking materials used is ⁵/₄ cedar decking. This has rounded edges so you will end up with virtually no splinters. But inspect this lumber for the qualities discussed earlier. Just because some company has labeled it "decking" does not mean it will suit your needs.

Use cedar with one smooth face and one rough face (called S1SE, meaning surfaced on one side and two edges) for fascia. With the rough side turned outward, it has a pleasing rustic appearance. However, water trapped between a fascia board and the lumber it is covering up can promote decay, so treat these pieces well.

Sometimes cedar will develop black, slimy spots. While this could be mold, chances are that it's just natural resin leaching out of the wood. It can be washed away with soap and water.

LUMBER GRADING STAMPS

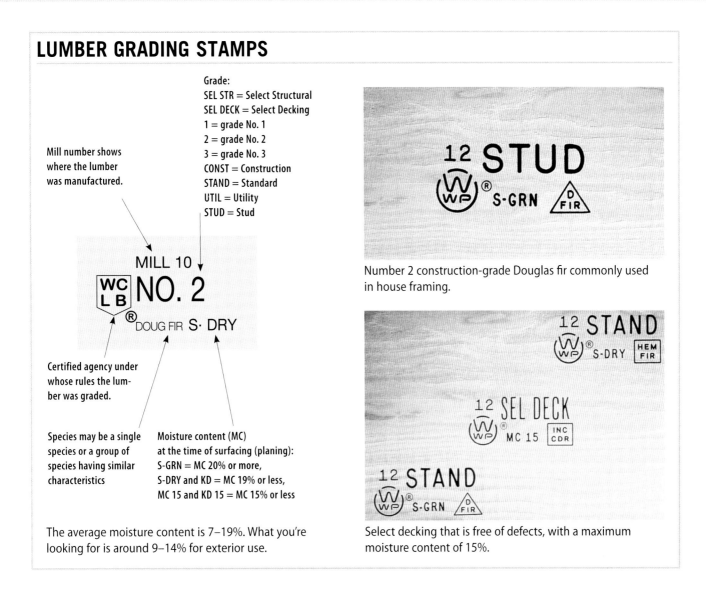

Mill number shows where the lumber was manufactured.

Grade:
SEL STR = Select Structural
SEL DECK = Select Decking
1 = grade No. 1
2 = grade No. 2
3 = grade No. 3
CONST = Construction
STAND = Standard
UTIL = Utility
STUD = Stud

MILL 10

WC LB | NO. 2
DOUG FIR S· DRY

Certified agency under whose rules the lumber was graded.

Species may be a single species or a group of species having similar characteristics

Moisture content (MC) at the time of surfacing (planing):
S-GRN = MC 20% or more,
S-DRY and KD = MC 19% or less,
MC 15 and KD 15 = MC 15% or less

The average moisture content is 7–19%. What you're looking for is around 9–14% for exterior use.

Number 2 construction-grade Douglas fir commonly used in house framing.

Select decking that is free of defects, with a maximum moisture content of 15%.

Cypress

Bald cypress is the South's answer to redwood. Native to the swamps and lowland areas throughout the Southeast, bald cypress is similar to redwood in hardiness and strength, although it is not as stable. In the southern United States, local sawmills can be a very economical source for decking lumber. It's hard to get cypress outside of its native region, but your lumberyard might be willing to order it for you.

Treated Wood Products

Preservative-treated (PT) lumber has been used to build wood decks for years. In the past, most lumber was treated with chromated copper arsenate (CCA), which gives the wood a greenish tint that fades over time. The treatment process provided a durable product that went into the construction of millions of decks. However, CCA contains arsenic, a known carcinogen, and safe use of the product required some special handling procedures.

The wood treatment industry has elected to stop producing CCA treated lumber for use in residential applications. Other types of preservatives are now used, including copper azole and alkaline copper quaternary. These and other types of preservatives can affect the look and structural characteristics of the lumber. Be sure to follow the manufacturer's directions for installation, safe handling, and proper uses.

There is nothing wrong with the millions of decks constructed with CCA treated wood. Properly maintained, they will last for years and do not present a risk to those who use them if they follow standard safety practices, including wearing a dust mask, gloves, and eye protection when cutting CCA treated lumber, and washing your hands after handling the wood. Do not sand or burn the wood.

South American Hardwood

If you have a big budget and a taste for the exotic, you may want to look into South American hardwoods (sometimes called ironwoods), such as ipé and pau lopé. This lumber is extremely strong and durable. In fact, some ironwoods have roughly twice the strength and load rating as similarly sized preservative-treated Douglas fir. And the resistance to rot and insects is often five times better than treated lumber found in this country.

As you may expect, these woods are quite expensive; using ironwood for only the decking and railings could well triple the materials cost for your entire deck. Ironwoods are also slow to install—cutting is arduous, and you may have to predrill for every screw or nail.

☐ SMART TIP

CROWNING

Most structural lumber you use for joists and girders has a natural bend, or crown. When you select these beams, sight down the edge to find the bend, and mark an X on the up side. Setting joists and girders with the crowns up counteracts any tendency for the frame to sag.

SELECTING LUMBER

Many lumberyards store structural lumber outside. When it's delivered, you will probably find some high-quality pieces, while others have open knot holes and other defects. Most lumber today is sold in mixed-grade shipments, and unless you're paying for a select grade, you have to deal with it by selecting the best boards for the most visible area of the deck. On the deck surface, don't worry about grain direction, and simply turn the bad side face down.

When purchasing mixed-grade shipments, separate the best-looking boards from the ones with knots; use the nicer ones on the most visible areas of your project.

LUMBER DEFECTS

You probably can't afford to buy clear, select lumber for every part of your deck, so most pieces are going to have some small defects. Some defects are cosmetic and won't affect the strength of the board; others will cause trouble. Here is a list of lumber defects, with descriptions that will tell you whether or not you can live with them.

Bow is a bend in the wood along the wide face, from end to end. It has no effect on strength, and you can use the board on your deck as long as you can straighten it as you fasten it in place.

Cup is a bend across the width of a board. If it's not severe, you can try to flatten it out with nails or screws (for decking) or blocking (for joists). A cupped decking board will hold water if installed cupped-side up, and this will promote rot, so be sure to turn the cupped side down before you flatten it.

Crook is a bend in the wood that makes a hump on the narrow face when you sight from one end to the other. The high portion is called the crown, and joists are always installed crown side up. Most long boards have a small crook, but excessive crooking makes wood unsuitable for framing. When a deck board has a moderate crook, you can usually push or pull it into position before fastening.

Twist is a slight corkscrew-shaped distortion of the wood, and if it's severe enough to be noticeable at first glance, the lumber is unsuitable for decking or framing.

Check is a rift in the surface caused when the surface dries more rapidly than the interior. It produces patches that look like small tears in the surface. These are usually only cosmetic and do not affect the strength. Kiln-dried wood checks less than green wood.

Split is a crack that passes completely through the board at the ends. This is a serious structural weakness. Don't use split lumber on any part of your deck.

Wane is the lack of wood along one edge of a board, usually in a tapered pattern along the length of the board. This occurs on boards cut from the outer edge of the tree—where the bark once was. Wane has little effect on strength. Remove any bark that remains on the lumber because it will promote rot if it stays there.

Knots are the high-density bases of limbs. The knots themselves are strong, but they have no real connection to the surrounding wood. Avoid large knots in decking, which may come loose over time. Large knots (anything over 1 inch) in the bottom third of a joist could weaken it significantly.

Decay is the destruction of the wood structure by fungi or insects. Don't use decayed wood on any portion of your deck.

Pitch Pockets are accumulations of natural resins on the surface of a board. They have little effect on strength, but will cause discoloration if you paint or stain the board.

SYNTHETIC DECKING

This is the fastest growing category of decking material due to the fact that manufacturers are coming out with increasingly attractive products that are generally easier to install than wood. Synthetics don't have the strength of wood and so are used only for decking and railings, not for framing.

Unlike wood, these products vary greatly from one manufacturer to the next. Also they are available in a range of prices and quality. However, there are three basic types of synthetic decking: composite, solid polyvinyl chloride (PVC), and composite capped with PVC. They all come in wood-like colors, and the more expensive products have color variations and embossed grain-like textures that are quite convincing to the eye, though they don't feel like wood to the touch.

Composite Decking. Wood particles mixed with plastic, sometimes recycled from beverage containers, are bound with epoxy to create composite decking. It is very stable and won't expand and contract nearly as much as wood. The color is permanent, but over the years it does fade. Faded composite decking can be coated with a stain specifically formulated for the purpose. The biggest problem with composite decking is that it can absorb moisture that allows mold to grow.

Solid PVC. This is the closest to maintenance-free of all available decking materials. Mold won't grow on PVC and periodic washing is all it needs. However, solid PVC is very expensive, more so because stainless steel fasteners are recommended simply to match the longevity of the PVC material, and not due to the performance of holding the decking in place. Also, solid PVC expands and contracts significantly along the length of board. Solid PVC also comes in ¾-inch-thick boards for use as fascia.

Capped Composite. Manufacturers came up with PVC-capped composite decking in an effort to combine the stability of composite with the mold-resistance of plastic. In appearance, it is indistinguishable from solid PVC. As the name implies, it consists of a hard plastic surface bonded to a composite board. In some products the plastic covers just the top and sides of the boards; high-end versions are fully capped all the way around, a better protection against mold. Capped composite costs more than composite alone but less than solid PVC and so has become a popular choice.

Composite decking is usually embossed with a pattern to mimic wood grain. Capped composite (left) can have color variations added to the plastic surface to make it look more like wood.

CONCRETE

In building your deck, you'll most likely use concrete for footings to support the posts.

Concrete is composed of three elements: portland cement, aggregate, and water. The aggregate is a mixture of sand and gravel that acts to bind the cement paste together, adding strength.

It is important to get the mixture right. Too much water will weaken the concrete; too little will make it difficult to work. So the general rule when mixing your own is to add just enough water to make it workable for your needs. If you use premixed bags, read the label to find out how much water to add, and add it slowly. The mix should be liquid enough to fill all the spaces in a tube form or hole, but if it gets soupy, it's too wet.

The compressive strength of concrete—the amount of weight you can place on it before it crumbles—is determined by the amount of cement in the mix.

FASTENERS

The nails, screws, bolts, and hardware you choose hold your deck together, transforming a pile of lumber into a useful, well-built outdoor structure. Some of these choices, such as what size bolts hold your girder to your post, are dictated by building codes; others, such as whether to use screws or nails to hold down your decking, depend more on personal preference than local codes.

Whatever type of fastener you choose, remember this rule of thumb for determining the length you need: the fastener's penetration into the bottom piece should be equal to or greater than the thickness of the top piece. So unless you plan to countersink the fasteners into the top board, they should be at least twice as long as the thickness of the top board. For example, when installing 1½-inch boards, you should use 3- or 3½-inch fasteners.

Deck Fasteners Applications

Joist hangers for preservative treated decks are required where the joist end meets a beam or ledger at 90 degrees and has no other means of bearing support, such as a beam below the joists. These hangers are required to be fastened with 10D joist hanger nails in each hole location approved for this application.

NOTE: No other nail types are approved for substitution. However, the use of a #10 x 1½" Strong Drive Connector screw can be used in each hole location.

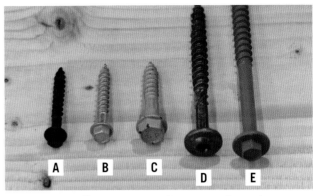

- A - #10 x 1½" Strong Drive Connector Screw hot dipped galvanized coating
- B - Heavy-Duty Strong Drive Connector Screw hot dipped galvanized coating
- C - Rugged Structural Screw 5⁄16" x 3⅛"
- D - LedgerLok Screw hot dipped galvanized coating (Replaces ½" diameter lag screws)
- E - Connector Screw Hidden flange type (Outdoor Accents)

Flashing is critical to prevent water penetration into any wood product. Even more so when decks are constructed because the wood decking boards are installed with gaps between them for water drainage and to allow for expansion and contraction of the decking boards.

The top of the deck floor joist framing is constantly exposed to moisture where the designed gaps occur and that leads to wood decay. In addition, water may be trapped under the decking boards attached to the top of the deck floor joist and rot will occur in an area you cannot see. To help with both above situations a self-adhere rubber flashing tape has been designed and recommended to be install along the top of all joists and ledger boards for prevention of contact with water.

NOTE: Even if your deck only requires rebuilding of the wood deck boards, it is highly recommended to install the self-adhere flashing tape before installing new wood or synthetic decking boards.

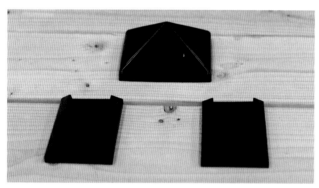

Tops of deck posts are subject to wood rot because water lays on horizontal surfaces and the end grain of every board is exposed at the end of the board or post after cutting. Preventative wood rot can be prevented by using a sealant on the exposed ends of the posts.

A better method is to install a decorative post cap that will cover the entire end of the post and provide long lasting protection against wood rot.

Composite decking over preservative treatment joists has a variety of concealed fasteners to eliminate unsightly exposed screws through the top of the deck board. The most common type of fastener used with edge grooved composite decking is type shown below.

This type of concealed fastener fits in the manufactured groove in the edge of the composite decking board and includes a stainless screw and when attached to the preservative deck joist provides a strong attachment point and proper spacing between the composite deck boards.

Outdoor Accent Accessories and Connectors

These types of fasteners and connectors are solely for use with non-preservative lumber such as red wood or cedar or other types of exterior wood products that do not have a preservative treatment process to prevent wood rot. These fasteners provide excellent structural support and additionally are aesthetically appealing to accent your construction.

> **NOTE: Using these accessories and connectors with preservative lumber will cause the accessory and connector to corrode severely over time. Consult your sales advisor at the point of purchase before buying to ensure the correct application with your wood type.**

Floor or ceiling joists that require a joist hanger but will be exposed to end users and NOT made of preservative lumber can utilize a Hidden Flange Hanger design for various size joists such as 2x6 or 2x10. To attach these hangers, use the Connector Screw (E) above.

Floor or ceiling joists that need to be attached to a vertical post can utilize the Deck Joist Tie connector. This is attached to a non-preservative joist and post utilizing 4 lag screws and washers.

Vertical boards that require to be attached to a ceiling joist and to the underside of a roof structure as a mean of vertical strength to support a span can be attached with the Tee Strap connector.

Wood deck rail attachments can be challenging. Some advanced applications have routed cut-outs to accept the ends of the wood rails. Some basic applications use screws installed at angles through the ends of the rails to attach them to the posts.

A more efficient way is to incorporate the use of rail attachments to a post. Start by cutting the horizontal rails to length and allowing for the thickness of each bracket. The brackets are secured to the ends of the horizontal rails with two flat head screws. Be sure to keep the top of the bracket flush with the top of the rail at both ends of the board.

Next the rails are secured to the posts through the side holes provided at the desired height. This not only ensures that the rails are secure but provides that finished look.

Next install the top rail that creates the T-Rail style, and the railing will be safely secure and will last a long time.

NOTE: For preservative wood rails substitute the supplied screws with exterior screws suitable for that application to avoid corrosion of the screws.

Deck fasteners also can be decorative as well as structural for constructing overhead porticos and other roof framing styles that can enhance your deck designs. These fasteners used below illustrate the best type and applications to ensure your project utilizes the best design for strength and durability.

DECK HARDWARE

Besides screws, nails, and bolts, many other metal fasteners are used in the construction of a deck.

Deck Fasteners

Specialized deck hardware allows you to securely install decking boards with no visible fasteners. There are several hidden-fastener systems, some designed to work with a specific decking product. All of these systems are more expensive than traditional fasteners and they take more time to install, but it may well be worth the extra time and expense to have a clean, nail-free surface, especially if your decking boards are beautiful cedar or redwood.

Flashing

Installing your flashing properly prevents water from getting into your home and helps ensure the integrity of your deck. Poor flashing installation is a major contributor to deck ledger failure and collapses. When possible, buy preformed pieces that are in the exact shape you need. You may have to buy a roll of flat sheet metal and form it yourself.

Aluminum flashing will last practically forever, but it has a tendency to expand and contract with changes in weather, causing nails to come loose and leading to leaks.

Make sure you use aluminum nails with aluminum flashing, or you'll have corrosion. In addition, aluminum flashing paired with preservative-treated lumber, which is high in copper content, can result in corrosion. Galvanized flashing might develop rust spots after some years, but it is thicker and stronger and does not react to temperature changes as readily as aluminum.

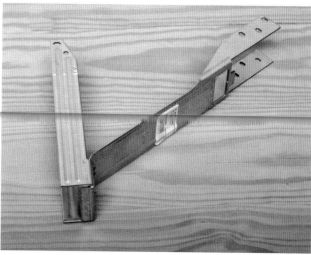

Tension ties. This hardware secures the deck framing to house framing to prevent the joists from pulling away from the ledger.

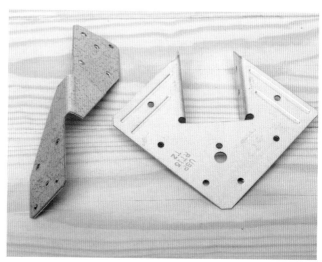

Hurricane ties. The one at left attaches to one side of the joist and beam. The other type slips under the joist and is attached to both sides of the joist and one side of the beam.

 SMART TIP

TREATED WOOD FASTENERS

There is evidence that some of the newer wood treatment chemicals are more corrosive than the traditional treatments for preservative-treated wood. (See "Treated Wood Products," page 33.) Check product information sheets for specific fastener recommendations. Some manufacturers of fasteners are recommending stainless steel nails or screws when using the newer types of treated lumber.

DECK CONNECTORS

All connectors shown require 10D galvanized hanger nails in each hole for proper attachment.

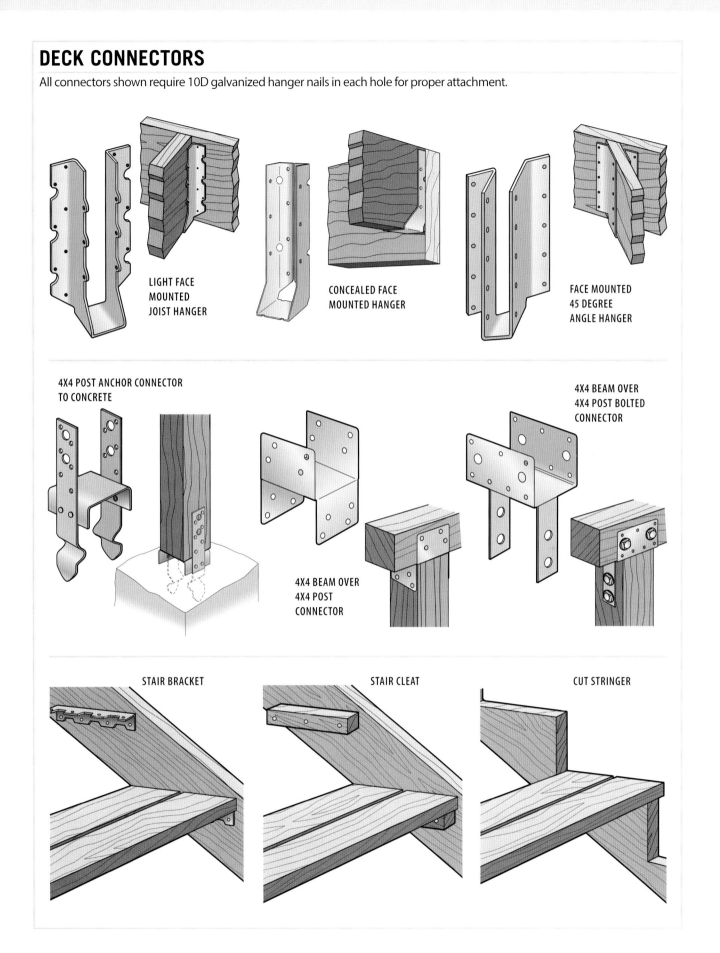

LIGHT FACE
MOUNTED
JOIST HANGER

CONCEALED FACE
MOUNTED HANGER

FACE MOUNTED
45 DEGREE
ANGLE HANGER

4X4 POST ANCHOR CONNECTOR
TO CONCRETE

4X4 BEAM OVER
4X4 POST BOLTED
CONNECTOR

4X4 BEAM OVER
4X4 POST
CONNECTOR

STAIR BRACKET

STAIR CLEAT

CUT STRINGER

CHAPTER 4

YOU AND YOUR DECK

For some people, the hardest part of building a deck, or having one built for you, may be coming up with a design that meets all of your requirements and suits the terrain of your yard. How will you use the deck? What's the best place in your yard to place the deck? Will it be on one level or do you want a multilevel design with separate activity areas? These questions have an impact on the costs along with many more you will need to consider during the design process. This chapter will guide you through the design process. You can also see pages 216 to 309 for more inspiration.

BEGINNING THE PROCESS

We all have different reasons for adding a new deck to our home. Most people find they want a new deck for a variety of practical and financial reasons. With a deck, you expand your living space and increase your home's value for a fraction of what it would cost to build an addition. You enhance your living style as well, gaining a new space for entertaining and socializing. But for a deck to do all these things, you need to start out with a good plan.

A well-planned deck will harmonize with the house in both size and shape and provide a smooth transition down to the yard. It can offer more exposure or more privacy, and either take advantage of a cool breeze or protect you from a stiff ocean wind.

What to Expect. Building a deck is a relatively straightforward project, as long as you have the proper tools, materials, and deck design suited to your area and skill level. The project won't totally disrupt your home life, either, as kitchen remodeling would. Most of the mess is kept outside, and as long as you have a good place to store materials, the project can stretch from weekend to weekend with no major problem.

During your initial planning, include the whole family and develop a wish list of features. Gradually, you will pare away the excesses and zero in on a design that works for your situation. Then you'll work through the project step-by-step, from drawing plans, getting permits, choosing a framing style, and selecting materials and patterns for your decking, railings, and stairs, to applying finishes and maintaining your deck.

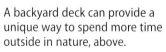

A backyard deck can provide a unique way to spend more time outside in nature, above.

A small pond adds an unusual feature to this deck, left.

The proportions of a well-designed deck fit with the house, top right.

A deck can be used to add to the modern character of a house, bottom right.

CHOOSING A DESIGN

While deck materials, shapes, sizes, and costs can vary widely, there are several design decisions common to almost every deck project. Although most decks are simply platforms raised above the yard, they are really an extension of the house—more like living space than yard space—even though they are outside. Because a deck connects to and expands the adjacent indoor space, deck additions are likely to be most appropriate and useful added onto living/family room areas and kitchen/dining room areas. For example, replacing a solid wall with sliding glass doors leading to an expansive deck is doable, as long as changes to the wall's load-bearing status, wiring, and exterior siding are taken into consideration.

Draw a series of rough sketches as you proceed. Expect to fill a wastebasket or two with these. Don't think of them as actual designs so much as focal points for conversations—it's usually easier to point to a place on your drawing than to walk around the house.

Feel free to steal ideas from online searching, books, magazines, and other decks in your neighborhood. When you see a deck that particularly pleases you and seems appropriate for your situation, talk to the owners about how their deck works for them. Jot down some notes, and ask permission to take a few photos. Most people will be flattered that you like their deck and will be more than happy to tell you all about it. And don't forget about the designs that begin on page 208.

You will probably discover lots of terrific deck ideas that you end up not using, either because you no longer like the way they look, you discover that they just won't work with your design, or the extra expense for exotic materials will blow the budget. Don't be discouraged. In fact, expect it to happen—and happen several times—before you come up with a design.

How You Will Use Your Deck

Everyone in the family probably has different visions of the ideal deck. Gather all their opinions, and figure out an overall design that will work for everybody. Consider the following items.

Entertaining and Barbecuing. Plan a convenient cooking area, probably somewhere near the kitchen. Figure out where you'll put tables for sit-down dinners as well as a good place to set up a buffet table. If you'll have a grill on the deck and plan to do a lot of barbecuing, you might want to add a small sink near the cooking area—as long as you can handle what comes with setting up water and sewer connections as well as freeze protection.

Begin the design process by settling on how you plan on using your new deck, left. Sharing meals was a prime consideration for this deck.

Decks are great places to entertain during pleasant weather, opposite top.

Built-in benches, opposite bottom, provide seating and design interest. A circular design helps promote conversation among people on the deck.

💡 SMART TIP

START AN IDEA SCRAPBOOK

Keep your ideas and your wish list in order by starting a design scrapbook, either in a physical scrapbook or online, using Pinterest or a Google doc, for example.

Lounging and Sunning. Pencil in space for a hammock or a swinging chair—a shady spot is often best. Sun worshippers will congregate on an expanse of deck that gets full sun.

Balancing Privacy and Openness. Think about whether you want the deck to feel airy and open to the world or cozy and secluded. A small deck will generally feel cozier than a large deck. Low benches and railings designed with large, open sections give a feeling of openness. A narrow deck that hugs the house will have a more sequestered feel than one that juts into the yard.

Decks are usually raised off the ground, which might mean that you and your family will be on display for all the neighborhood to see. Existing fences may be too low to shield you from view. Sometimes the problem can be solved by stepping the deck down in stages or by planting trees and shrubs.

If you feel overexposed, a well-placed trellis or pergola added to the deck can give you some nice climbing plants to look at as well as provide a pleasant enclosure and screen.

Enjoying the View. Plan your landscape along with your deck to get the best view. Orient the deck so that you will be looking at the best features of your yard and to take advantage of a nice view beyond your property line.

Planning for Children's Play. A jungle gym will probably look better in the yard, but your deck design should provide an inviting place where kids can play. Build the stairway extra wide or have a series of descending platforms, and children will spend hours playing with dolls and trucks and letting their imaginations run wild. Plan a spot for a comfortable chair where you can relax while keeping an unobstructed eye on the kids in your yard.

Lighting for Nighttime Use. Plan some appropriate lighting if you want to use the deck after dark. Whether you choose standard 120-volt wiring or a low-voltage LED option, plan to run the wires somewhere out of sight, maybe even underground.

Including a Pool or Whirlpool. Built with a surface of rot-resistant wood or composite material, a deck makes an ideal surface next to a pool or spa. Both materials are softer than tile or concrete and wood, making the deck a pleasant place to sit or lounge when you get out of the water. An inexpensive aboveground pool gains a lot of class when you surround it with a deck. If your design includes a spa or hot tub, position it for privacy as well as an unobstructed view of the stars.

Container Gardening. It is almost impossible to put too much foliage on or near a deck. Find planters that will go well with your deck and your house, or plan to build some from the same material as the decking. With enough sun, tomatoes, peppers, and all sorts of vegetables do well. An herb garden flourishes without a lot of work and still looks great after a bit of harvesting. If you're an avid gardener, you might even consider putting a greenhouse on the deck. Just be sure that water from planting containers doesn't get trapped on the deck—standing water invites rot.

Plan a lighting scheme if you plan on using your deck after dark, left.

Closed designs tend to make a deck feel cozier than one that is open, opposite. This design also provides a certain amount of privacy.

Traffic Patterns

Make the deck easy to reach by installing French doors or sliders—the more entrances, the better. Large windows that look onto the deck will entice people outside. If you plan to eat a lot of meals out on the deck, make sure it's close to the kitchen.

Also take the time to plan the approaches to the deck. Plan a clear, unobstructed path to the deck from indoor entertainment areas and from areas where your family spends a lot of time. A door out to the deck near the kitchen and another near the living room help avoid bottlenecks during parties. A landing at the bottom of the stairs down to the yard reduces wear and tear on the grass and is usually required by code.

Weather Considerations

Think about how the weather and the seasons will affect the ways you use the deck, and plan accordingly. For example, a deck with a greenhouse on a southern exposure will help extend the growing season in a cold climate. The three main weather variables with which you need to concern yourself are sun, wind, and rain.

Incorporate the flow from house to deck to yard into your design.

TRAFFIC PATTERNS

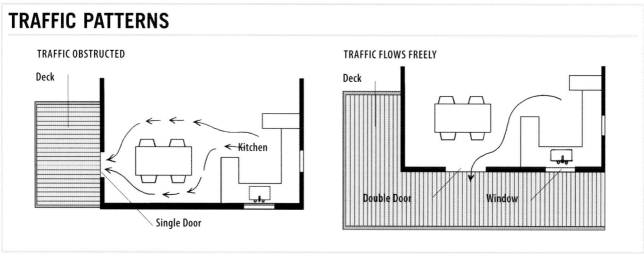

TRAFFIC OBSTRUCTED

Deck

Kitchen

Single Door

TRAFFIC FLOWS FREELY

Deck

Double Door

Window

SEASONAL CONDITIONS

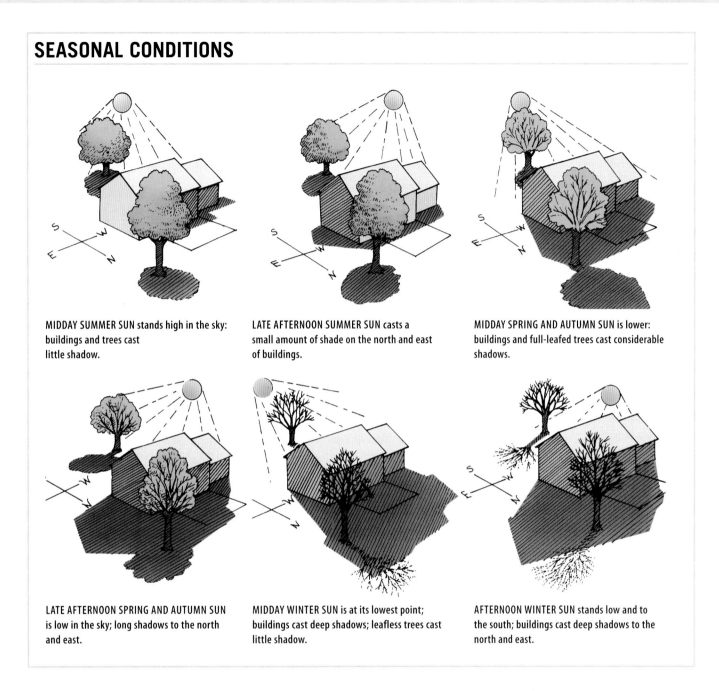

MIDDAY SUMMER SUN stands high in the sky: buildings and trees cast little shadow.

LATE AFTERNOON SUMMER SUN casts a small amount of shade on the north and east of buildings.

MIDDAY SPRING AND AUTUMN SUN is lower: buildings and full-leafed trees cast considerable shadows.

LATE AFTERNOON SPRING AND AUTUMN SUN is low in the sky; long shadows to the north and east.

MIDDAY WINTER SUN is at its lowest point; buildings cast deep shadows; leafless trees cast little shadow.

AFTERNOON WINTER SUN stands low and to the south; buildings cast deep shadows to the north and east.

Sun. Decide how much sun and how much shade you want, and take this into account when siting the deck. A deck on the north side of a house will be in shade most of the day. This can be an advantage if you live in a very hot climate and a disadvantage for most everyone else. An eastern exposure gives the deck morning sun and afternoon shade; this is often the best choice in warm climates. In cold climates, a southwest exposure provides full late afternoon sun, making the deck warmer on cool days in the spring and fall.

Also consider the angle of the sun above the horizon. The sun is highest in the summer and lowest in the winter. This means that in the winter a south-oriented deck will receive less direct sunlight than during the summer. A fence or tree that does not block out the high summer sun may block out sunlight during other times of the year when the sun is lower.

You may want continuous shade for a hammock, afternoon shade only for an eating area, and as much sun as possible for potted plants and a sunning area. You may need to change your foliage, pruning branches or planting more trees and shrubs.

Wind. If heat is a problem and you want to maximize the breeze, plan to prune trees or remove shrubs. If you have more wind than you want, you may need to plant new foliage. A raised deck will be windier than one near the ground.

For extreme conditions, you may need to construct a windbreak of some sort. A louvered or lattice wall covered with climbing plants is much more attractive than a solid fence and does a good job of diffusing a strong wind.

Rain. Most people think of sunny, clear weather as the best time to enjoy life on the deck, but you may live in an area where it rains much of the year, or perhaps you just like to watch the rain. You could install a large set of sliding glass doors between the deck and the living room, so you can open the doors and enjoy the patter of rain as it falls on your deck and potted plants.

Envisioning the Contours

You'll find that areas defined on sketches tend to look larger than they actually are in real life. To avoid disappointment later in the project, transfer the scale drawings to the actual building site. You can drive stakes into the ground and connect them with string to outline the deck.

Arrange lawn furniture inside the deck's planned outline, and try it on for size. Imagine yourselves doing what you hope to do on your new deck, and ask some obvious questions: Is there enough room for a planter here? Is this the right-size space for a buffet table if you have a party with 15 guests? Is there room for a table and chairs here, and room for people to get to their seats? Will the hammock fit over there? Where will the barbecue be? Would an L- or T-shape work better? What if you put some hanging planters or large potted plants over there, to give a sense of separate spaces? In this way, you will come up with some fairly specific ideas about the shape and size of your deck.

If it feels cramped, consider extending the deck in logical increments. Using 12-foot-long joists instead of 10-footers, for example, has little effect on labor costs and increases material costs only marginally, but may dramatically increase the deck's usefulness and sense of space.

If you have the space and the money, you may be tempted to build a very large deck. If you've got a large house and plenty of deck furniture, this can work well, but a jumbo deck can sometimes overwhelm a smaller home. Plan deck areas that feel comfortable and are scaled to the size of your house.

💡 SMART TIP

PREVIEW THE DECK CONTOURS

To help you visualize the actual size of a deck plan that's sketched out on a drawing, measure the rough dimensions on several of the potential building sites and stretch out an extension cord or a garden hose to mark the contours.

The surrounding area will play an important role in determining how popular the deck becomes.
Create designs that enhance the views.

IMPROVING YOUR HOUSE AND YARD

A deck usually does not stand alone; it is attached to your house and sits on top of your yard. So consider not only how the deck itself will look but also how it will fit in with its surroundings. This does not necessarily mean striving to make the deck blend in and disappear, but any contrasts should be pleasing to onlookers rather than jarring.

Although the decking boards are probably the most visible element when you look at the deck from the house, the structural elements may loom large from other perspectives. Railings, stairways, and fascia boards are often the things people see first. If the deck is raised far above the ground, the posts, beam, and even framing hardware may become the most prominent visual features.

Basic Elements

There are four basic elements to consider when matching your deck design with your house and yard: shape, mass, color, and texture.

Shape. The shape you choose for the deck should harmonize with the lines of your house. The alignment of a deck should in most cases be much more horizontal than vertical. This will give it the light, breezy feeling that you want from an informal space. However, if you are building a raised deck, the posts will define strong vertical lines. If your house is tall and narrow, some of this vertical sense will be welcome, and you may want to repeat these lines. In many cases, you will want to soften the vertical aspect with a series of horizontal lines, using decking and railings.

Think about the deck's overall shape, as well. If your house has a pleasing L-shape, for example, you can repeat that shape with a deck. A house with a confusing shape can be softened with a deck that is simple, and a plain-looking house can be jazzed up with a deck that has a bold shape.

Most people choose to have a deck that is attached to the back of the house and leads to the backyard. You may want to consider other options, such as a wraparound deck, a deck that incorporates a tree, or an island or peninsula deck. You may also need to consider an unattached deck if the design of your home won't allow you to attach the deck to your house safely, such as if you have masonry veneer.

Also examine your house and your yard for existing lines: rectangles, curves, projections, even triangles. Use these as starting points, and think of your deck as providing variations on those themes. If your existing lines are a bit boring, you will want to liven

Unusual angles and mixed materials can be used to complement the style of your house.

A curved deck provides the setting for a graceful railing design.

things up a bit with some new angles—octagonal and other rectilinear shapes are good choices, as are curved lines. But if you already have a good variety of lines, adding complex shapes with your deck will only make for a muddled general impression. Usually, simplicity is best: two or three lines artfully repeated are more pleasing than a jumble of shapes.

You probably can't change the shape of your house to suit your deck, but it is often possible to change your landscape in conjunction with building a deck. You can also design garden edgings or patio surfaces to complement the lines of your deck.

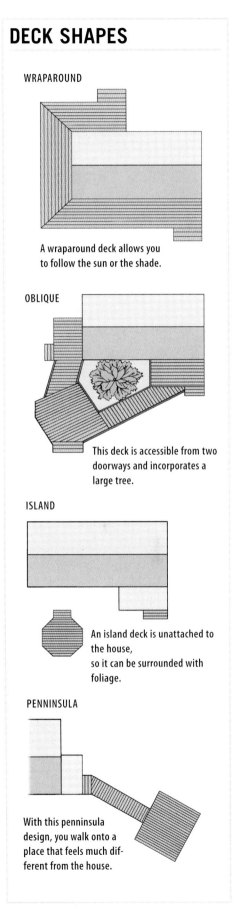

DECK SHAPES

WRAPAROUND

A wraparound deck allows you to follow the sun or the shade.

OBLIQUE

This deck is accessible from two doorways and incorporates a large tree.

ISLAND

An island deck is unattached to the house, so it can be surrounded with foliage.

PENNINSULA

With this penninsula design, you walk onto a place that feels much different from the house.

Mass. The size of a deck should suit the house. The most common problem is a deck that is too massive and overpowers a small house, making the house appear even smaller than it is. Decide which vantage points are the most important, and think about how your deck will appear from the yard and the house.

Many factors affect the visual mass of a deck. For example, building low to the ground or designing railings that are low or light-looking will help the deck recede and thus appear smaller. Large visible beams, railings that are densely packed with boards, and wide fascia boards all will make a deck seem more massive.

Thick 6x6 posts supporting an elevated deck might be the most obvious feature, but an interesting pattern of cross bracing draws attention to thinner wood. And the longer these posts are, the less thick

they appear. **Color.** When people think of a deck, they automatically think of exposed wood. The colors of wood and patterns of wood grain project a relaxed, casual mood. Redwood or cedar decking has beautiful color and looks great right away, but some people find the green tint of some preservative-treated decking unpleasant. All of them will gradually fade to gray after a few years of exposure to the sun unless you stain the deck regularly.

Deck stains come in a wide range of colors, so you can easily find a stain that complements the color of your house. Often a combination of natural wood and stain works—one option is to stain the entire deck except for the cap piece that sits on top of the railing. Another option that avoids a lot of maintenance is to use composite decking and railings that are made to look like wood.

Texture. Wood has a fairly rough texture: Knots, minor cracks, and rough spots are usually considered part of the charm of a deck. Such casualness goes well with almost all landscaping, but it may be unsuitable beside your house. If you need to clean up the lines a bit, buy more-expensive wood with fewer knots. Some synthetic decking materials have an embossed surface that imitates clear wood grain. Some of the better synthetic products have color variations that do a very good job of imitating the look, if not the feel, of wood. (See Chapter 3, page 26 for more on these products.) Other options include metal railings, glass windscreens, latticework, and rough-sawn lumber.

Plan the size and shape of your deck so that it works with the design of the house.

This decking, complements the textures of the garden.

PLAN FOR A BETTER VIEW

Avoid one of the common flaws in many deck designs: a railing that blocks your view. Because most railings rise at least 36 inches above the deck surface, it's wise to place them far away from glass doors and windows. Even on a sloping site where you want the main deck area close to the ground, you can add platform steps near the house, and install the railings around the perimeter of the main deck area. Place shade structures close to the house where they won't block the views.

Built-in benches are a popular option.

Consider how the deck will form a transition from the house to the yard or garden beyond.

Bridging House and Yard

Your deck will be a destination for outdoor living, but it will also be a bridge linking your house and your yard. In fact, a well-designed deck will feel something like a bridge, not only because it is suspended over the ground but also because it balances the amenities of the indoors with those of the outdoors. In addition to the basic elements of mass, shape, color, and texture, here are some specific ways to ensure that your deck makes a graceful transition:

Stepping Down. Where possible, avoid long sections of stairway. Use a series of landings on multiple levels to step down in a way that feels more natural and graceful. Often the challenge is to make sure that each level is a usable and visually pleasing space. Solve this by making the levels cascade—falling off each other at different points or even at different angles—rather than just progressing downward in a straight line like huge steps. But take care: stairs have strict geometric provisions in the code; the landings in this case would have to each be at least 36 inches in the direction of travel to not be considered stair treads.

Deck stairs look best when they are wider and more gradual than you'd typically find indoors. A standard 36-inch-wide stairway starts to look like a ladder if it is more than six steps long. An accurately scaled drawing can help you visualize the best design.

Patio Transition. The stairway from your deck might lead down to a lawn, but a patio or path at the bottom of your steps might work better. Materials that echo your house—bricks, concrete pavers, or colorful crushed stone—are good choices because they strike a nice balance. Patio materials can be rustic or formal, ranging from rough landscaping timbers to mortar set tiles. Natural stone and brick, which are midway between formal and rustic, often work well. Plan the lines of your patio carefully—they are a continuation of the lines in your deck, which in turn should be tied to the lines of your house.

Configuring Planters. It's hard to go wrong with foliage, as long as you can keep it healthy. Any color combination looks great—nature doesn't agonize over paint chips. You can make a planter of the same

material as the deck, and use plants in it that are similar to those in your yard to create a tie-in between deck and yard. And if you can build a planter that harmonizes with the house's exterior, then you can tie in all three elements.

Incorporating Trees. If you have a tree that looks great next to your house, don't cut it down. Build your deck around it, instead, to take advantage of the shade and help the deck blend into the site. Trees near the edge of the deck work well too, forming a sort of arch from yard to house, with the deck in the middle.

💡 SMART TIP

DESIGN FOR SAFETY

Don't forget these elements when designing your deck:
- A railing system that complies with building codes
- Adequate lighting for nighttime safety

A series of broad deck levels, opposite, guides people from the main area down to the pool.

An open deck includes a planting area, right top. Decks give you the option of incorporating shrubs and trees in the design.

Wide steps, right, provide plenty of room for placing container plants and other yard and garden accents.

This deck was built before the current deck code. Handrails are required on stairs with four or more risers (three treads).

immediatly grabs your attention. Perhaps you already have one—a beautiful tree, a lovely view, an inviting pool. Or you can supply a new eye-catcher yourself—a hot tub, a huge potted plant, a series of flower boxes, a well-kept greenhouse, or a statue. Play to your strengths, and position the deck and furniture to accentuate your focal point.

DESIGN CHALLENGES

Every design project hits a snag now and then, whether it turns out that your railing hits the house in the middle of a window or the stairs end in the middle of the driveway, but learn to see these challenges as opportunities to create pleasing points of interesting detail. Solutions to some of these problems are given later in the book, but now is the best time to start thinking about them.

Storage Space. Add storage space by providing access to the area under your deck or by building an attached shed. List the things you need to store, and make sure you have enough room, or they will clutter up your deck.

Lighting. Installing a lighting system adds a lot of charm to your deck, and if you plan now, you can hide at least some of the wires by running them through parts of your deck framing. This is much easier to do before you put the decking down.

Drainage Problems. Drainage will only be a problem in the future if it is a problem now. For minor problems, plan a gravel-filled trench in the ground to collect runoff from your deck and direct it away from the site. If you have major water problems, such as frequent standing water or significant erosion, be sure to deal with them before you build the deck.

Adding an Outbuilding. If a gazebo, shed, or play structure is in your future, include it in your plans now. There may be a simple way to tie it to the deck and the house. For example, make the roof of the same materials as the roof on your house and paint the rest of the structure the same color as your house. Play structures can usually be built of the same woods used to build the deck.

Theme and Variation. The best decks take one or two great ideas and then work out variations on those general themes.

The theme could be a gently curved line that you use in several places, such as the edge of the decking, the railings, and a path next to the deck. Or you may experiment with a unique decking pattern: have three or four sections that break off of each other at similar angles, for instance. If you have a large octagonal-shaped projection, you may be able to add a smaller version of it elsewhere on the deck, or you can echo the shape by building an octagonal table or bench.

The most visible elements of a deck are often those that project vertically. Choose railings or benches to harmonize with the overall structure. Planters should echo the deck structure.

A great deck usually has a stunning focal point, something that

The designer of this deck extended the railing design up to the trim on the gazebo roof, opposite.

If you are planning on adding a shade structure, incorporate it into your plans from the beginning, right.

Pergolas and arbors add vertical visual interest to deck designs, below.

In addition to being compatible with the surroundings, this deck conforms to the site.

Sloping Sites. A sloping site makes the construction process more difficult but also presents an opportunity for an interesting, multilevel deck.

Trees. Trees on a deck site also present a chance to do something stunning, such as building the deck around the tree. Consider the age of your tree and how fast it will grow, and plan to leave ample space.

Pools and Hot Tubs. Building a deck with a pool, hot tub, or spa requires precise planning, engineering, and cutting. Think carefully about how high and wide you want the decking around pools and tubs for maximum sitting and sunning pleasure. Hot tubs either have to be placed on a slab on grade, with the deck built around them, or they are placed on the deck. If they are placed on the deck, the deck structure is engineered to accomodate the tub and its weight.

Shade and Access. If you want some shade but don't have foliage overhead, add some louvered structures or brightly colored awnings. For areas with heavy rainfall, build a roof extension.

Plan access hatches so you can get at plumbing or electrical service junctions underneath the deck, just in case something needs repairing someday. Little trap doors and hatches that would look tacky inside are charming on a deck. But check your local building code, as various electrical equipment—service panels, receptacle outlets, GFCI devices, etc.—each have their own specific clearance requirements.

Guards are usually required on any deck over 30 inches above the ground, as measured 36 inches horizontally from the edge of the deck. This is to address a sharp slope or cliff right at the edge of the deck at grade. Plan now if you want to include any custom design features or unusual patterns in your railings. A built-in bench adds visual interest to a long expanse of railing as well.

OVERLOOKED DECK LOCATIONS

Decks aren't always found hugging the ground right next to the back door. An island deck isn't attached to the house at all, so it can go virtually anywhere on your property. However, roofs typically only have to resist a 20 pounds-per-square-foot load, whereas a floor has to resist, at minimum, a 40 pounds per square foot load. This means that you have to ensure your roof will be able to support that kind of weight if you want to build a rooftop deck. This is not typically a DIY project.

Another popular option is to build a private deck off the master bedroom and change a window into a door.

A new deck need not be built tight against the house. This section of deck juts out into the garden for a better view of the surroundings.

This deck was built before the current deck code. Handrails are required on stairs with four or more risers (three treads).

When planning, think of the various uses for your deck. Here, having a shaded spa was an important consideration.

FINAL DRAWINGS

Once you have made all your decisions regarding site, substructure, decking, stairs, and railings, you are ready to finalize your plans. The finished drawings should be clear: do not rely on scribbled-over and often-erased sheets—take the extra time to draw a clean set of plans because they will be easier to follow.

The set of deck plans at the end of this chapter is a good example of what you'll need to produce in order to get your building permit. After reviewing these drawings and your site plan, your building department will either issue you a permit or ask for some changes.

Plan Drawings

Plan drawings show the deck framing from above. For these drawings, it is common to leave out the railings and decking. Be sure to include the following:

- Correct dimensional drawing of the perimeter
- All joists, beams, posts, and footings
- Dimensions for all lumber
- The distance spanned by beams and joists
- Indication of size and direction of decking (It's not usually necessary to draw this.)
- Hardware, such as joist hangers, angle brackets, and bolts
- Exact locations of doors and windows
- Any electrical and plumbing fixtures and lines

Elevation Drawing

An elevation drawing shows the deck in cross-section from the side. Draw at least one elevation, including these elements:

- A detailed drawing of the railing system, including all dimensions that pertain to local codes
- Views of the concrete footings, with dimensions showing how deep and wide they will be
- Hardware list, including sizes of post anchors, tread cleats, and bolts
- Height of the tallest post
- A rough approximation of the site's slope

Detail Drawings

Draw close-up views of complicated spots on your deck. Sometimes you will need to make a detail drawing to satisfy the building department. At other times, you may need it yourself in order to figure things out. Draw details for situations like these:

- Where the stair railing meets the rest of the deck railing

- Hatchways for access to electrical and plumbing
- Framing around trees or hot tubs
- Changes in level
- Any area of the deck with special framing, such as extra joists under a section of deck that will support a portable hot tub
- Flashing around ledger

Deck Location Considerations

- Overhead electrical service cables
- Windows adjacent to stairs, ramps, hot tubs need safety glazing (tempered glass)
- Below-grade egress window wells from basements
- Electrical service panel and AC condenser and disconnect clearances
- Foundation vents, combustion air openings, dryer exhaust vents, other vents

SAMPLE DETAIL DRAWING

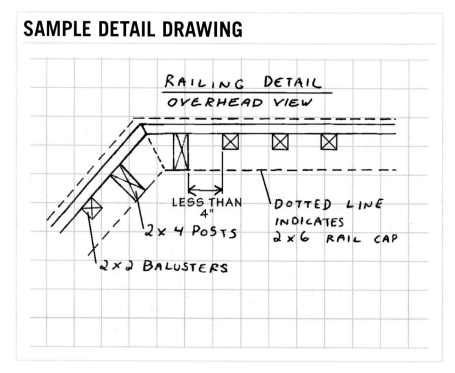

RAILING DETAIL
OVERHEAD VIEW

LESS THAN 4"

2x4 POSTS

2x2 BALUSTERS

DOTTED LINE INDICATES 2x6 RAIL CAP

SAMPLE PLAN DRAWING

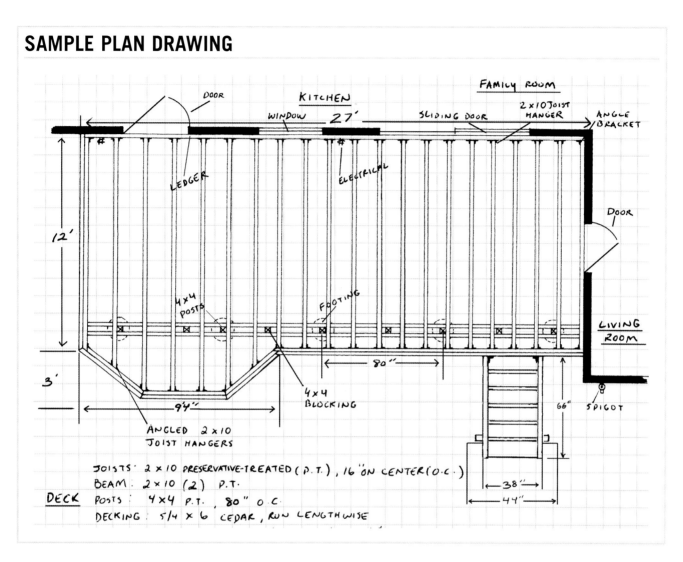

SAMPLE ELEVATION DRAWING

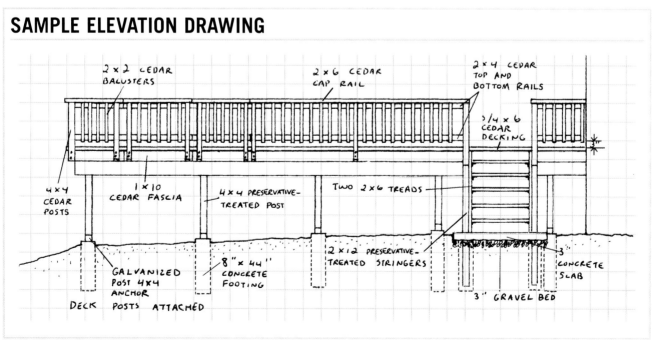

There is no one way to build decks—except the correct way. While inspection methods vary, all inspectors tend to zero in on one area: the ledger, to make sure the deck is securely attached to the house. Of course, there is more to building a deck then simply passing the inspections. The techniques you use will not only make the deck functional but will also contribute to the overall appearance of the deck. This chapter covers basic building techniques, including the laying out and the cutting of curved surfaces on the deck.

MEASURING AND MARKING

Good carpentry begins with accurate measuring and marking. Get in the habit of using the same techniques every time, and your work will be much more precise.

Using a Measuring Tape

You'll use your measuring tape for taking most of the measurements on your project. You will notice that the metal hook at the end of the tape is a bit loose. It is made that way on purpose: it moves back and forth ⅛ inch, which is also exactly how thick it is. This means that you will get the correct measurement both when you hook the end of your measuring tape over the end of a piece of wood, or when you butt it up against something to take an inside measurement.

Make sure you pull the tape straight before you measure. If it curves in any way, you'll get a bad reading. If a helper is calling out measurements for you to cut, make sure that their measuring tape agrees with yours—sometimes the hook gets bent, which can throw your cut off by ⅛ inch or so.

Scribing in Place

When possible, the easiest and most accurate way to measure is not to measure at all, but rather to hold the lumber in place and mark it for cutting. This usually involves butting one end of the board exactly to the spot

💡 SMART TIP

STEP-AHEAD LAYOUT

To inexperienced DIYers, the carpentry technique of marking a step-ahead layout may seem a little simpleminded—after all, you just measure for a modular framing layout (usually 16 inches on center), draw a guideline with a pencil and a square, and then take the extra step of marking a large X beside the line, working in the direction of your layout. However, this way there will be no confusion when it comes time to place joists. If you always cover the X and align the joist to the line, you'll never stray from the on-center layout.

ACCURATE LEVELING

Here are some popular leveling tools.

1. A carpenter's level normally has bubbles. This one displays a digital readout.
2. Laser levels used to be only for contractors, but some new models have come down in price. The red beam projects a level line against any surface on your site.

where it will rest and marking a cut line on the other end.

If you must cut a number of boards to the same length, cut one and use it as a template for making cuts on the others. Mark a "P" for pattern so every board is to this length and install it last when done using it.

Sometimes it's best not to precut the boards at all, but instead let each piece run wild. It's common to let the decking boards run wild initially, then snap a chalk line and cut them all off in place.

Marking for Cuts

When you make that little pencil mark on the wood indicating the exact length to cut, be sure you know which part of the mark indicates the cut line. Most carpenters make a V, with the bottom point indicating the precise spot. Using your square, draw a line through the V, and make a large X on the side of the board that will be waste. (See "Smart Tip," opposite.)

To mark long lines, snap a chalk line. Have a helper hold one end, or tack a nail and hook the clip onto it. Pull the line very taut, be sure it's in position on both ends, pick the line straight up several inches, and then let go. For long lines or a wavy surface, you may need to first snap your end and then have your helper snap theirs.

For very long lines, tack the far end and have your helper put a finger on the center point, then snap both sides.

There are usually a variety of ways to complete a building task; just be sure the way you pick will meet the local building code.

CUTTING USING A CIRCULAR SAW

For all saw adjustments and checks below, be sure the saw is unplugged. You'll use your circular saw so much in the course of building a deck that you'll soon become comfortable with the tool. But don't let that make you overconfident. When it comes to power tools, complacency can be very dangerous. A circular saw can injure you in a fraction of a second if you are careless.

So take basic safety precautions: know where your power cord is at all times; be sure your retractable blade guard works properly. Avoid kickbacks by correctly positioning the board you are cutting. Don't stand directly behind the saw when cutting—position your body to one side. And keep your blade sharp so that it's less likely to bind.

Test for Squareness

You can't always trust the degree markings on your saw's bevel gauge, so take the time to verify them before you make many cuts.

Set your saw for zero-degree bevel, and crosscut a scrap piece of 2x4. Roll one of the cut pieces over, and butt them together on a flat surface. If your blade is not square to the base, you'll see a gap at the bottom or the top of the cut equal to twice the amount your blade is out of square. (See "Test for Squareness," page 73.)

If you see a gap, unplug the saw, turn it upside down, and loosen the bevel adjustment. Set a square on the base and hold it against the blade. (See "Smart Tip," right.) Hold the square against the body of the blade, not the teeth; the teeth are offset and will throw off your adjustment. Tighten the bevel adjustment when the blade and base bear evenly on the square.

Making Accurate Square Cuts

Work on a stable surface that won't move during the cut. To avoid kickback, make sure that the cutoff can fall away without binding.

Position the Workpiece. If the cutoff will be long, don't just let it fall to the ground. If you do, the weight of the unsupported cutoff might cause the board to break off before you finish the cut, leaving a jagged piece sticking out at the end of the board. Provide something for the cutoff to fall onto that is only an inch or two below it.

Align the Blade to the Line. A spinning saw blade carves a groove through the wood—that groove is called a kerf. One edge of the kerf lines up on your cut line;

💡 **SMART TIP**

SAW SETUP

To use a circular saw safely, avoid blade binding and kickback by supporting lumber so that the cut opens and the pieces fall away as you saw. Install a new carbide-tipped blade for best results, and check the saw shoe for square.

An arbor lock freezes the blade.

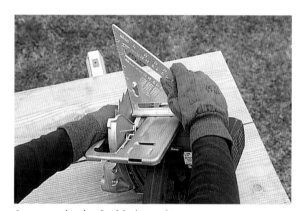

A square checks the blade angle.

the rest of the blade's width should be on the waste side of the line. Standard saw blades cut a ⅛-inch-wide kerf, though you might find thin-kerf blades at the store, too. These blades cut kerfs around 1/16 inch wide. Because they are removing less wood, they require less force to make the cut.

Whatever size kerf you cut, be sure you cut to the waste side of the line so that your board will not end up shorter than you marked it.

Remember that the teeth on a circular saw blade are offset. One tooth veers to the left, the next to the right, and so on in an alternating pattern. Take this into account when you line up the blade to the cut line: first, select a tooth that's offset toward the cut line, and align the saw so that the tooth just touches the line. Then look at the front edge of your saw's base to find the alignment notch. Pivot the saw body until the zero-degree mark in the notch lines up with your cut line.

Make the Cut. Always wear safety glasses when using poser tools. To operate the saw, squeeze the trigger and saw with a light, steady pressure, allowing the blade to set the feed rate. You might want to use a cutting guide when making your first few crosscuts until you have a feel for the saw, but if you want to make a lot of cuts quickly, you should also learn to cut freehand.

This actually takes only a bit of practice. Get in the habit of keeping your eye on the leading edge of the blade, and become acquainted with the best way to align your saw. When you cut, push through smoothly, without micromanaging the cut by making little turns back and forth. Soon you will easily be making accurate cuts.

For precise cuts, use a guide. An angle square works well. (See page 70, photo 2.) Make sure your saw's base butts up well against the guide and won't easily slide over on top of it. Hold the square in place against the edge of the board, and set the base of your saw so that its edge bears firmly against the edge of the square. Slide the square and saw until the saw blade lines up with the cut line. Make sure the square doesn't slip during the cut.

SAFE CUTTING TECHNIQUES

1. WITH THE SAW UNPLUGGED, adjust your cutting depth so that just the teeth of the blade extend below the wood. This is the safest way to cut efficiently.

2. PLACE THE STOCK on 2x4 scraps to raise it off the work surface. Clamp the board in place so you can use two hands to make a safe and accurate cut. Always run the base of the saw along the supported side of the cut so that the waste can drop away at the end of the cut.

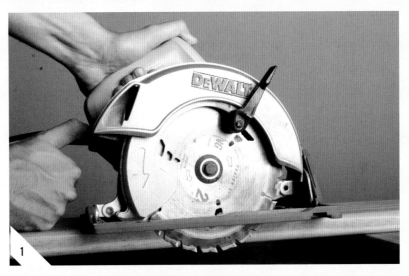

Cutting Miter Angles

A mitered cut doesn't go straight across the board—it is a bisect angle across the face to leave one edge of the board longer than the other. The most common miter angle used in deck construction is 45 degrees, and it's typically used where the decking or handrails meet at a right-angle corner.

Miter cuts can be hard to get exactly right. Sometimes the blade guard hangs up on the edge of the board at the beginning of the cut, making it difficult to start straight. Cutting from the long point of the miter angle to the short point can eliminate this issue. And you're working in an unusual position, which takes some getting used to. If your decking or railing design calls for a lot of miter cutting, you may want to consider renting a power miter saw.

Cutting using a miter saw comes in handy when railings or decking meet at a right angle.

SQUARE CUTTING

Whenever possible, keep two hands on the saw during a cut.

1. Use a square to mark the cut line. Place an "X" on the side of the line that is the waste side. Then set the saw with the shoe parallel with the line, align the front guide notch, and start cutting.

2. You can use a square guide to help with precise cuts, but this method leaves only one hand on the saw.

3. Use a rip guide to control long cuts in line with the wood grain. The T-shaped guide is available for most circular saws.

TEST FOR SQUARENESS

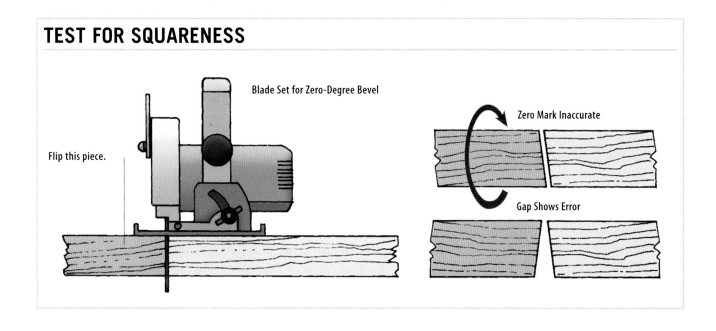

Blade Set for Zero-Degree Bevel

Flip this piece.

Zero Mark Inaccurate

Gap Shows Error

Ripping

When ripping lumber with a circular saw—that is, cutting it the long way to make a board narrower—a ripping guide comes in handy. (See photo 3, page 73.) The guide has a shoe that runs along the side of the board as you cut it along its length. This is a steel guide designed to fit your particular saw and usually attaches to the base with a thumbscrew.

Cutting Dadoes and Rabbets

Technically, a dado is a groove cut across the grain of a piece of lumber. A rabbet is similar to a dado, except that a rabbet is on the end of the member. In deck building, there are not many places where you would use rabbets and dadoes, but you might cut a rabbet at the top of a support post to receive a beam. Be sure to set the blade depth the correct distance when cutting these features or the post may be damaged with too deep of a saw kerf.

Cutting Notches

A notch is essentially a dado or rabbet, but in a board instead of a post or beam. The most common reason you'll need to cut notches in deck building is to fit a decking board around a railing post. The first step is to mark for the notch.

Mark the Notch. Start by putting the board you need to notch on top of the last full board you installed next to the

Use your circular saw to cut angles, dadoes, rabbets, notches (as shown here), and more.

post. Then slide the board over against the post, and mark the width of the notch, defined by the edges of the post, on the face of the decking board. Now measure how deep the notch needs to be, and lay out the notch with your square. Remember to include the spacing between your decking boards as you lay it out. Keep the board in position while you make your marks so that you can visualize as you go, and you will be less likely to make the common mistake of measuring on the wrong side of the board.

USING A WATER LEVEL: THE OLD-SCHOOL METHOD

A water level is a low-tech tool that uses a basic principle of physics: that water always seeks its own level. The inexpensive tool consists of a clear, flexible plastic tube and a couple of clips to fasten the tube in place. To use it, simply fill the tube with water (and a dye to make the level easier to read), and wait for the water to stabilize at the ends of the tube. The center portion of the tube can snake up and down over the site in any direction, and the water at each end will still be dead level.

Find level over distances.

Dyed water is easier to read.

Complex deck designs are attractive, but they usually require the know-how to make a variety of cuts. Practice on scrap lumber before making a new cut.

Make the Shoulder Cuts. Start the shoulder cut or cuts by cutting in with a circular saw until the kerf just hits the seat cut layout line. Because the saw's circular blade cuts a curved path through the wood, there may still be some wood to remove at the bottom of the cut. You'll need to finish the shoulder cuts using a handsaw, reciprocating saw, or saber saw. If the cut is a little uneven when you're finished with the notch, try smoothing the cuts with a chisel.

Finish the Notch. For a notch at the end of a board, make the seat cut in the same way. If the notch is in the middle of the board and the wood is straight grained with no knots in the way, make the seat cut with your chisel. Place the chisel along the seat cut line with the flat side facing away from the waste. Make sure the chisel is perpendicular to the board, and give it a sharp hammer blow.

Otherwise, make the seat cut with a saber saw or reciprocating saw. Another option is to nibble away the waste with repeated circular-saw cuts into the seat cut as you did for the shoulder cuts; then clean it up with a chisel.

Making a Plunge Cut

Occasionally you have to cut a hole in the middle of a board. You could drill a pilot hole and use a saber saw, but for a straighter line, use your circular saw to make a plunge cut (sometimes called a pocket cut).

Make sure your power cord is out of the way, and grasp the saw with both hands. Position the saw and raise up the back, using the front of the foot plate as a fulcrum. Now hold the blade guard so that the blade is exposed, and lower the saw until the blade is just above the right spot. When you are sure everything is safe and aligned, squeeze the trigger, and slowly lower the blade down to make the cut. If you do not twist as you go, you will be able to move forward with the saw after you have plunged through the board, but be sure the foot plate is resting fully on the board before you do so.

ATTACHING A LEDGER

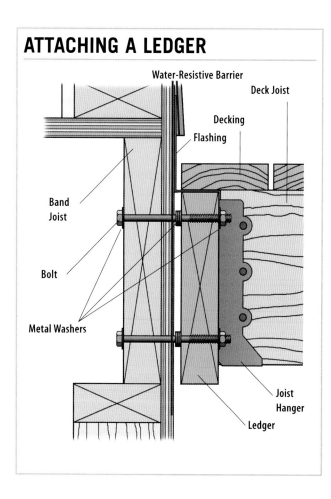

Water-Resistive Barrier
Deck Joist
Decking
Flashing
Band Joist
Bolt
Metal Washers
Joist Hanger
Ledger

💡 SMART TIP

LEDGER CHECK

To check the flatness of a ledger or house wall, nail two same-thickness blocks at each end and string a line between them. A third same-sized block should just tuck under the string. Where it doesn't fit, you'll see the margin of high and low spots.

CUTTING POSTS

Most do-it-yourselfers don't have a circular saw with enough capacity to cut through a 4x4 support post in one pass. That leaves two options. You can use a handsaw to cut straight through, or make two passes (from opposing sides) with a standard circular saw. Take the time to make square marks around the post to serve as a guide. And because posts typically are treated lumber, remember to wear a respirator mask, gloves, and safety glasses.

Cutting 6x6 posts, which are even more common, will likely require a reciprocating saw to finish the cut after using the circular saw to start the cuts.

Cutting 4x4s

A 7¼-inch circular saw will not cut all the way through a 4x4 in one pass, so you'll need to cut from two opposing sides. Using a square, draw a line all the way around the 4x4: if the last line meets up with the first, you know your layout lines are square. Then make cuts on two opposite sides. If your blade is square and you cut accurately, the entire cut will be fairly smooth, but don't expect perfection. In nearly every case, the top of a 4x4 gets covered up by other pieces of wood anyway.

If you are cutting off a 4x4 that has a piece of lumber, such as a built-up girder or outside joist, attached to it, first cut whatever you can get at with a circular saw to remove most of the waste; then finish the cut with a handsaw or reciprocating saw. In many cases you can use the second piece of lumber as a guide for the saw.

NAILING

Some contractors have a one-question test for new carpenters: they just hand the prospective employee a hammer and watch how he grips it. If the guy wraps his thumb around the shaft, he's in, but if he extends the thumb up the handle toward the head, he's out. The second grip puts less power in each swing and can result in serious damage to the tendons in the wrist. Good nailing technique, once learned, becomes second nature.

💡 SMART TIP

PREDRILLING

Where you have to make a butt joint between boards, predrill each end at a slight angle to avoid splitting the wood as you drive nails. On a long deck, be sure to stagger butt joints so that they don't line up and fall on only one or two joists.

Predrill each board at butt joints.

Nails won't split predrilled boards.

PNEUMATIC NAILING

To make sure your compressor can handle a framing nailer, check out the specs. A nailer needs 3 cubic feet per minute (cfm) of air at 90 pounds per square inch (psi). There are now battery powered nail guns, making this technology an increasingly viable option for the do-it-yourselfer.

1. Air-powered nailers speed work by firing nails from a clip that you slip into a slot below the handle. An air compressor powers the tool.

2. The most important safety feature on a pneumatic nailer is a lock-out safety tip. This keeps the tools from firing accidentally, even if you squeeze the trigger.

Reducing Stresses and Misses

Many handymen and even some pro carpenters do not have good nailing technique. A common mistake is to hold the hammer too stiffly, with the wrist locked in place. Instead, let your wrist flex a little, and finish each stroke with a snap of the wrist. Spend some time practicing; as you gain confidence, you will become more relaxed, and letting the wrist flex will come naturally.

Start with a hammer weight that feels comfortable when you swing it, weighing maybe 16 or 20 ounces. Hold the nail in place, and hit it once or twice until it can stand on its own. Then drive it home with several powerful strokes.

Avoiding Splits

Whenever you are nailing near the end of a board (or near what will be the end once the board is cut off), take precautions to minimize splitting. Remember that any little split you see now will only get larger in time; and some spots that look OK now can develop splits later.

There are two techniques. First, you can predrill each hole. This may seem bothersome, but if you can do a whole row of nails at once, it really doesn't take much time. And the extra 15 minutes you spend now will mean a much better-looking deck for years to come. Use a drill bit that's slightly smaller than the diameter of your nail shaft.

Another less effective but easier technique is to blunt the nail before driving it. Hold the nail upside down against a solid surface, and tap the tip a few times with your hammer to blunt it. This reduces the outward strain that the nail puts on the board.

Skewing

If you're driving two nails through a decking board and into the joist below, skew the nails, or angle them toward each other a little. This creates a stronger connection by hooking the boards together and reduces the possibility of splitting.

Toenailing

Most of the time, when two boards need to be joined at a right angle, you drive a nail through the face of one board into the other.

But sometimes the face into which you would prefer to nail is inaccessible, or the piece you have to nail through is too thick. In cases like this, toenail the pieces together.

Toenailing means nailing at an angle through the end of one board into the face of another. Position an 8d or 10d nail about 1½ inches from the end of the board. Get the nail started; then adjust it to a steep angle so the tip will come out near the center of the board's end grain. If possible, drive two nails on each side of the board.

The code only requires toenailing of joists down to a 2-ply or larger beam below. This connection is for lateral restraint. You can also toenail a rafter down and the code allows it to resist uplift loads up to a limit. Reinforce the joint with framing hardware whenever possible. Do not use toenails to connect the ends of joists to a flush beam.

SMART TIP

TOENAILING

When you can't nail through the face of one board into the end of another, drive toenails. Start the nail at a slight angle, and after a few blows increase the angle to drive the nail in. Don't rely on toenails solely to make structural connectors. Be sure to include a baluster at each end of all handrails.

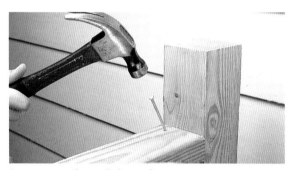

Start a toenail at a slight angle.

Increase the angle as you nail.

DRILLS AND SCREW GUNS

Though nailing has its advantages, there's a lot to be said for fastening with screws. They hold more firmly than nails and are easier to remove or tighten. Screws generally cost more, but the extra expense is usually a small part of your materials budget. And once you get the hang of using them, screws can actually be easier to use than nails.

With practice, anyone can master the art of driving screws. A screw gun or a special attachment for your drill can help: it sets the depth automatically and makes it difficult for the driver bit to slip completely off the screwhead.

A screw gun is different from a regular drill, either corded or cordless. The chuck will only drive screws—you can't put a regular drill bit in it to drill holes. The depth of drive is adjustable.

Drive all your screws to a uniform depth, just below the surface of the lumber. A deeply sunken screw head is a place for water to collect, leading to decay.

FASTENING TIPS

Nailing decking boards requires some delicate work with the hammer to avoid damaging the wood. A nail set eases the process, but also slows it down. The best bet with screws is a screw gun with an adjustable depth-of-drive feature. Various types of hidden fasteners leave the face of the board untouched.

1. When driving nails, the final blow should seat the nail without leaving a mark.

2. Dents create pockets that hold water.

3. When using a pneumatic nailer, the force of the gun should match the density of the wood to seat the nail flush.

4. Too much force can cause splits that will trap water.

5. As with nails, screws should seat flush.

6. Use a drill/driver with torque control for best results. A poorly driven screw will damage the surface.

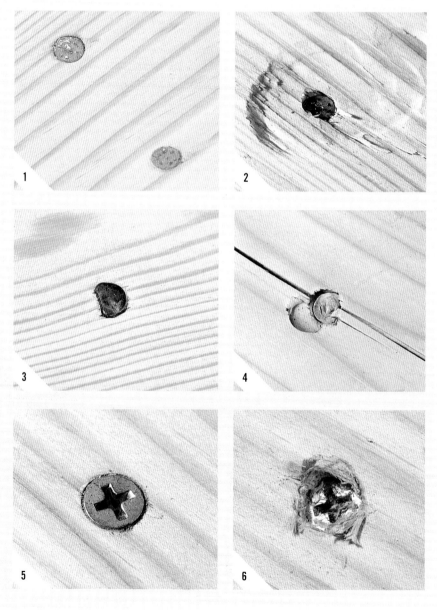

DECAY-RESISTANT DESIGN

In addition to choosing the best wood possible, construction methods such as those that follow will help reduce decay and minimize the effects of wood shrinkage over time.

Protecting Open Grain

When you look at the end of a board, you are looking at the open grain, also called end grain. Open grain soaks up rainwater—and any other liquid—like a sponge, making it the most vulnerable part of a piece of lumber.

For this reason, cover up open grain whenever it is possible. This is especially important when the open grain is horizontal, or facing up, so that water can sit on it. Plan your deck railings carefully to eliminate exposed horizontal open grain whenever possible.

Avoiding Trapped Water

Of course, a certain amount of open grain is unavoidable—the ends of decking boards typically have exposed end grain. This usually isn't a problem as long as the boards can dry out quickly after they get wet. In fact, covering vertical open grain with wood or butting it against the house often increases the likelihood of decay. Unless the wood stays tightly butted against the house for years, which is unlikely, there will be small gaps in which water can collect and sit.

CONCEALING END GRAIN

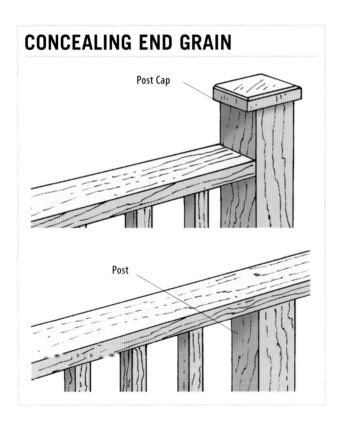

Post Cap

Post

AVOIDING TRAPPED WATER

There are often small gaps between attached decks and walls. Water can become trapped against the house and the open wood grain of the deck, increasing the chances of decay. Correctly installed flashing will allow water to flow out and away from these gaps, keeping it from becoming trapped and decreasing the likelihood of decay.

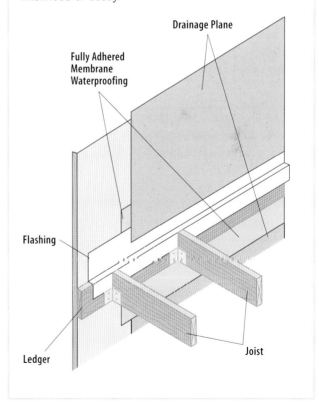

Drainage Plane

Fully Adhered Membrane Waterproofing

Flashing

Ledger

Joist

Tightening Butt Joints

If possible, plan your decking pattern to minimize butt joints. This may mean spending extra money for longer boards, but you will end up with a deck that has fewer problem spots.

When you make butt joints, take steps to ensure that they will remain tight for years. Choose dry lumber to minimize shrinkage. After you have installed the first board, firmly tap the second toward the first before you fasten it. Drive your nails or screws at an angle so that they pull the decking boards tightly together.

Treating Open Grain

The code requires that cut ends, holes, and other abrasions in preservative-treated lumber be field treated with preservatives.

For boards that will get a lot of contact with moisture, the most effective way is to set the end of the board in a container of preservative and let it soak for a few minutes. A more common solution is to brush it on. Plan ahead: in some places you can brush on preservative after the deck is built, but in other places, such as where the decking meets the house, you won't be able to get at it.

LAYING OUT AND CUTTING CURVES

For short curved edges, mark the cut line with a compass—don't just eyeball it and expect it to come out right. For longer curves, make your own compass out of a pencil, a length of string, and a nail driven into the deck.

Experiment with centers and compass openings until you find the curve that pleases you. (**Step 1**) Tack a nail at that point, and tie your string to it. Tie the other end to your pencil, and experiment to be sure you've got it right. It's easy to make mistakes, so do a dry run without making any marks on the deck boards. Be sure to hold the pencil at the same angle at all times. (**Step 2**) When cutting out a curve, be sure you have a heavy-duty saber saw, one that cuts with ease and does not wobble. (**Step 3**) Spend some time practicing on scrap pieces of lumber first—a mistake here might be difficult to correct. Don't force the saw through the cut—let it proceed at its own pace. Pushing too hard could deflect the blade and leave you with a bad cut.

Smoothing and Rounding

It's a good idea to spend time smoothing rough spots and rounding off sharp edges of decking and railings. For a small amount of time and effort, your deck will take on

💡 SMART TIP

WHEN TO CAULK

Most decks require little if any caulk because they are designed to drain. But you might need some caulk where elements of the deck meet the house—for example, where a railing joins the house siding and where a ledger board or ledger flashing meets the foundation. If you do apply caulk, choose a type that combines long life with good adhesion, either straight silicone caulk or a siliconized latex caulk.

a more finished, handcrafted look. And your family and friends will be less likely to encounter splinters.

The best way to round off decking and other parts of the deck is with a router and roundover bit. (**Step 4**) If set properly, this is a nearly mistake-proof method of rounding. But the router will probably not be able to reach every part of your deck that needs rounding, and you will have to finish some spots by hand using a file.

Some good places for rounding are the edges of decking, rail caps, built-in benches, and exposed posts and beams. You can do most of the rest of your smoothing with a sander or sanding block. (**Step 5**) You may have to start with a rough-grit sandpaper and then go over it all again with medium-grit paper. (80-grit is fine for finishing; a finer paper is rarely needed.) Whenever possible, use long, smooth strokes rather than short quick ones. And it doesn't pay to press down hard; a moderate amount of pressure usually lifts off just as much. Usually, the only areas on a deck that you should consider smoothing are those places that people often handle or against which they rub, such as rail caps, seats, tables, and play areas.

For rounding off, the trick is to decide how much you are going to round off, and then stick with the same pattern. If some parts are only slightly rounded while more wood is removed from other places, the deck will look sloppy and haphazardly built.

For softer woods, the sanding block will do a moderate amount of rounding off. Though it may take some fairly heavy work, the advantage of a sanding block is that you can't make a big mistake. For more extensive jobs, consider a belt sander. But be careful—it's easy to make a deep gouge very quickly if you hold a belt sander in one place for too long.

PROJECT: 🐾🐾🐾
CUTTING CORNER CURVES

Curved edges on a deck add lots of visual interest but require careful framing. (See page 137.) A perfect layout is crucial, so take your time with the setup and the cutting.

TOOLS & MATERIALS
- Measuring tape
- Pencil
- Nail
- Hammer
- Saber saw
- Router & bits
- Sander

1 Think of the curve you want as part of a circle. Find the center by measuring the radius from each edge.

2 The intersection of the lines is the center. Use the nail, string, and pencil to draw a curve on the deck.

3 Use a saber saw to cut the corner curve. Support large waste pieces while cutting.

4 For a finished appearance, smooth the edges with a router fitted with a roundover bit.

5 Sand the edge for a final finishing. You can use a random-orbit sander or a sanding block.

6

FOOTINGS AND FOUNDATIONS

Decks are only as strong as the foundation on which they rest. Deck foundations consist of footings that reach below the minimum frost line depth required by code and that support strong posts. If the footings are strong, the joists, decking, rails, and stairs they support are likely to stay where you put them. Footings are the basis of every good deck, and building them begins with some heavy-duty digging.

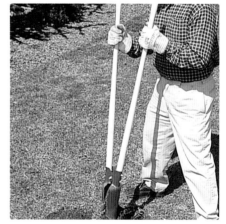

LAYING OUT THE DECK

The footings will be the least visible element of your deck, so there is a temptation to treat them with nonchalance. But if footings are not set accurately, correcting those mistakes during the rest of the job could be a colossal pain. So take the time to check, cross-check, and recheck every step of the way.

It's best to have a helper for this, not only because you need someone to pull strings taut, hold one end of the measuring tape, and help make adjustments, but also because two heads are usually better than one when working.

Locate the Ledger. The ledger board is usually the primary reference point for the deck. You may even want to install the ledger first and then go on to laying out and digging the foundation. (See "Preparing for the Ledger," pages 104–105.) In any case, to lay out the footings, you first need to mark the ends of the ledger. Account for the outside joists and the fascia board, if there will be any

Draw a Reference Line. Once you have marked the ends of the ledger on your house, use a level or a plumb bob to bring the line down to a place on the house near the ground. If your yard slopes appreciably downward from the house, place this mark near the ground. If the yard is fairly level, make the mark a foot or so off the ground. Attach a screw or nail to this spot so that you can tie a string line to it.

PROJECT:
LAYING OUT LINES

You can tailor the 3-4-5 method for determining a square corner to suit your project: use multiples of those numbers, such as 9-12-15.

TOOLS & MATERIALS
- 1x4 lumber
- Saw
- Drill-driver
- Layout strings
- Measuring tape
- Level
- Plumb bob

1 Construct batter boards from the 1x4 lumber. Make pointy ends to drive the boards into the ground.

3 To be certain that your angle will be 90 degrees, use the 3-4-5 technique: with a measuring tape, measure the short side of the triangle to be 3 ft.; the adjacent side should measure 4 ft.; and the longest leg will be 5 ft. This will create a right triangle, and thus, give you a square corner.

4 You could also measure the diagonals. If they are equal, the corners are square. Be sure all the lines you are checking are level with each other.

Assemble Batter Boards. For each outside deck corner you will be locating, construct two batter boards. **(Step 1)** Make these by attaching a 36- or 48-inch-long crosspiece squarely across two stakes. You can buy premade stakes at the lumberyard, or simply cut pieces of 2x4 or 1x4 to a point on one end. Although they are temporary and will be used only to hold string lines, the batter boards must be sturdy—there is a good chance they will get bumped around.

Lay Out the Perimeter. Measure from the house to determine the approximate location of your posts, and roughly mark lines, using a string or long pieces of lumber. You want this measurement line to run through the center of the posts, meaning that you have to take into account thicknesses of beams and outside joists: a

2 Set the batter boards in pairs a few feet outside of the actual contruction zone. Attach lines.

5 Use a plumb bob or level at the intersection of your lines to determine the location of the corner pier.

two-by is 1½ inches thick, and the center of a 4x4 is 1¾ inches from each edge. Pound a stake into the ground or otherwise mark the location at the (again, rough) intersections of the lines.

Establish Centers at Corner Footings. Firmly pound two batter boards into the ground 16 inches or so beyond the stake in each direction. Run string lines from the house to the batter boards and from batter board to batter board in the other direction if necessary. **(Step 2)** On the ledger, the string line will usually be run 1¾ inches in from the outside ends of the ledger location.

Now check for square using the 3-4-5 method: measure along your house or ledger board, and mark a point 3 feet in from the nail holding the string. Now measure along the string and use a piece of tape to mark a spot 4 feet from the house. Finally, measure the distance between the two marks. If this is exactly 5 feet, then you have a square corner. **(Step 3)** If you have the room, you can be more accurate by using multiples of 3, 4, and 5 feet—for example, 9, 12, and 15.

Double-check the layout for square by taking three pairs of measurements; the two lengths of your rectangle should be equal to each other, as should the two widths and the two diagonals. **(Step 4)** Once you have established that your lines are square, attach them securely to the batter boards using a nail or screw to make sure that they cannot slip sideways when someone bumps into the string.

Mark for Postholes. Use a plumb bob or chalk-line box, which can double as a plumb bob, or a level to mark the spot on the ground that will be the center of each post— and therefore the center of each posthole. For the corner posts, bring a plumb line down from the intersection of your lines. **(Step 5)** Hold the line until the bob (or chalk-line box) stops swaying, and mark the spot with a small stake.

The next step is to clear the area of plants and sod that may get in the way of your deck. Be sure to mark the post locations before tackling the landscape work. Of course, you could also remove plants, lawn, and the like before laying out for the deck's posts. If you remove too much lawn or plants, you can go back and fill in with plantings along the deck's perimeter later.

DISTRIBUTING THE LOAD

A deck's footings must support not only the dead load of the deck—the total weight of the framing, decking, railings, benches, and planters—but also the nonpermanent weight called live load—things like snow, people, and furniture. Building codes mandate a residential deck support 40 pounds per square foot, but in some regions they require 60 pounds per square foot. Dead load must be supported, whatever it is. Code assumes 10 pounds per square foot is the maximum dead load, and if you use heavier decking—a paver system, for example—then you need an alternative design, since this would exceed what the code assumes. So your footings must be strong enough to handle 50 pounds per square foot of deck (8,000 pounds for a 10 x 16-foot deck).

This load is distributed through the framing structure to the footings set in the ground. Typically, the ledger will shoulder its portion because it's bolted to the house and transfers its load to the house's foundation. However, if the house wall itself is cantilevered over the foundation, it may not be designed for additional load. In this case, you will need access underneath the cantilevered floor of the house in order to attach the floor joists of your deck to the rim joist of the house.

You cannot bear a structure on disturbed soil, or loose soil, you must excavate to undisturbed soil in its natural density. Then the code provides assumed bearing capacities for different soil types.

SITE WORK

The shade provided by your deck will usually discourage plant growth, but to be safe, lay down plastic or landscaping fabric and cover it with gravel because it will be difficult to do so after the deck is built. But first make sure the earth slopes away from the house—it would be a bad idea to put plastic down if there was drainage toward the foundation of the house. Landscaping fabric is usually a better choice than plastic because it does not trap moisture. If you live in an area where vegetation is extremely lush and tenacious, consider removing the grass, plants, and roots from the site by digging up all of it and hauling it away. Then fill the area with landscaping fabric and gravel. (See "Removing Sod" and "Preparing a Gravel Bed," pages 90 and 91.)

PROJECT: 🐾🐾🐾
REMOVING SHRUBS

You may need to remove vegetation to make way for your new deck. Save valuable shrubs and other plants by transplating to another area.

TOOLS & MATERIALS
- Shovel
- Burlap
- String
- Wheelbarrow

1 Use a shovel to dig under the root of the shrub. Mature plant roots can be difficult to remove.

2 Lift the plant and roots free of the hole, and place the root ball on a piece of burlap.

3 Tie the burlap with string to protect the root area, particularly if the new planting site is not ready.

Solutions for Wet Sites

You may find that your chosen deck site presents you with some extra challenges, usually in the form of water. Here's a list of common problems and typical solutions:

A Site That Is Already Wet. You can build over a moderately soggy site, once you provide drainage to prevent standing water under the deck. The deck may reduce the amount of rain that falls on the ground, but a deck also puts the site in shade, so water will evaporate more slowly, especially if your deck is very near the

ground. Any water standing under a deck for more than a few days breeds mosquitoes and can start to smell horrible on hot summer days.

The simplest way to deal with this problem is to grade the site—to make sure it is sloping uniformly away from the house with no valleys or pits. This can usually be handled simply by shifting dirt with a shovel and rake, although it is back-breaking work. You may find it useful to measure the slope using a tape measure and line level.

Deck height plays a role in the type of piers and posts needed, opposite. A low, pond foundation wall is found with flat stones, while a higher foundation wall is found with clear plexi and blocks. Check with the building inspector for code requirements in your area.

PROJECT: 🐾🐾🐾
REMOVING SOD

You can reuse sod if you are able to replant it in a day or two. Keep rolls of sod moist and in a cool place in the yard. The sod will dry out, so replant it quickly.

TOOLS & MATERIALS
- Square-bottom shovel
- Work gloves
- Wheelbarrow

1 Starting about 1 ft. outside of the layout lines, score 16-in.-wide strips of sod with the shovel. Use the shovel to cut the roots, otherwise you won't be able to roll up the sod.

2 Roll the sod out of the way. Include about 2 to 3 in. of soil as you roll.

3 Sod rolls can get heavy, so work with sections that you can easily manage.

For more severe problems, dig a drainage ditch to collect water and carry it away from your site. Dig the ditch about 12 inches deep at the high end, and angle it down about 1 inch for each 10 feet of trench. Put approximately an inch of gravel in the bottom of the ditch; install a perforated drainpipe (with the holes down); cover with more gravel; and top it off with soil. The far end of the pipe can emerge from the ground if you have a good slope on your property and somewhere to direct the water, or it can pour the water into an underground dry well—a large hole filled with stones and topped with gravel and soil.

Runoff from Heavy Rains. If you have downspouts that dump water on your deck site, plan to change your gutter system so that it will empty out elsewhere.

As a heavy rainfall runs off the deck, you may end up with a little water-filled moat all the way around. This is a problem that's hard to predict before you build, but it's also fairly easy to fix. For minor puddling, try ringing your deck with plants in a wood-chip bed. For larger problems, you may need a bed of gravel 6 inches deep, or you may even need to install a drainage ditch as described previously.

PROJECT:
PREPARING A GRAVEL BED

This method will stop weed growth, but you can also use a general herbicide in addition to these steps. Be sure to follow the instructions on the label.

TOOLS & MATERIALS
- Rake
- Shovel
- Perforated plastic or
- landscape fabric
- Gravel
- Wheelbarrow

1 Clear away rocks, roots, and other debris. The ground must slope away from the house.

2 Roll out the plastic. Overlap the edges by 6 in. shingle-style so that water runs away from the house.

3 Dump the gravel in several piles around the site. Rake it out to create an even surface.

Erosion from Water. On a very hilly site, you might have erosion problems; little gullies left where the rain has carried away soil are the usual telltale signs. Severe erosion can undermine your footings, causing them to sink, tip, or fail completely.

Limit erosion by planting suitable foliage to stabilize the site. Check with a local nursery for the best type of plants to use. Or you may need to provide drainage: simple trenches might solve the problem, or you may need to dig a drainage ditch.

Unstable Soil. Any concrete footings or posts sitting in a posthole must sit on undisturbed soil, which is usually reached by 16 inches below grade. However, in cold climates you'll be required to dig deeper to below the local frost line to prevent the deck from heaving in the winter. Check with your building department for the required depth in your area.

Footings placed in unstable or loose soil will settle along with the soil, sometimes unevenly. Swampy soil is likely to be unstable, as is any area that's recently been excavated and backfilled, including within 5 feet of house foundation walls. If you are unsure about your soil's stability, talk with a local soil engineer, an architect, or the local building department. Experts such as these should know a good deal about local conditions and what sorts of foundations work best in the kind of soil on your site.

💡 SMART TIP

MARKING FOR UTILITIES

Before you start digging piers for your deck, check into the location of underground utility lines, such as a natural-gas main or sewer line. On a big project where you're using a contractor to do the digging, the excavation contractor should plot the exact location of underground utilities. But even then it pays to check on them yourself with the local utility company. In most areas, a company representative will come to the site and locate the lines so you can mark them with flags. To check your area for underground services, call 811 or go to call811.com.

You don't see it, but a well-designed foundation will provide years of reliable service.

CANTILEVERS

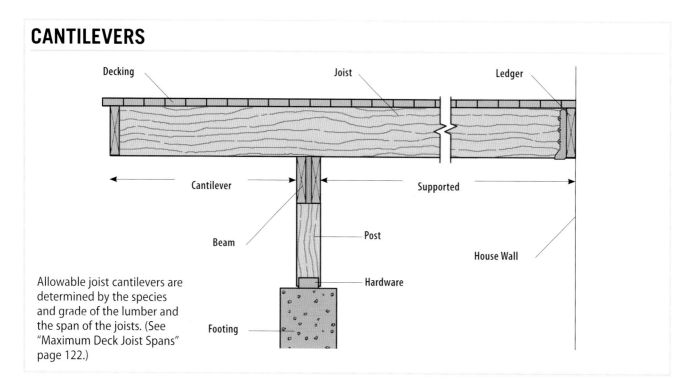

Decking Joist Ledger

Cantilever Supported

Beam Post

House Wall

Hardware

Footing

Allowable joist cantilevers are determined by the species and grade of the lumber and the span of the joists. (See "Maximum Deck Joist Spans" page 122.)

FOOTINGS

Most likely you will need to pour concrete and make new footings. Consult local codes.

Precast Piers. If you have a stable site with little sand and no wintertime frost or you don't connect the deck to the house, you may be able to simply set precast concrete piers directly on top of undisturbed soil instead of using footings. Remove loose soil, and provide a spot where the piers can rest on level, undisturbed soil. Make sure that this system is code-approved in your area.

Hole-Dug Piers

No Frost Line. In stable soil, you can simply dig a hole that will act as a concrete form. For areas with little frost, a hole that is 8 inches in diameter and 12 inches deep, for instance, will yield a substantial footing. Fill the hole completely with concrete, and taper it upward so that the center is an inch or two above the ground. Insert an anchor or bolt directly into the concrete.

Below the Frost Line. Another option is to dig a cylindrical posthole that is at the frost line or extends several inches below your area's frost line, and fill it with concrete. Flare the bottom of the hole a bit for stability. This method works best for footings with wide diameters. Be sure to check your local code to find out the frost line requirements.

Hole-Dug Forms

The top of a footing formed by pouring concrete into a hole is usually flush to the ground, which means that the bottom of the post is near ground level and subject to moisture. You can modify this technique by extending the form above the ground using 1x6s or pieces of plywood.

Plan pier locations carefully.

TYPES OF FOOTINGS

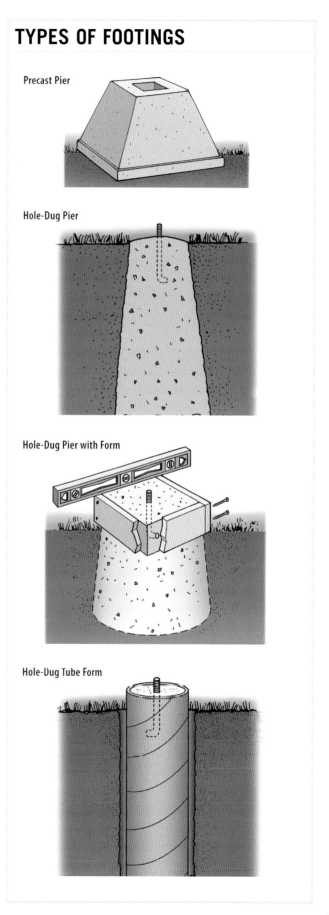

Precast Pier

Hole-Dug Pier

Hole-Dug Pier with Form

Hole-Dug Tube Form

Precast Pier on Concrete. You can purchase a precast concrete pier and set it on a footing below grade.

Pouring Into a Tube Form. This is an easy and accurate way of pouring a footing. The tubes come in a variety of sizes, though 8 inches in diameter is the most common. The forms are made of fiberboard and are easy to trim to the exact length you need. A tube form has great advantages over just digging a posthole and filling it with concrete: it can be easily extended above the ground to whatever height you desire; it makes your job easier because you don't have to mix extra concrete. You need to fill the soil in around the tube and compact it. The tubes are waxed, so after the concrete sets you can easily strip away the part that shows above ground.

Post Anchors

With most anchors, you embed one part of the metal in the concrete while it's still wet. Often you just insert a J-bolt or an anchor strap and attach the rest of the anchor later, but some anchors come in one piece and you embed just the lower portion. Look for an anchor that you can adjust laterally. Adjustable anchors give you an inch or two of play in all directions so that you can compensate for small layout errors.

💡 SMART TIP

ALIGNING PIER HARDWARE

When you set and pour concrete piers, you may set the anchoring pin slightly off line. That's one good reason to use adjustable post hardware. Most types have a slot in the base instead of a hole. That allows you to adjust the hardware slightly in any direction to place the base of the post exactly where you want it.

POST HARDWARE

ADJUSTABLE

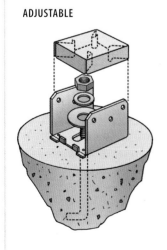

PINNED

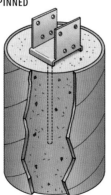

BRACKETED

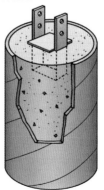

PRONGED

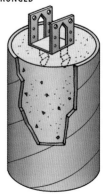

Use these methods only for an upper-level deck that you can frame on temporary braces and then plumb bob down to find the exact post location.

Continuous Posts

You can also extend posts down into postholes. It may seem that doing this adds a lot of strength to the structure, but in the case of a mostly horizontal structure such as a deck, that is rarely the case. You will probably gain rigidity by tying the deck to your house. So unless you are building a freestanding deck that is raised more than a couple of feet above the ground, concrete-set posts do not add significant lateral strength. But for low-level decks, concrete-set posts do indeed offer some resistance to lateral loads—there are ways in the building code for calculating how much.

And there are drawbacks to posts sunk in concrete or gravel: first, there's no correcting of mistakes. Second, posts set into the ground are more likely to rot. And third, they are very difficult to replace in case they get damaged. So unless you have special reason to use them elsewhere, use this type of post only for the stair rails, which often need a little extra lateral support.

However, continuous posts are required in some areas subject to earthquakes. They are also sometimes called for when the deck is raised high above the ground to make sure the post bottoms won't move. But sunken posts are not used as often for tall decks because there are better ways to keep the post bottoms from swaying. Continuous posts are often simply set into postholes that are backfilled with concrete. They can also be inserted into a large-diameter, concrete-filled tube form.

To determine when a post should be sunk into the ground versus kept aboveground, refer to the code.

💡 **SMART TIP**

CONTINUOUS POSTS

In some situations you can set posts directly into a concrete form—for example, to help support the end of a stairway railing where it's not practical to pour another pier. But the most durable design is to set posts in hardware on top of piers.

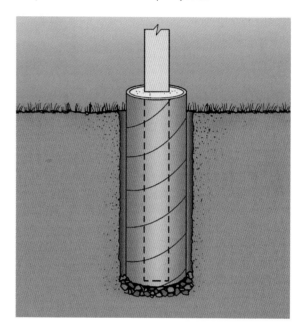

FOUNDATION OPTIONS

There are prefab products that can help you build footings and piers faster. Concrete deck blocks (left) simply sit on the ground, and the deck frame tucks into cuts in the tops of the blocks. The system meets many local codes because the deck floats. It's not actually attached to the house and may even be considered a temporary structure. Be certain to check this kind of system with your local building department. The concrete tube footing form (right) is a high-density plastic form that attaches to prefab pier tubes. It adds strength because it creates more bearing area to distribute the load over more soil.

DIGGING POSTHOLES

If there are just a few holes to dig, you can do the work yourself using a posthole digger. For larger projects, however, you'll thank yourself for renting a power auger to speed up the job. Some are designed for one-person operation (though it certainly wouldn't hurt to have a helper), and the larger ones require two fairly brawny people.

Dig the Holes. Once the marker stakes are all firmly established, remove the string lines to give yourself room to dig. Whether you are using the auger or a posthole digger, if you run into a rock, you'll need a wrecking bar (also called a breaker bar or a crowbar) to break up stones or pry them loose. If you run into roots, chop at them with your posthole digger or shovel, or use branch pruners. In extreme cases, you may have to go in there with a handsaw.

Tamp the Bottom and Reattach String Lines. The bottom of your footing hole should be firm. Even if you have reached undisturbed soil, an inch or two of dirt crumbs will be left over from the digging process, so tamp the soil down with a piece of 4x4. Put your string lines back in place, recheck them for square, and double-check your footing locations.

Install the Forms. Once you have dug the holes, install the concrete forms of your choice, making sure they are secure. If you are using a fiberboard tube form, you can usually just backfill outside it with dirt to keep it stable. Some designs call for leveling all the footings with each other. To do this, first backfill all the tubes, then mark them with a water level and cut them off with a handsaw.

Add Rebar. If your local codes require reinforcing bar, this is the time to add it. There is no need to pour gravel into the bottom of the concrete form. And before buying rebar, first be sure to check the building code—the International Residential Code (IRC) does not require rebar.

If you do need to use rebar for reinforcement, do not pound it into the ground. Rather, you must encase the rebar completely in concrete.

Do it carefully so the rebar will be at or near the center of the concrete. Be sure it does not stick out of the form and will not interfere with the part of your post anchors that you'll embed into the wet concrete. Consult the code and/or ask the building inspector to specify a size for the rebar; also inquire about rebar spacing.

DIGGING OPTIONS

Working in rocky soil, you will find it handy to have a pickax, or at least a heavy-duty wrecking bar to help dislodge rocks.

1. Using a shovel is the basic and sometimes back-breaking way to dig piers. But you'll wind up moving more dirt than you need to.

2. A posthole digger has two handles that work in a scissors action to cut and scoop dirt. They make a neater hole with a smaller diameter.

3. The power auger is a tool you can rent. There are one- and two-person models that churn through the dirt. Both are a handful to operate, but they are efficient.

1

2

3

POURING CONCRETE

Now it's time to begin forming a permanent part of your deck. Though backfilled footings aren't too impressive looking, they are important to the overall stability of your deck.

Estimating

Concrete is sold by the yard; a cubic yard is 3 feet by 3 feet by 3 feet, or 27 cubic feet, and there are 1,728 cubic inches in a cubic foot.

For box forms, multiply the inside length times the inside width times the depth, all measurements in inches. Divide the result by 1,728 to convert into cubic feet, then divide by 27 to convert into cubic yards.

To find the volume of cylindrical footings, the formula is: volume = $\pi r^2 h$. That means that you multiply pi (3.14) times the radius squared times the height to get cubic inches. Then you convert that into cubic feet by dividing by 1,728; then divide by 27 to obtain cubic yards.

Getting Concrete

There are two basic ways to get concrete ready to pour on site: you can add water to premixed bags or mix your own from piles of raw materials.

Using Premixed Concrete. You can buy bags that have the cement, sand, and gravel already mixed. A wheelbarrow makes a good container for adding water and mixing. Each bag yields about ⅔ cubic foot, so an 8-inch-by-42-inch cylindrical footing, for instance, will take two bags, and ½ cubic yard will require about 20 bags.

PROJECT: 🐁🐁🐁
MIXING CONCRETE

To make this dusty work go smoothly, pour in about two-thirds of the water to start; then mix and add the rest slowly. Follow the directions on the bag for mixing.

TOOLS & MATERIALS
- Concrete mix
- Work gloves
- Wheelbarrow
- Hoe
- Bucket
- Water

1 Whether you use premixed ingredients or combine them yourself, do the mixing in a wheelbarrow.

2 Mix the dry ingredients with a hoe. Create a crater in the center of the pile.

3 Pour in the water slowly, following the directions on the bag. Too much water ruins the mixture.

Mixing Your Own. For in-between amounts or for sites where truck delivery would be difficult, consider mixing your own concrete in a wheelbarrow or on a sheet of plywood. Or, for larger amounts, you can rent an electric mixer.

Mixing and Pouring

The basic technique is the same here whether you are using premixed concrete in bags or combining your own dry ingredients. You can build or buy a mixing trough, but the easiest method is simply to mix right in the same wheelbarrow you will use to transport the concrete. (See "Mixing Concrete," page 97.)

Mix Dry Ingredients. If you're mixing your own dry ingredients, shovel them right into the wheelbarrow. Use three shovelfuls of gravel, two of sand, and one of cement.

Mix the dry ingredients thoroughly with a concrete hoe even if you are using premixed bags. In any case, though, mix only one bag at a time, as concrete is very heavy.

Add Water. Hollow out a hole in the center of the dry ingredients and pour in some water. Mix thoroughly, then slowly add more water, testing the concrete as you go for the right consistency. Don't make it soupy, even though more water makes mixing easier. It should be just fluid enough to pour into your form.

Pour and Strike Off the Concrete. Pour the concrete directly from the wheelbarrow, or scoop it into your forms with a shovel. Clean up any excess as you go. Poke a 2x2 or a piece of rebar deep down into the concrete in several places to get out any air bubbles. Once you have filled the form, strike it off with a scrap piece of 2x4 to obtain a smooth, level top surface.

PROJECT: 🐦🐦🐦
BUILDING PIERS

Backfill fiberboard forms once they are in the hole to hold them steady, eliminating the need for braces.

TOOLS & MATERIALS
- Form tubes
- Level
- Concrete
- 2x4
- Post anchor hardware
- Wrenches

1 Place a cut tube in the hole. The top of the tube should project 6 in. above grade.

2 Level the tube. Then brace the tube while the concrete sets up. Once it is solid, you can compact and wet the backfill around it more densely to provide greater lateral support to the pier. Check for level while backfilling.

3 Pour concrete into the form. Insert the J-bolt that comes with the hardware into the center of the form. After the concrete cures, attach the rest of the post anchor hardware.

ALTERNATIVE METHODS FOR SECURING POSTS

Engineered helical piers

Surface deck block

Install Post Anchor Hardware. Install your J-bolt or post anchor immediately. Wiggle it a bit as you place it to get rid of air bubbles. Then line up the hardware with your string line and a plumb bob to ensure it will be in the center of the post. Be certain that it is sticking up the right distance out of the concrete, and use a torpedo level to make sure it's plumb. Loosely cover the top of your footings with plastic so they won't dry too quickly. You can start to build on the footings after 24 hours. But remember that concrete takes three weeks to fully cure, and it will be prone to chipping if you bang into it during the first few days.

Installing Posts in Postholes

If you choose to sink your posts into the ground, give the buried section an extra dose of preservative, especially the open end grain. Field treatment of cut ends of treated lumber is required. There are multiple topical treatments available, such as copper naphthenate–based preservatives and oxine copper–based preservatives. Regardless of which preservative you choose, a brush (paintbrush) is needed to apply it to the ends of the lumber.

Dig Flared Holes. For additional bearing capacity, flare your holes so that they are 3–4 inches wider at the bottom than at the top. Use a large-diameter concrete tube form and put the post inside before pouring the concrete. This makes more efficient use of concrete and makes it possible to bring the concrete several inches above grade.

Check and Brace the Posts. You will let the posts run wild and cut them to their exact height after the concrete is set. For now, however, use a line level to make sure that all the posts are sitting high enough. Align them with your layout strings, and plumb them in both directions. Then attach two braces to each post.

Pour the Concrete. As you pour, poke a long pole or piece of reinforcing bar into the concrete on all four sides of the post to release any air bubbles. This is especially important when the post extends down inside the footing and the concrete forms a long, narrow ring around the post. Stop pouring and do this a few times until the form is filled with concrete.

Use a 2x4 to slope the top of the concrete upward, creating a small incline so that rainwater drains away from the wood.

The ledger, posts, and beams are the components that secure the deck to the house and the ground. They carry the structural load of your new deck. In most cases, looks are not important because these components are usually hidden, but what is important is selecting the right materials to do the job and installing these elements correctly.

Once you have the ledger and beam in place, the deck's joists should go down smoothly. Install a solid layer of joists, and the decking that rides across them will be solid underfoot.

For help with selecting the right tools and materials for the project or to brush up on some of the construction techniques deck building requires, see Chapters 2, 3, and 4.

FRAMING BASICS

In nearly every case, preservative-treated lumber is the best choice for framing a deck. Treated wood is infused with chemicals that resist rot, and it costs only a little more than untreated framing lumber. For highly visible areas such as outside joists, you can pick the best looking boards in the pile. Or you can hide treated outside joists behind fascia boards made of redwood, cedar, or composite boards.

Redwood and cedar are occasionally used for framing. These woods are naturally rot resistant and more attractive than treated wood. But they are more expensive and not as strong, so these woods are typically reserved for visible areas such as decking and railing.

A basic deck frame is made of posts, a beam, joists, and a ledger. Posts rest on your footings and are usually 4x4s, though 6x6s are often used for upper level decks. The main beam usually rests on top of the posts, although to create a ground-hugging deck, it can also rest directly on level footings. This main support beam can be a solid four-by or two or more two-bys. Joists that support the decking are either connected to the side of the main beam, or rest on top of the main beam on one end, and are attached to the ledger board at the other end. Joists and ledgers are made of two-by lumber and are generally of the same width. The ledger is attached to the house.

SIZING AND SPACING FRAME MEMBERS

The required span for a piece of lumber is the distance it can safely traverse without being supported underneath. If you exceed a required span, your deck will feel flimsy and there is a good chance it will sag over time.

The charts "Maximum Deck Beams Span" and "Maximum Deck Joist Spans" on pages 120 and 122, are based on the International Residential Building Codes (IRC), which have been adopted by most building departments in the United States. The IRC allows 4x4s and 6x6s up to 14 feet tall, depending on how much load they carry.

Use the span charts to help you plan the deck. Before designing the structure of your deck, however, check with your local building department to make sure your municipality adheres to the IRC—while unlikely, it is possible your municipality has different code requirements.

Also remember that the same sizes of different wood species can have different requirements. Not all 4x12s have the same ratings. Generally, stronger woods such as Douglas fir can span greater distances than weaker woods such as cedar.

You'll also find that the suggested spans in this book (and in literature from your building department) are

Connections at the ledger, posts, and girders will determine the stability of your new deck.

💡 SMART TIP

SPACING OPTIONS

Spacing of framing members must be permitted by the locally adopted building code, but you have a lot of leeway in the design stage. Refer to the standardized span tables implemented by the International Residential Code (IRC) to figure out the spacing requirements for your deck.

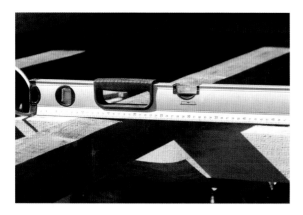

based on normal loads. If you plan to place heavy objects on your deck, such as soil-filled planters, you'll need to reduce the spans or beef up the lumber sizes, or both.

You will need to determine the span of the beam and the span of the joists. Then you can select the right materials for the job. Once you have determined the spans, spacing, and species of your beams and joists, include this information on the drawings you'll submit to the building department to get your permit to build the deck.

Joists

In planning your joists, keep in mind the size and lumber type of the joists, as well as how far apart they will be spaced. This is called the on-center, or o.c., measurement.

Cantilevering. It's common practice to have joists cantilever over a beam by a foot or two as a way to get more deck area with less joist size. It also hides the beam and its supporting posts, or at least makes them less prominent. Codes specify maximum joist overhangs based on the wood species, spacing, and dimensions of the joists with a maximum cantilever of one-quarter of the joist's allowable span—the distance between the beam and the other end of the joist. As a practical matter,

there's usually no good reason for a long cantilever. The chart "Maximum Deck Joist Spans" on page 122 specifies the cantilevers allowed by the International Residential Code, but check with your local building department in case it adheres to a different code.

Beams

House framing may contain several types of major beams, although on almost all decks there is only one that supports the outer ends of the joists. You can sometimes reduce the beam size by adding a post or two or by cantilevering the beam beyond the post, thereby saving money in lumber. But that savings is likely to be overshadowed by the extra labor of digging and pouring additional piers. Allowable beam spans depend on the size and type of the lumber, as well as the span distance of the joists that rest on it.

Bear in mind that the building department may consider a beam made of two 2x8s to be just as strong as a 4x8, or they may consider it weaker. Built-up strength also depends in part on how the built-up beam is constructed.

Posts. Unless your deck will carry an unusual amount of weight, 4x4 posts will work if your deck is 4 feet or less above the ground. Larger 6x6 posts may be required for decks over 4 feet high, and code in some areas now require posts to be at least 6x6 in all cases.

Ledger

The ledger usually makes the best starting place for laying out the whole deck, so you may want to install it before you dig your footing holes. It is a major supporting member, so it must be firmly attached to the house. Make your ledger of the same two-by material as your joists. Pick a straight board that is not cupped, so the joist ends can fit snugly against it. This piece of lumber is crucial because it does two jobs. It carries a lot of weight and connects the deck to the house. There are several ways to install a ledger, but the most important consideration is safety. You must be sure that the ledger is securely bolted to the house framing, typically to the system of floor joists. You can't secure deck ledgers to siding or sheathing alone. And you can't secure ledgers through siding unless it is flat plywood.

LEDGER DESIGNS

The ledger can be a trouble spot because rain and snow can collect between it and the house and damage both. In particular, if you have beveled horizontal siding or shingles, simply attaching the ledger onto the siding is an invitation for trouble because water will collect in the V-shaped channel between the siding and the ledger. To prevent these problems, make sure you install your ledger properly.

The point is to avoid having moisture trapped against the ledger or the house framing for long periods.

Preparing for the Ledger

If any of the following steps do not apply to the method of installing a ledger that you're using, just skip to the next step.

Locate the Ledger. It may sound like a good idea to have your deck surface level with your interior flooring, but if you do so, you will be inviting rain and snow to seep under your threshold and into your house. So plan to have a small step down. Even 1 inch will go a long way toward keeping your home drier in most regions. You can make a larger step, but it should be no more than the step in a standard interior stairway. Steps can be up to 7¾ inches.

But the main consideration should be to locate the ledger where it will be easy for you to bolt it directly and securely into the house floor framing. This should be possible with a step down of only an inch or two. If the step is much greater, the ledger may line up against the house foundation instead of the floor framing. You can still attach it securely.

To locate your ledger, measure down from the level of your house floor to the level of the decking. This is the amount of your step. Then add in the decking thickness: 1½ inch for nominal two-by decking; 1 inch for nominal ¾ decking. Mark this level, and extend it along the house wall to mark the length of the ledger. You want this line to be perfectly level. (See "Smart Tip" on page 111.)

To make marks that will ensure that your ledger is level throughout its length, either use a water level or set your carpenter's level atop a straight board. (Because few boards are perfect, it is best to place the level near the center of the board.) Better yet, use a laser level: these devices stand on their own and so are much more error-proof.

Once you have made several marks, snap chalk lines between them, and double-check those lines for level.

Mark for Outer Joists, Fascia, and Decking. It helps to visualize all the dimensions of your finished deck, so

LEDGER OPTIONS

No matter what kind of siding you have, there is a way to attach a ledger board securely. But you need to be sure that water will drain past the ledger, and not into the house. Do this by flashing the ledger so that water drains off the front face or by adding spacers between the ledger and the house so that water drains straight through. You also need to be sure that the ledger is solidly connected to the framing of the house.

DIRECTLY ON SIDING

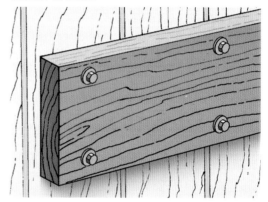

This is not much of an option, because it only applies where there is ½-inch board siding and no sheathing behind it.

FLASHED ON SHEATHING

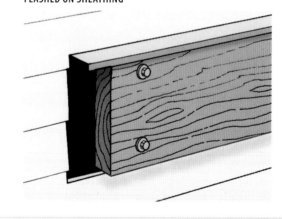

mark for every lumber piece that will go up against your house. This means adding 1½ inches for the outside joist, plus ¾ inch for fascia (if any), plus the distance you plan to overhang your decking (if any) on each side of the deck.

Cut Out the Siding. If the ledger installation requires removing some of your siding, mark an outline for the cutout, taking into account everything that will fit into it: the ledger, the end of the outside joists, an extra ⅛ inch

SMART TIP

LEDGER SETUP

You can tack joists to marks on the ledger and install hangers later or set hangers ahead of time.

in width for the flashing (if any), and possibly the end of the fascia—but not the decking. Marking will be easier if you tack a piece of ledger-width material in place and draw a pencil line around it.

Be sure to follow the manufacturer's directions for removing or cutting the type of siding you have.

Check for Straightness. Check the surface against which you will be placing the ledger by holding a string against its length. If anywhere along the length, there is a gap of more than ¼ inch between the string and the wall, tack shims to the house so that when you attach the ledger it will be straight. You can also use a string with blocks to check the flatness of your ledger once it's installed. (See "Smart Tip" on page 111.) Remember that unless you cut every joist to fit (a job that you don't want to do), the front edge of your deck will follow the contours of your ledger.

Install Flashing. If you have cut out a section of siding, install flashing that is the same length as the cutout. (It will cover the top of the outside joists as well, so snip the front edge to make it fit over them.) Tuck the flashing up under the siding—the flashing should be integrated in behind the water-resistive barrier. Before you slide the flashing in, make sure you have a clear path for it by prying the upper siding piece loose and removing all nails in the flashing's path. Handle the flashing carefully

because it bends easily. Gently renail the siding back into position to hold the flashing in place.

A variety of ready-made flashing is available. One of the most practical has a Z-shape that bends twice— once to slide up under the siding and once to cover the face of your ledger. This last, front-most portion of the flashing need only be wide enough to keep water from wicking between the flashing and the top of the ledger. Remember that the joists will be smashed up against it, so it is best if the flashing comes down the ledger at a right angle to protect the horizontal surface of the ledger.

Cut and Mark the Ledger. Cut the ledger, which runs at one end of the joists, and the header joist, which runs at the other, to the same length. (A header is usually a type of beam, but header joist in this context is also called a rim joist or band joist.) If your deck is not rectangular, they will not be the same length, of course.

Because the ledger and header joist run parallel with each other, and the joists are perpendicular to them both, it makes sense to cut the header joist and ledger at the same time, and to mark them both for the joist locations before you install the ledger. After marking the tops, use a square to extend the lines down the faces of the ledger and header. Don't forget to make an X indicating on which side of the line the joists will be installed. (See "Smart Tip," above.)

LEDGER INSTALLATION

WEATHERPROOF DESIGN

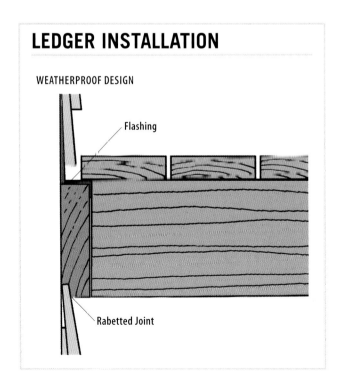

Flashing

Rabetted Joint

PROJECT:
REMOVING SIDING

You have some leeway in placing your ledger on the wall. The step down from house level to deck level can be between roughly 1 inch and 7¾ inches. Set the ledger where you can bolt it securely to the house framing.

TOOLS & MATERIALS
- Water level
- Pencil
- Circular saw
- Wood shims
- Gloves
- Hacksaw
- blade
- Pry bar or hammer

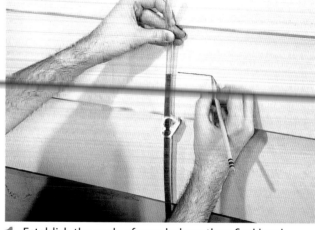

1 Establish the ends of your ledger; then find level points at each end and snap a chalk line.

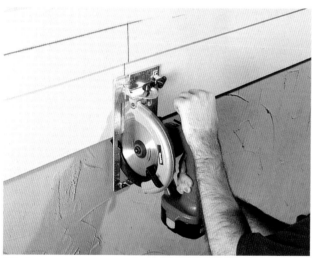

2 Set your saw to cut through the siding but not the sheathing. Make cuts at each end of the ledger.

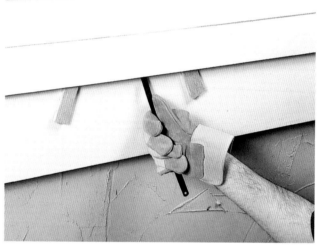

3 Pry the siding up, and insert wedges to hold it up. Use a hacksaw blade to cut nails.

4 Make the horizontal cut with your saw. Set the blade to siding depth to avoid cutting the sheathing.

5 The siding should come out easily. If it does not, use a pry bar and hammer to ease it out.

ATTACHING LEDGERS

Whether you are attaching to wood, masonry, or stucco, it is important to fasten the ledger securely. If you cannot attach your deck to your home (for example, if you have masonry veneer), you may be able to build a floating deck (see "Smart Tip," below) that does not need a ledger. Remember that the ledger bears a lot of weight. While about half of the entire deck load away from the house may bear on the main beam and support posts, the remaining load bears on the ledger. Without a strong beam and a row of posts for support, the ledger must be strong enough to transfer the load to the house

foundation. It is a critical connection—most deck failures occur because of a faulty connection to the ledger.

Because decks are typically slightly below the house's interior floor, there is almost always a continuous rim joist to provide solid attachment anywhere along the ledger. This is true of wooden houses coated with stucco. The only exception is a building that is made of masonry rather than supported by a wooden frame.

Attaching the Ledger to Masonry

If you are planning to attach your ledger to a concrete or masonry wall, always check your local code to ensure that it allows attaching a ledger to a concrete or masonry

LEDGER BOLTS

Unless you increase the number of ledger lag screws in order to offset the load, do not countersink the lag screws. You'll need to plan your bolt locations so they don't fall behind joists. Also, code often requires predrilling to two diameters—first with a ⅜-inch bit all the way through the rim joist so the bolt threads will bite into the joist. And then with a ½-inch bit so the bolt will slip through the ledger without a chance of splitting it.

💡 SMART TIP

FLOATING DECKS

Some decks, including decks built next to cantilevered house walls, don't have a ledger and aren't connected to the house, although they might look as though they are. An island deck built right next to the house gives the illusion of a standard deck but skips the ledger work and adds an extra beam near the house. Be sure to check local codes about floating decks.

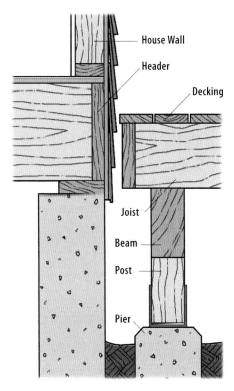

wall and that you are following the code requirements. If you cannot attach your deck to your wall, you may be able to build a floating deck that does not need a ledger. (See "Smart Tip" on page 107.)

Attaching the Ledger to Wood Framing

Whether your wood-framed house is sided with wood, aluminum, vinyl, or stucco, you need to attach the ledger through the sheathing and into the wood framing of the house. Attaching a ledger to a frame house at the level of the floor frame (or just below it to allow for a small step) is the safest approach. (See "Installing Ledgers on Wood," page 110.)

Depending on the direction of the floor framing, you are most likely to find one of two conditions. If the joists run parallel with the house wall, there will be a solid joist running the length of the deck. If the joists run perpendicular to the house wall, you still should find solid material because the joist ends are covered with a rim joist, also called a belt or header joist.

If you are putting the ledger elsewhere on a frame house—for example, on a raised deck—you will be able to tie into the wall studs. In any case, you should verify the location of solid framing and be sure that your lags or bolts fall directly over them. You may get a tipoff from siding nails that are driven every 16 inches. But to be safe, you

---

PROJECT: 🐦🐦🐦
INSTALLING LEDGERS ON STUCCO

For stucco over concrete, use lag shields in predrilled holes. For stucco over wood, use bolts or screws.

TOOLS & MATERIALS

- Ledger
- Circular saw
- Clamps
- Combination square
- Pencil
- Saw
- Flashing for stucco
- Drill and bits
- Props
- Ratchet wrench
- 4-in. lag screws
- Scrap wood
- 1½-in. concrete or deck screws
- Caulk

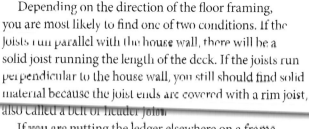

1 Use a temporary guide board to cut a level line where the top edge of the flashing will fall.

2 Insert the flashing into the groove. Note the lip on top of the flashing.

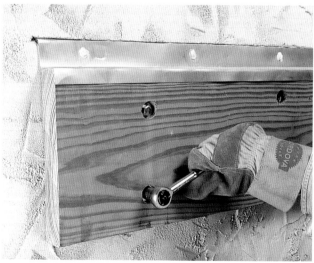

3 Predrill holes in stucco and in ledger. Fasten ledger to the house with lag screws.

CHECKING LEDGER LOCATION

The connection between the ledger and the house is crucial. That means fastening the ledger to the structure of the house. To locate the framing, measure its position off the foundation inside and transfer the location outside. Then double-check by cutting out a piece of siding and testing for hollow areas and solid framing with a nail. The ledger bolts should reach into or through the house framing.

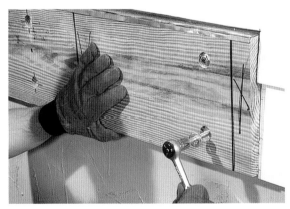

LEDGER SCREWS

While lag bolts are still used to attach ledgers, many professional deck builders now use specially designed ledger screws, which also meet code. The screws require no predrilling and have a washer integrated into the hex head. They usually come with a hex-head driver and you just drive them in with a drill/driver. Ledger screws typically must be installed with two at each interval, unless using larger fasteners like lags and bolts, which require a staggered V-shape. The number of screws required is determined by the span of the joists, so you'll need to refer to a chart on the technical sheet for the screws. Select screws that are long enough to pass through the house rim joist.

should strip off a piece of siding, a section of tar paper or house wrap underneath, and a section of sheathing if need be to be certain of the framing pattern.

Most codes allow you to use ½-in. lag screws or ledger screws. Select screws that are long enough to pass 1½ to 2 inches into the framing member. Use a washer for each to increase the strength at the lag head and to keep the head from digging into the wood.

If you have access to the framing inside, in a basement, for example, you may be able to use bolts instead of lags. This allows you to be absolutely certain of the connections, and to lock up the ledger with a bolt head and washer outside and a nut and washer inside.

Position the ledger, check again for level, and drill pilot holes according to code. Drill pilot holes for lags and clearance holes for bolts. Then install the fasteners, and be sure that they have locked into solid wood framing.

POSITIONING THE POSTS

When installing posts you have choices to make about how they will be supported at the bottom and how they will be attached to beams. At the bottom, you can either sink posts into holes the way you might with fence posts and secure them with concrete poured into the holes, or you can set them on concrete piers. Local codes may specify one method over another, and of course that's the final word. But using concrete piers generally provides more stability and durability. It's the way most houses are built, with a concrete footing and foundation to support the structure above. Concrete piers also keep the post a few inches above ground, which reduces the possibility of rot.

The most common method is to cut the posts to height so they form level supports directly under the beams. Here is a rundown of the basic procedure for the most common and probably the most durable system.

Check for Rough Length. In most situations, you will cut the post to exact height later. But first make sure that every post will be tall enough. Use a line level, water level, or long piece of lumber with a level on top to find out how high each post needs to be. (It is best to slope your deck slightly down coming away from the house, but this measurement is too small to worry about at this point.) Give yourself at least a few extra inches and you won't have to worry.

PROJECT:
INSTALLING LEDGERS ON WOOD

For the most secure connection, bolt through or lag into framing. Don't secure the ledger to the siding alone.

TOOLS & MATERIALS
- Ledger board
- End joist
- Clamps
- Combination square
- Pencil
- Saw
- Flashing
- Drill and bits
- Props
- Ratchet wrench
- 4-in. lag screws

1 Transfer the layout marks for the joists from the ledger to the end joist.

2 Predrill holes for fasteners. This will guarantee clearance for joist hangers later.

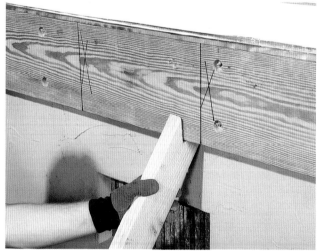

3 Prop ledger into position, and drive lag screws with a ratchet, or install bolts if possible.

ATTACHING BEAM TO NOTCHED POST

When beams are attached to the side of a post, they must be fastened with a bolt that goes all the way through the members with a nut on the other side. Traditionally, ½-inch bolts were used for this purpose. Now you can use screw-bolts that require no predrilling. You place a special washer over the screws then drive them through the beam and post (top). Then you place a cap on the other side (bottom). Drive the screw a bit more and the cap tightens without putting a wrench on it.

SMART TIP

LEDGER CHECKS

You need to check for level, of course, but also for flatness against the wall. Do this using three blocks. Tack one at each end, connected by a tightly drawn string. Use the third to check the margin between the string and the ledger. If the ledger is flat, the margin will be the same all along the ledger.

Check the ledger for level.

Check the ledger for flatness.

Locate and Attach Post Anchors. If you are using adjustable post anchors, now is the time to fine-tune their positions. Most hardware has a slot or some other way of making an adjustment. This way, if the threaded anchors fixed in the concrete piers are not exactly in line with each other, you can slide the post hardware one way or the other before fastening them in place.

The best way to do this is to confirm your measurements from the house wall and double-check for square. Then string a line or snap a chalk line between the outermost piers. Center one post anchor (which may not be exactly centered relative to the anchor bolt), and tighten it in place. Most hardware has a platform inside the bracket, which keeps the post slightly elevated and out of standing water. Typically, you fasten down the base plate before inserting the platform. But you should follow the manufacturer's directions. Then repeat the process at the other end, and use your string line to make sure that any intermediate anchors fall into line.

Insert and Fasten the Posts. Make a square cut on the bottom of each post to be sure that it seats firmly in the anchor. If you are not using preservative-treated lumber, even though that is the best policy on posts, it will help to flood the freshly cut end grain with wood preservative.

If the posts are short, they may stand by themselves in the hardware. But on most projects, you'll need to attach a few temporary braces. You don't need to plumb the posts exactly at this point; just keep them roughly plumb and stable as you fasten the anchors.

The procedure may vary from one manufacturer to another, but a typical anchor has one open side (so you can slide in the post). When the post base is in position, you simply bend up that metal flap with pliers. Then drive a few nails through the perforated holes in the hardware flaps to lock the post in place. Even though the post is roughly in place, you may want to wait until it is ~~anchored~~ ~~fully~~ ~~locked~~ ~~down~~ ~~with~~ ~~nails~~. (See "Anchoring Posts," page 114.)

You don't want to pound away on the nails and possibly dislodge the anchor or, worse yet, crack the concrete pier. To guard against this, you install the anchors with structural wood screws. Or you can back up the post with a heavy hammer as you nail on the other side. The extra weight, say, from a sledgehammer that you hold in one hand, absorbs a lot of the impact and keeps the post from shifting as you use a standard hammer in your other hand.

Plumb and Brace the Post. This job is easiest with two people because there is a lot to do at the same time. You need to release the temporary braces, fine-tune the plumb position of the post (checking and rechecking in two directions), and lock up the final position with a clamp before securing the braces.

Ideally, you can have one person check the level and, once the post is perfectly plumb, tell the other person to drive in a screw attaching the brace. Do this again for the other brace, and then recheck the first direction. Don't be surprised if you have to redo things once or twice. But once you have achieved perfect plumb, drive in more screws for stability—at least two for each attaching point. Then you can drive in the rest of the nails to hold the post anchor to the post.

If you are working solo, set up ground stakes and 2x4 braces at 90 degrees to each other. Drive a screw through the base of the 2x4 into the stake, pivot the brace onto the post at about a 45-degree angle, and secure it with a clamp. The idea is to use the clamp as your helper. Keep enough tension on the clamp to prevent the brace from falling, but not so much that you can't tap the post slightly one way or another as you make minor adjustments to bring the post plumb. When the post is plumb, tighten the brace, work on the other side, and finally lock the braces with several screws to hold it secure. Remove the clamps. (See "Smart Tip" on page 114.)

💡 SMART TIP

PLUMBING POSTS

Plumbing posts can be challenging because you need to manage a level, a brace, and a clamp at the same time. In most cases, you must adjust a pair of braces while adjusting the posts and the level. A handy tool called a post level clips onto the post and reads in both directions at once, so you can make adjustments and add braces with both hands free.

PROJECT:
PLACING RAISED-DECK POSTS

Ground contact can foster rot; use treated wood that is rated for ground contact, even if you plan on installing post anchors to hold the post above ground level.

Keep in mind that this is just one way to build a deck. Many pro builders today do it a bit differently: they build the deck floor perimeter, square and level it on temporary braces, and then place the posts underneath.

TOOLS & MATERIALS
- 2x4
- Level
- Pencil
- String
- Batter boards
- Posthole digger
- Posts
- Clamps
- Drill & bits
- Stakes & braces
- Sledgehammer
- 2½-in. screws

1 To locate the posts, start from a reference point on the house and plumb down.

2 Extend layout strings from plumb marks to batter boards. Mark the hole locations.

3 Remove the strings, and start digging the hole. Dig below the frost line.

4 The type of footing that supports the post will be determined by the local building code.

5 To brace the post, attach a 2x4 to a ground stake and clamp it to the post.

6 Brace the post in two places to keep it steady. Plumb the post and secure the braces to the stake with 2½-in. screws.

PROJECT:
ANCHORING POSTS

With pier and post anchors, wood stays off wet ground that can cause rot. It is important to square off the bottom of the post so that the post is plumb when in position.

TOOLS & MATERIALS
- Post
- Sawhorses
- Square
- Circular Saw
- Post hardware
- Wrenches
- Hammer
- Nails

1 Square off the bottom of the post so that it seats securely in the post anchor.

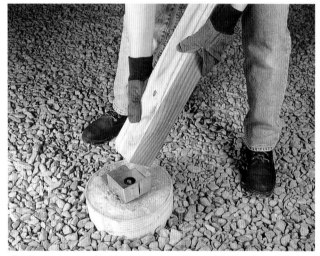

2 Set the post in the anchor. Adjustable hardware provides some play in the anchor position.

3 Close the anchor around the post, and drive nails through the anchor into the post.

💡 SMART TIP

BRACING

Even short 4x4 posts for a deck beam near ground level need to be braced securely in two directions. Drive pointed stakes into the ground about 2 feet away from the post as shown. Attach a 2x4 to each stake, and extend it up the sides of the post at a 45-degree angle. Secure with screws.

PROJECT:
ESTABLISHING POST HEIGHT

Few homeowners have levels long enough to span from the house to the posts. Extend your 4-ft. level by placing it on top of a straight board. Note that this project depicts a way of building a deck that may be overly intricate for a casual DIYer.

TOOLS & MATERIALS

- 2x4
- 4-ft. level
- Joist & beam stock
- Pencil
- Combination square
- Circular saw
- Post-cap hardware
- Drill & bits
- 1¼-in. deck screws or 8d nails
- Hammer

1 Use a straight 2x4 and level to mark the elevation of the ledger on the posts.

This photo shows a deck pier against the house foundation. This can be a problem due to the backfill and depth of the foundation.

2 Use a section of joist stock to measure down from the mark to find the bottom edge of the joist.

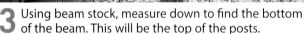

3 Using beam stock, measure down to find the bottom of the beam. This will be the top of the posts.

4 Mark a cut line with a square. Use a circular saw to cut the posts.

5 Install the post caps to each post, and secure with screws or nails. Predrill nail holes.

MAKING AND INSTALLING BEAMS

There are several things to consider when you choose the main beam for your deck. Sometimes one characteristic outweighs all others. For example, if it will be difficult to dig through rocky soil on your site, you may want the largest possible beam and only two piers. More often, several factors go into the final decision about how big and what kind of beam to use.

Beam Size. First, think about space, particularly the amount of vertical room that the beam and joists will use together. If your deck is built close to the ground, you may not have room to put a large beam on top of posts with a layer of joists on top of it. If you need to save room, it can make sense to use more posts and a smaller beam or to bolt the beam to the posts.

Another option is to use the beam itself as the header joist. You might need a large beam made of several 2x12s, for example. But instead of resting the joists on top of it, you can use framing hardware and butt the joists into its side. This way the beam is at the same level as the joists. You'll save almost a foot of vertical space.

Beam Appearance. Next think about whether the beam will be visible, and if so, what it will look like next to a stairway or an entrance to the house. No matter what type of wood you use, an evenly spaced layout and nicely installed bolts on a built-up beam can look good.

Lattice panels hide the beam in this deck.

A massive timber can have a classy yet rustic look. But availability comes into play. It may be that you can't get a good-looking 4x8, for instance.

But you have many ways to dress up a beam. You can cut a 45-degree angle off the bottom corners to create a floating effect or chamfer or rout the edges in a decorative detail. You can coat the lumber with stain to dress up the appearance of treated wood or cover the rough construction lumber altogether with a finished fascia board.

If the beam needs bracing but you don't want to use galvanized hardware in an exposed location, you can add 2x4s or 2x6s to the sides of the support posts and extend them up along the sides of the beam. This makes a neat structural sandwich that you can lock up with bolts.

Beam Weight. Lastly, consider weight. A 16-foot length of treated southern yellow pine 4x12 can be a real backbreaker. And things can get downright dangerous if you have to lift the beam high in the air. So in some cases, it is simply easier and safer to use a built-up beam.

Types of Beams

You can use several types of beams as a main support beam under deck joists. Here is a rundown of some of the most common types.

Solid. This is a beam made of a solid piece of four-by lumber, generally set on top of 4x4 posts. This has a classic, clean look, but there is little leeway for correcting mistakes, and it can be difficult to find a straight, good-looking piece of four-by lumber.

Built-Up. This is a beam made of two two-bys (photos page 121), sometimes with spacers sandwiched between (photos page 118). Before you add spacers, be sure to check the thickness of the posts on which the beam will sit—actual post thicknesses can vary a bit. This built-up assembly can actually be stronger than a solid-timber beam and is usually less expensive. But it does take some extra time to fabricate. Once you assemble the pieces, it may be just as heavy and difficult to maneuver as a conventional solid beam.

Spaced. While the code does not provide for using spaced beams, for simple ground-level decks, spaced beams are okay. This is another two-part beam consisting of two pieces of two-by lumber attached to opposing sides of the posts. Though time-consuming to build, this beam may be best for the do-it-yourselfer because it involves little heavy lifting and is easily correctable during construction.

(photos page 121), ... (photos page 118).

SMART TIP

CLAMPING CROWNS

While most structural lumber has a crown, or slight hump along one edge, it's not likely that you will find two with exactly the same curved shape. Even if you nail together a girder with both crowns up, one board may be a little higher than the other. To bring the top edges into alignment and provide a uniform base for the joists, you can drive a few toenails. But you are likely to get better results with a clamp. Set one end on the low board, the other end on the high board, and tighten to bring the two boards into line.

Laminated. This is likely to be a special-order item because the beam is made of many two-by boards that have been joined together with glue. You can build one yourself, of course. But this option is best reserved for special load conditions where you need a very large beam that is easier to assemble board by board than to buy in one piece.

There are other types of manufactured beams—for example, large timbers made from interwoven strips of wood. Because they are built and not grown, you can order one in almost any size.

Also available is the very common laminated veneer lumber, or LVL. LVL refers to beams made from the gluing together of many sheets of veneer, each sheet only a couple of millimeters thick, produced by rotary peeling of logs. The end product has strength comparable to high-end solid lumber.

Let-In. This is a beam set into notches in the posts—usually with the top of the beam flush to the top of the posts. Notching allows the beam to bear directly on the post while also allowing you to bolt through the side of the beam into the post.

Beam Locations

Joists can either rest on top of a beam (usually the simplest solution because you can hide the beam by cantilevering the deck) or be attached to the side of the beam with just hangers. Both attachment approaches will meet codes if you use large enough lumber with the proper spacing

Attaching to the Top. Where joists cross the top of a beam, you can space them out on your layout lines and tack them in place with a few toenails. This keeps them from shifting, although being attached to a ledger, header, and bridging makes it difficult for them to shift at all. But there are small pieces of hardware (galvanized straps with a twisted shape) that you can use to tack the joist to the beam without toenails. In some areas, your building department may require these tie-downs to help resist special loads.

Attaching to the Side. By attaching joists to the side of the beam, you can run the joists at the same level as the beam. In fact, the beam takes the place of the header joist and so will be cut to exact length and marked for joists in conjunction with the ledger. As always, make sure the beam is crown side up when you mark for the joists. All beams have a tendency to sag when they are loaded, and installing the crowns up provides some extra resistance to sagging.

Beam Assembly

You can use lag screws and washers to assemble the components of a beam, or predrill and bolt all the way through. But most carpenters simply nail them, and reserve lags and bolts for attaching the ledger and connecting beams to posts.

In most cases, if you drive nails with a hammer, you'll be fine with rows of three fasteners about 12 inches apart. For even more strength, you can flip over the beam and install some fasteners through the other face as well. Best of all, though, is to use a three-ply beam and fasten from both sides into the middle.

Be sure to use nails or screws that penetrate all the components without poking through on the other

PROJECT: 🐾🐾
PACKING OUT BEAMS

Use treated lumber for the spacers.

TOOLS & MATERIALS
- Beam stock
- ½-in. treated spacers
- Clamps
- 10d nails
- Hammer

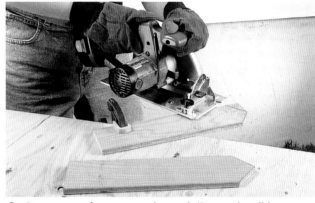

1 Cut spacers from treated wood. (Per code, all beams must be treated or naturally decay-resistant.)

2 Tack the spacers to one side of one beam. Set the spacers 16 in. on center.

3 Place the other board on top to create a spacer sandwich. Secure with 10d nails.

side and that align with code requirements.

Installing a Beam

The following is the basic sequence you can use to place your main beam in the right position.

Mark the Corner Posts. Use a level and a long, straight piece of lumber, a line level, or a water level to mark the location of the beam on the posts. It's wise to mark the two corner posts first, and check and double-check your marks from the ledger and between the posts themselves. Once the corner posts are marked, you can string a line between them to mark any other posts in line under the beam. You want to find the spot on the post that is level with the top of the ledger. If you want the deck to slope slightly for drainage, measure down from that mark ¹⁄₁₆ inch for every foot of joist travel. But most builders do this only on decks with closed surfaces—for example, tongue-and-groove boards you might be more likely to use on a porch floor.

Because typical decks have spaces between the boards, there is more than enough area for water to drain. From the mark that indicates where the tops of the joists will be, measure down the depth of a joist to find the top of the beam. Follow these steps on both corner posts, and check the post marks for level.

If you plan to butt the joists into the main beam, remember not to make the last measurement. When you level across from the top of the ledger, you will be marking the tops of the joists and the top of the beam at the same time.

Mark the Rest of the Posts. Use a chalk line to extend lines between the marks you made on the corner posts. You might double-check the line marks with a level to be sure you will be cutting in the right place. Take the extra time to verify your level lines.

Once you are certain of the marks, use a square to extend lines onto all the faces of your posts. You'll need these when you cut because most circular saws can't cut

deeply enough to go through a 4x4 post in one pass. (See "Cutting Posts" on page 77.)

Cut Off the Posts. To make your cuts safely and accurately, be sure that the posts are securely braced. Double-check your circular saw to make sure it cuts at a perfect right angle.

Because this is an unusual cut and you have to hold the saw sideways, get into a comfortable position with solid footing. Try to keep the same margin along the marked lines—for example, leaving the pencil line on and cutting just up to it. This will help you get a flat surface on the post even though you need to make two or three passes.

Cutting the Beam. If the beam will be low to the ground, you don't want to let the piece run long and cut it in place. You should probably recheck your measurements. But at this point your posts should be locked in proper plumb position in a line that is squared up with the ledger on the house.

If you are using a spaced-type beam and plan to build it up in pieces along several posts, be sure that the splices will fall over the centers of the posts. You'll need to be careful making these connections. Predrilling is essential to avoid splitting the beam pieces and the post.

If you need to make multiple splices on your beam, plan the lumber lengths so that you splice one side of the beam on one post and the other side on another.

Attach the Beam. If you have a heavy beam to set, arrange for plenty of help and be sure that any ladders you use are stable. There is an extra step you can take to be sure that the beam won't topple off your posts during assembly.

The idea is to temporarily but securely screw a piece of 2x4 or 2x6, called a scab, onto the corner posts

WAYS TO ADD STRENGTH TO A BEAM

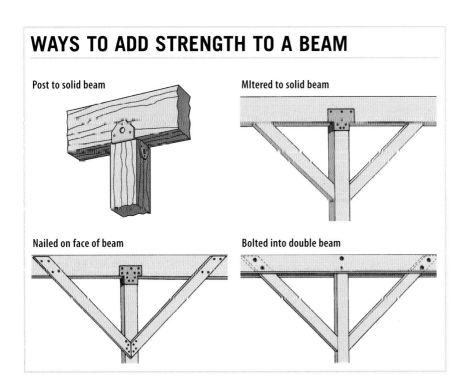

Post to solid beam

Mitered to solid beam

Nailed on face of beam

Bolted into double beam

with at least 6 inches projecting past the top. As you get the beam into position, it will bear down on the posts, of course, and now it won't tip because of the scab. You can have a clamp at the ready and use it to pin the beam to the scab as soon as you set the heavy timber in place. This approach can help even if you install galvanized

hardware connectors on the posts. This hardware will likely be required by local codes.

A typical connector has two flanges that fit over the post, and two that rise up around the beam. When the timber is in place, you can tack through perforated holes in the fastener to lock the pieces together.

MAXIMUM DECK BEAMS SPAN — 40 PSF LIVE LOAD

BEAM SPECIES	BEAM SIZE	EFFECTIVE JOIST SPAN LENGTH (FEET)					
		6	8	10	12	14	16
		MAXIMUM DECK BEAM SPAN LENGTH					
Southern Pine	One 2x6	4' 7"	4' 0"	3' 7"	3' 3"	3' 0"	2' 10"
	One 2x8	5' 11"	5' 1"	4' 7"	4' 2"	3' 10"	3' 7"
	One 2x10	7' 0"	6' 0"	5' 5"	4' 11"	4' 7"	4' 3"
	One 2x12	8' 3"	7' 1"	6' 4"	5' 10"	5' 5"	5' 0"
	Two 2x6	6' 11"	5' 11"	5' 4"	4' 10"	4' 6"	4' 3"
	Two 2x8	8' 9"	7' 7"	6' 9"	6' 2"	5' 9"	5' 4"
	Two 2x10	10' 4"	9' 0"	8' 0"	7' 4"	6' 9"	6' 4"
	Two 2x12	12' 2"	10' 7"	9' 5"	8' 7"	8' 0"	7' 5"
	Three 2x6	8' 6"	7' 5"	6' 8"	6' 1"	5' 8"	5' 3"
	Three 2x8	10' 11"	9' 6"	8' 6"	7' 9"	7' 2"	6' 8"
	Three 2x10	13' 0"	11' 2"	10' 0"	9' 2"	8' 6"	7' 11"
	Three 2x12	15' 3"	13' 3"	11' 10"	10' 9"	10' 0"	9' 4"
Douglas fir-larch Hem-fir Spruce-pine-fir	One 2x6	4' 1"	3' 6"	3' 0"	2' 8"	2' 5"	2' 3"
	One 2x8	5' 6"	4' 8"	4' 0"	3' 6"	3' 2"	2' 11"
	One 2x10	6' 8"	5' 10"	5' 1"	4' 6"	4' 1"	3' 9"
	One 2x12	7' 9"	6' 9"	6' 0"	5' 6"	5' 0"	3' 9"
	Two 2x6	6' 1"	5' 3"	4' 9"	4' 4"	3' 11"	3' 7"
	Two 2x8	8' 2"	7' 1"	6' 4"	5' 9"	5' 2"	4' 8"
	Two 2x10	10' 0"	8' 7"	7' 9"	7' 0"	6' 6"	6' 0"
	Two 2x12	11' 7"	10' 0"	8' 11"	8' 2"	7' 7"	7' 1"
	Three 2x6	7' 8"	6' 8"	6' 0"	5' 6"	5' 1"	4' 9"
	Three 2x8	10' 3"	8' 10"	7' 11"	7' 3"	6' 8"	6' 3"
	Three 2x10	12' 6"	10' 10"	9' 8"	8' 10"	8' 2"	7' 8"
	Three 2x12	14' 6"	12' 7"	11' 3"	10' 3"	9' 6"	8' 11"
Redwood Western cedars Ponderosa pine Red pine	One 2x6	4' 2"	3' 7"	3' 1"	2' 9"	2' 6"	2' 3"
	One 2x8	5' 4"	4' 7"	4' 1"	3' 7"	3' 3"	3' 0"
	One 2x10	6' 6"	5' 7"	5' 0"	4' 7"	4' 2"	3' 10"
	One 2x12	7' 6"	6' 6"	5' 10"	5' 4"	4' 11"	4' 7"
	Two 2x6	6' 2"	5' 4"	4' 10"	4' 5"	4' 0"	3' 8"
	Two 2x8	7' 10"	6' 10"	6' 1"	5' 7"	5' 2"	4' 10"
	Two 2x10	9' 7"	8' 4"	7' 5"	6' 9"	6' 3"	5' 10"
	Two 2x12	11' 1"	9' 8"	8' 7"	7' 10"	7' 3"	6' 10"
	Three 2x6	7' 8"	6' 9"	6' 0"	5' 6"	5' 1"	4' 9"
	Three 2x8	9' 10"	8' 6"	7' 7"	6' 11"	6' 5"	6' 0"
	Three 2x10	12' 0"	10' 5"	9' 4"	8' 6"	7' 10"	7' 4"
	Three 2x12	13' 11"	12' 1"	10' 9"	9' 10"	9' 1"	8' 6"

Note: Be sure to check all allowable spans between supports and all lumber requirements with your local building department.

PROJECT: 🐾🐾🐾
MAKING AND SETTING A BUILT-UP BEAM

Find the crowns on your lumber, and assemble the beam with the crowns up.

TOOLS & MATERIALS
- Clamps
- 10d nails
- Hammer
- Level
- 2x4 braces
- Stakes
- Drill & bits
- 1¼-in. deck screws

1 Sight down the stock and locate the crown. Place the crowns side by side.

2 Nail the boards together; use groups of 3 fasteners 12 in. on center.

3 Put the beam in the post caps crown side up. You may need a helper.

4 Plumb the beam. Braces help keep the posts from shifting.

This photo shows a deck pier against the house foundation. This can be a problem due to the backfill and depth of the foundation. NOTE: Piers and footings supporting deck posts must bear on undisturbed soil and cannot bear on backfill material around an existing foundation.

5 Secure the beam with a series of braces. Drive screws through the post caps into the beam.

JOIST LAYOUTS

Every part of a deck needs careful layout, of course. But when it comes time to plan out and install the joists, you need to be sure to account for the decking that will cover them. Because you will most likely be using decking in stock lengths, generally in 2-foot increments, you want to make a modular layout that makes the most efficient use of the materials you buy.

Modular framing layouts for most decks (and for most house frames) work in multiples of 16 inches. That's the distance from the centerline of one joist to the centerline of the next one in line. Two units make 32 inches, and three make 48 inches, which is another basic building block of construction that matches the width of drywall panels, plywood, and other sheet materials.

You would end up wasting a lot of wood if you didn't maintain the 16-inch module. There wouldn't be a joist where you needed one at the end of a deck board.

Planning Lengths of Deck Boards. Oftentimes your deck boards won't be long enough to reach from one end joist to another. If for example, the deck is 29 feet, 2 inches wide, you might use a 16-foot deck board and a 14-foot deck board for each course. In this case the boards meet at the center of a joist. That's why the modular layout is from center to center, so that each board is supported by half a joist's width. Stagger the joints in this situation—start one course with the longer board and the next course with the shorter board so the joints fall on different joists. This looks better and also knits the deck together more strongly. Typically you'll let the ends of the decking boards "run wild" when you install them, then snap chalk lines to cut them all to final length with a circular saw. Many people pitch the deck away from the house very slightly so that the water runs away from the house.

Spacing the Joists. Because the joists are 1½ inch thick there will be 14½ inches between each set of joists. The exceptions, as you will see in the next paragraph, are the rim joists and the joists closest to each one.

MAXIMUM DECK JOIST SPANS				
		JOIST SPACING (O.C.)		
		12"	16"	24"
SPECIES	SIZE	ALLOWABLE SPAN		
Southern Pine	2x6	9' 11"	9' 0"	7' 7"
	2x8	13' 1"	11' 10"	9' 8"
	2x10	16' 2"	14' 0"	11' 5"
	2x12	18' 0"	16' 6"	13' 6"
Douglas Fir-Larch Hem-Fir Spruce-Pine-Fir	2x6	9' 6"	8' 4"	6' 10"
	2x8	12' 6"	11' 1"	9' 1"
	2x10	15' 8"	13' 7"	11' 1"
	2x12	18' 0"	15' 9"	12' 10"
Redwood Western Cedars Ponderosa Pine Red Pine	2x6	8' 10"	8' 0"	6' 10"
	2x8	11' 8"	10' 7"	8' 8"
	2x10	14' 11"	13' 0"	10' 7"
	2x12	17'5"	15' 1"	12' 4"

Note: Be sure to check all allowable spans between supports and all lumber requirements with your local building department.

💡 SMART TIP

JOIST ASSISTS

When large joists are too heavy to set yourself, this add-on makes the job possible. Temporarily screw on a strip of wood that overhangs the joist. When you wrestle the joist into place, the strip rests on the ledger and carries the weight.

No matter how beautiful the finished project looks, all well-built decks start with a carefully constructed post, beam, and joist support system.

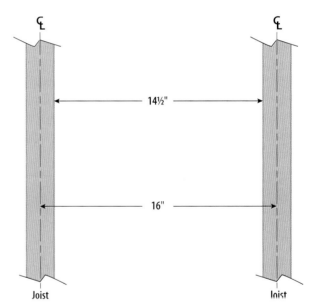

With the exception of rim joists, joist spacing should be 16 inches apart on the center line. Since joists are 1½ inches thick, the space between the joist edges will actually measure 14½ inches.

Although you want the joists to be 16 inches on center, a centerline would be covered by the end of the joist, so you'll actually strike a line at the location for one side of each joist, and then mark an X at the side of the line where the joist will be. Because the joists are 1½ inch wide, the side marks will be ¾ inch from the center of each joist. Fortunately no math is needed to allow for this when doing your layout. Just hook your tape measure over one end of the ledger or beam and strike a line at 15¼ inches to mark the side of the first joist in

from the outermost joist. (The 16-inch on center spacing starts from the outside of the rim joist, so the spacing between it and the next joist will be 13¾ inches.) Tape measures have special marks to indicate 16-inch intervals, so all you need to do is strike a line ¾ inch to the same side of each interval to indicate the side of each joist. The distance between the second-to-last joist and the other rim joist will be whatever is left over—for example, for a 31-foot-2-inch-wide deck, it would be 11¾ inches.

USING PRACTICAL TOOLS

Up to this point on a typical deck project, there has been no production work where you have to turn out dozens of members. You had to set a few posts and hammer some nails, of course. But getting joists is different. On most decks there are a lot of them, which means creating a DIY version of contractor-style production work when it comes to cutting and fastening them in place.

Saws. A handsaw will work, naturally, and you will need one to finish some cuts. But a circular saw is easier and faster. A 7¼-inch model is good for overall framing work. Smaller saws can't cut through a 2x4 in one pass, and larger ones are unwieldy. Use a combination blade for cutting with and across the grain—a blade with about 24 teeth is included with many saws when you buy them.

Hammers. With hammers, the reverse is true for most people: the hand-powered version works best. Air-power may not be for every do-it-yourselfer, since they are often more comfortable using a tool with which they are familiar, but an air-powered nail gun makes building a whole deck go much easier and faster.

In most cases, a 16-ounce claw hammer is the right choice. It's maneuverable in tight spaces and light enough to use for more than a few minutes. Heavier hammers pack more punch—on mishits as well as on nails—but a big hammer with a straight ripping claw can be cumbersome and wear you out if you're not used to hammering. Try handles of fiberglass or steel with special inserts and grip rings and rubber sleeves—whatever feels best.

💡 **SMART TIP**

CARRYING EXTRA LOADS

A large spa or hot-tub spa loaded with water and people can weigh, on the high end, about 10,000 pounds. You'll need additional strength in your framing if you install one on a deck. Check the manufacturer's installation specs and consult your local building department to be sure that your framing is designed to adequately support this extra load. Consult your local building department with all equipment and usages of your proposed deck to ensure proper design and load capabilities. These applications may require a structural engineer to certify the design. You may be able to double up the adjacent joists, or you might be required to install additional posts and beams.

This deck was built before the current deck code. Handrails are required on stairs with four or more risers (three treads).

Most decks require only the use of basic hand tools.

PROJECT: 🐾🐾🐾
SETTING THE INNER JOIST

On decks that tuck into a corner, you need only one ledger, generally on the long side of the deck. The inner joist might look like a ledger from a distance, but it actually is the first joist and is not attached to the house.

TOOLS & MATERIALS
- Joist material
- Gloves
- Hammer
- 16d galvanized nails
- Framing square
- Corner bracket
- Joist-hanger nails
- Twist fasteners

This photo shows a deck pier against the house foundation. This can be a problem due to the backfill and depth of the foundation.

1 When you set the first joist in place, sight down its length to find the crown. Install it crown side up.

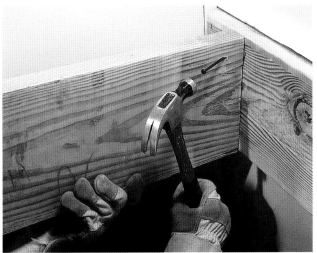

2 Tack the edge of the joist to the ledger by toenailing the two together.

3 To provide added strength, nail on a hurricane tie where the joist crosses the main beam.

Even many contractors who routinely use pneumatic tools also carry the old-fashioned version.

Drill-Drivers. While nails, often in conjunction with hardware such as joist hangers, still make most of the framing connections, screws are used for many of the connections in a modern deck, including installing deck boards and constructing railings. Thanks to improvements in battery technology, cordless drill drivers are light in weight and powerful enough to make corded drills all but obsolete. One option is an impact hammer which has an impact option that easily drills screws into tough material without stripping the screw heads.

You can fit the drill with a screwdriving bit, or a boring bit to drill pilot holes for screws if you have trouble driving them. One way to simplify the operation and get a taste of production work is to use a quick-change accessory. It fastens into the chuck of the drill and has a snap-in-and-snap-out sleeve that accepts boring bits and screwing bits. You don't have to loosen the chuck and refit a new bit every time you switch from drilling pilot holes to driving screws.

Another handy option is an extension sleeve that fastens into the chuck around a screwdriving bit. The idea is to fit the screwhead onto the driving head of the bit, then slip the sleeve over the screw so that you can drive it in a straight line. The little gadget keeps the bit from jumping off the screw—and maybe onto your finger. There are also drill attachments that feed strips of screws into a standard drill so that you don't have to reload. But the preloaded strips are much more expensive than buying screws by the box.

PROJECT: 🐦🐦🐦
SETTING THE OUTER JOIST

It is important to have a good, clean, square cut on the outer joist—if only because it will probably be the most prominent on the deck.

TOOLS & MATERIALS
- Joist material
- Measuring tape
- Pencil
- Framing square
- Circular saw
- Hammer
- 16d nails
- Corner bracket & nails

1 Measure out from the beam to determine the amount of overhang.

2 Use a framing square to draw a cut line on the joist. Leave beam and post braces in place.

3 Cut the outer joist using a circular saw. This is usually a prominent area, so make a clean cut.

4 Before nailing, make sure the deck frame is square and the two outside joists are equal.

5 Drive a toenail through the joist into the beam. Reinforce this with a twist fastener.

FRAMING HARDWARE

Galvanized metal connectors play a big role in making modern decks strong and safe. In fact, in some applications connectors are required by code. For example, building codes usually require joist hangers to be used to attach joists to ledgers. Joist hangers may or may not be required to connect joists through the header. When the joists are cantilevered over a beam, local code may allow you to nail through the face of the header into the end of the joists. Always check your local code.

To meet code, joist hangers must be installed with the approved fasteners. Hurricane ties are connectors that usually are required on any deck that has joists resting on a beam. There are two types, both of which are installed with 1½ in. approved connector nails. One type has two flat surfaces at right angles to each other. One surface is nailed to the side of the joist and the other to the side of the beam below. The other type slides up over the joist and has flanges that are nailed to the joist and the header. (See page 40.)

INSTALLING FLOOR JOISTS

In the majority of decks, joists are attached to the ledger on one end and are cantilevered over a beam with a header joist nailed to their ends to form the outside of the deck frame. There are various approaches to installing joists in this situation. One of the most common is to first install the two joists that meet the ends of the ledger, cut them to length, make sure they are square to the ledger, and then tack them in place by toenailing into the beam. (See "Setting the Inner Joist," page 125 and "Setting the Outer Joist," page 126.)

Then you can install all the other joists, letting the lengths run wild past the beam. After squaring those joists, you'll tack a temporary brace across them to hold them in position while you'll stretch a chalk line between the two joists you already cut (the inner joist and the outer joist if you are building into a corner of the house). Next snap a line on the top of all the other joists. You'll transfer this line to the side of the joists. By cutting them all off at this line you'll know they are the right length without having to measure each one.

(See "Setting the Inner Joist," page 125 and "Setting the Outer Joist," page 126.)

⚲ SMART TIP

STRAIGHTENING JOISTS

It's likely that you will get a few twisted timbers in a load of deck joists. You may be able to return the worst of them. But there will be some twists and turns that won't line up with your square layout lines. To get rid of a small twist, secure a clamp near the end and use the handle for leverage. To increase your leverage, use several clamps to attach a 2x4, and use it as the handle.

A twisted joist won't square up. Use a clamp to pull it into position.

Nail the joist into its final position.

Attach the Header Joist. If your end joists sit on top of the beam, attach them flush to the ends of the beam. Attach the header to the joists with three 16d galvanized nails through the header into the ends of the joists. Remember that stock-sized lumber does not always have

spots or cracks that can be trimmed away to create tight joints at the critical corners of the frame.

Install Joist Hangers. You should install joist hangers on the ledger and on the beam and according to your local code. You can install each joist and joist hanger as shown in "Setting Joists," opposite, or you can install all of the hangers and then go back and install the joists.

Take a short block of joist material, and hold it in place—it should touch the line and cover the X, but most importantly, its top edge must be flush with the top of the ledger or header. Slide the joist hanger up against it so that it touches on one side only. There are pointed tabs on the hanger; pound them in to hold the hanger position. Drive two nails through one side of the flange to secure the hanger. Double-check to make sure the block is still accurately in place, then close the hanger around it and fasten the other side with the recommended number of hanger nails.

Slide the Joists in Place. The joist ends may butt tightly against the ledger or header at all points. However, joist ends are permitted to have a ⅛-inch gap between them and the header. It's okay to have a larger gap—the joist hanger may still work—but that comes with reduction in load-bearing capacity, as the manufacturer's information may point out. Cut the joists to length.

Right now you're probably itching to make some real, visible progress in a hurry. But at this point it's a very good idea to take a little time first to seal the open grain of the cut ends with some sealer/preservative. In fact, per the code and the AWPA M4 standard, you must seal the cut ends.

Install each joist crown side up. This is a two-person operation. If things are tight, you may have to slide both ends down at the same time. A little pounding is fine, but if a joist is so tight that it starts to bend, take it out, measure again, and recut it.

If you have the kind of flashing that makes a 90-degree turn to cover the face of the ledger, just set the joist against the turned edge. Your flashing should have a down-turned edge; otherwise, water will wick under the flashing on top of the ledger. But don't dislodge the metal (or tear it) by bending the flashing up as you install joists.

Finish Fastening. Eyeball the framing to see that everything looks straight and parallel. Joist hangers and other metal connectors must be installed in accordance with the manufacturer's installation instructions and the specific size and length of nail and/or structural screws specified. Where joists rest on a beam, drive a nail to minimize twisting. Hurricane ties provide extra hold-down strength. They may be required by code, but even if they are not, it's a good idea to install them for under $100.

PROJECT: 🐿️🐿️🐿️
SETTING JOISTS

Make the joists and ledger flush; then install joist hangers. Some codes require the use of joist hangers.

TOOLS & MATERIALS

- Joists
- Square
- Pencil
- Gloves
- Horses and saw
- Hammer
- Scrap wood
- Joist hangers
- Twist fasteners
- Measuring tape
- 1x4 brace

1 Make a square cut on the ledger-end of the joists. Allow the other end to run long for now.

2 To help support the joist, nail a strip of wood with a small overhang to the joist.

3 Slip the joist hanger around the joist. Check for level and drive nails through the joist hanger.

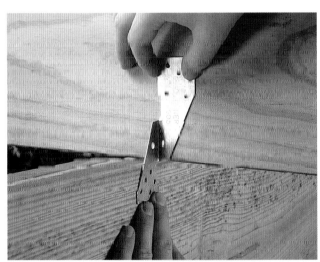

4 Add a hurricane or strong tie where the joist crosses the beam.

5 Copy ledger layout lines to a brace. Tack to joist at midspan, bringing joists to your marks.

Bracing

Decks that are raised above the ground need extra lateral support to keep them from swaying. An on-top solid beam has less lateral strength than a bolted-on beam and may need bracing even if it is lower.

Bracing can add a finish, hand-crafted look, and for less work than you might think. The only tricks are making accurate 45-deg. cuts and making sure that the braces are in symmetrical relation to each other and are exactly the same size, for a uniform look.

Y-Bracing. In most cases, simple Y-bracing is sufficient. To brace a solid beam on top of a post, cut pieces of post material (4x4 or 6x6) to go under the beam and against the sides of the post, or use 2x4s or 2x6s and attach them to the face of the post and beam. For beams attached to opposing sides of a post, sandwich the braces between the beams, and secure them using lag screws, bolts, or carriage bolts.

Y-braces add lateral support.

PROJECT: 🐾🐾🐾
TRIMMING JOISTS

Snap a line, and the cut joists will form a dead-straight line. Trim the joist ends using a circular saw.

TOOLS & MATERIALS
- Measuring tape
- Pencil
- Chalk-line box
- Framing square
- Circular saw

You will need to trim the joists because they do not come from the lumberyard in exact lengths. This is to get them to the same length.

1 Measure out from the ledger on each of the end joists. Mark the top of the end joists.

2 Line up the chalk line; the string should touch each joist. Snap the line.

3 Draw a cutting line with a framing square. Trim each joist using a circular saw.

Raised Decks

If you are building a deck that's 8 feet or more above the ground, most of the layout will be the same, but your work methods might differ dramatically. Most operations will take twice as long to perform, as you spend lots of time wrestling with ladders, carrying things up and down, and being extra careful.

Decking, ledgers, joists, and beams have all the same requirements as decks built low to the ground. However, there are a few key differences that you should take into account. For example, decks near the ground may not need a railing, which could alter your plans for post and joist placement. You should always check your local code to confirm railing and other requirements.

Bracing the Posts. To prevent shifting, you also may need lateral bracing, such as an X-pattern of 2x4s or 2x6s that ties together several long posts. Generally, concrete piers that extend below the local frost line offer the most solid and durable support for deck posts. And with this system, the posts sit a couple to several inches aboveground (locked in place with galvanized hardware), which greatly reduces the possibility of rot due to ground contact. (See "Anchoring Posts," page 114.) Use 2x4s or even 2x6s for temporary bracing. Pound the stakes deep into the ground.

Wait until the framing or even the entire deck is completed before pouring the concrete around the posts.

PROJECT: 🐁🐁🐁
SETTING THE HEADER JOIST

Adding a header joist is the last step before installing bridging. Save time and keep an accurate layout by marking the ledger and the header joist at the same time. They should be the same size.

TOOLS & MATERIALS
- Joist material
- Clamps
- Scrap wood
- Hammer
- 16d nails
- Corner brackets
- Joist hangers
- Joist hanger nails

1 The header joist holds the ends of the joists in place and helps maintain proper spacing.

2 Create a temporary shelf for the header by clamping strips of wood to the bottom of three or four joists.

3 Making sure the top edge of the header and the tops of the joists are flush, nail the header in place.

This will make your footing stronger because it will not get banged around during the construction process, which could loosen the concrete's bond with the post or with the earth. Also, doing it this way gives you the luxury of being able to make small adjustments to the posts, if necessary.

Notching the Post. Though not recommended elsewhere, notching the post for a beam is the best method when you have 6x6 posts. This approach provides better attachment than setting the beam atop the posts, and it helps prevent the beam from twisting. After you have cut the post to height, use your angle square to mark for the beam; the minimum requirement is to notch it completely in, so that the face of the beam ends up flush with the face of the post. That way, the beam is fully supported for its width. To do this, first set your circular-saw cutting depth to equal the thickness of the beam—for example 3 inches for a beam made of doubled two-bys. Make the seat cut first. Then, with the circular saw set to the same depth, run the saw down each side.

Attach the beam with through-bolts such as screw bolts rather than lag screws. Apply siliconized latex caulk to the joints, and give the exposed end grain of the post a healthy dose of a preservative-sealer.

SMART TIP

NAILING THE HEADER JOIST

When you box in the free ends of the joists, you may find that some are a little high or a little low, even though they all sit on the same beam. Help bring them into line by working with a helper who can raise or lower the free end of the header joist as you work down the row. Even a small amount of leverage will help you align the tops of the opposing timbers. And the tops need to be flush for your decking to lie flat. You will lose leverage as you connect more joists, but this trick can save you some planing or trimming work.

Step Decks

Some decks can have several levels, which means you'll have at least one step where deck platforms meet. These steps must be comfortable. Generally, each step should be no greater in height than a 7¾-inch stair rise. This maximum height, however, is amended differently in different local codes across the country, so be sure to check your local building code. Because the actual width of a 2x8 is 7¼ inches, often the easiest way to accomplish a level change is to place a 2x8 joist on top of the frame below. Remember that even a simple step-down between two large platforms can count as a step and be governed by building codes. As always, be sure to check the specifications for level changes with your local building department.

When planning and building a change in level, take care that no decking pieces will be left unsupported at their ends. One approach is to make a second framing box. For small raised areas, the simplest method is to first build the main deck, then construct a box of framing that sits on top of it. This is not cost-effective for larger raised areas, however, because double framing is under the raised section.

Another approach is to create shared beam support. This way, the upper level partially overlaps the lower so that they share the support of the same beam on one end. The end joists of the upper platform can fall directly over the end joist and beam below or it can overlap the level below by about 12 inches. Each level will have its own support at its other end. (See "Changing Levels," page 134.)

Multi-step decks can add a lot of beauty and functionality to a home. Remember if designing and building a multi-step deck that all decking pieces must be supported through their ends.

BUILDING AROUND TREES

Before you frame in a tree, find out how quickly your tree will grow, and leave enough room for the next ten years at least. But remember that trees can blow in the wind, too. The point is not to crowd the trunk too much. Instead, frame a roomy square or octagonal opening. Add extra bracing, you can cut a circle in the decking if you'd like.

The framing plan is relatively simple. When a joist in the basic framing structure is interrupted, you have to build a structural bridge to carry loads around the opening. It is one of the most basic operations of construction.

Start by laying out the rough opening and seeing where the joists in your modular layout fall. Chances are, you'll have to add at least one more joist to make an even box around the tree. You may have to add two.

But instead of adding a full joist, even if the tree isn't in the way, add two headers at right angles to the deck framing. (As always, check these header requirements with the local building department. You may need only single headers, but in some cases you might need to double them up.)

Once you have set the headers in place and secured them with galvanized hangers, you can fill in the layout with two pieces of joist lumber. Where the load that would have been carried on one continuous joist is interrupted by the tree opening, the load is shifted by the headers to the adjacent joists. In some cases where you make a large opening, you may also need to double up both full-length joists beside the opening. Your decision about whether to double up or not is also determined by where within the length of the span the headers are connected.

FLOOR BRIDGING

The joists will be pinned at each end but float freely between the house and the outer edge of the deck. You may want to treat the deck like a floor frame inside the house and add bridging. This is a series of short boards or metal braces, typically set along the midspan of the joists.

There is some disagreement about just how much strength and stability bridging adds to a floor frame. Some reports suggest that it isn't really necessary. But those findings generally refer to indoor framing where the joists are covered with a plywood subfloor, tying the joists together. Regardless, bridging greatly stiffens a deck.

Outside on a deck, most people find that bridging does stiffen the frame. The top edges of the joists will eventually be secured with deck boards, but the bottom edges won't be. That's another area where bridging can help: it helps to keep joists from twisting. And keep in mind that composite decking doesn't stabilize joists as much as wood does, another reason to consider using bridging.

Several types of bridging include old-fashioned wood cross braces installed in an X-pattern, the same basic setup in metal, and solid bridging cut from the same lumber as your joists. On decks, solid bridging often is the most practical system, particularly if you have cutoffs from your joists.

Bridging Layouts

Solid bridging cut from floor-joist material is easy to install. In a nutshell, you snap a chalk line across the center of the joist span and add bridging in a staggered pattern, alternating from one side of the chalk line to the

CHANGING LEVELS

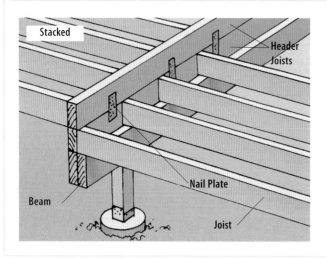

Stacked — Header Joists — Nail Plate — Beam — Joist

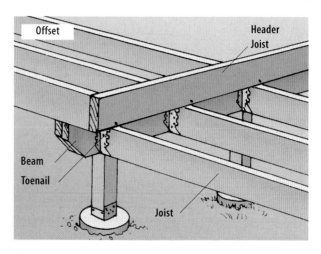

Offset — Header Joist — Beam — Toenail — Joist

other so that you can drive end nails instead of toenails. (See "Installing Bridging," page 136.)

In theory, every piece of bridging should be the same length. But you may find small discrepancies in the joist layout. If you simply add the same size piece of bridging in each bay, you might build in an accumulation of errors.

That's one good reason for temporarily tacking a brace across the tops of the joists. You can use a long 1x4, for example. The idea is to set the brace along your ledger and transfer the joist layout. Then set the brace near your chalk line and bring each joist into line on your layout marks.

You should be able to rely on the measurements, but it pays to take a look down each joist from the outer end of the deck to make sure it's straight. You need only one nail through the brace into each joist, and you don't need to drive it home.

Framing to allow a tree or shrub to grow through the deck adds design interest to the project. It also eliminates the need to remove large trees, an expensive and difficult process.

SMALL FRAMED OPENINGS

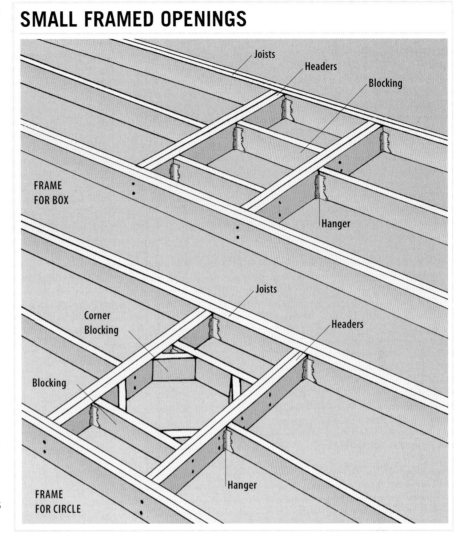

PROJECT: 🐿🐿🐿
INSTALLING BRIDGING

The best material for bridging is often the material used for the joists. Offset the placement of bridging for easy nailing

TOOLS & MATERIALS
- Measuring tape
- Pencil
- Chalk-line box
- Combination square
- Saw
- Joist stock
- Hammer
- 16d nails

1 Find the centerpoint of the two outer joists. Snap a chalk line between them.

2 Transfer the marks to the sides of the joist. Use a square that will reach the bottom of the joists.

3 Each joist bay will get a section of solid blocking, but you will need to offset them for nailing.

4 Cut bridging from joist stock, and install between joists. The brace helps maintain proper spacing.

5 Drive two nails into each edge of the bridging. Remove the brace when bridging is installed.

For blocking out the bridging, eyeballing them is sufficient. It's not a big deal if the bridging lumber isn't perfectly vertical. Remember that in one bay the bridging needs to ride on one side of the lines, and in the next bay it needs to ride on the other side.

The final step is straightforward once you have prepared the job. Just cut the blocks, tap them into position on your marks, and drive at least two nails into each end. If you find that the bridging blocks are not exactly the same size as the joists, keep the tops flush with the tops of the joists. That's where the decking will ride, so you want all the framing components to be in one flat plane.

Moving Joists

There may be one or two joists that have a big twist that is difficult to correct. You probably should have left them at the lumberyard, but sometimes a crooked board or two slips by, and you have to find a way to use it.

To push or pull a joist into place on the layout marks of your temporary brace, you can use other joists as a backstop for a 2x4 and force the crooked timber into place.

If you need to untwist a joist, say, to line it up with your square mark on a header, use a lever to help with the untwisting. One approach is to securely clamp a short 2x4 onto the joist and simply pull it to one side or the other until the joist corrects. You may need a helper to hold the position while you drive several nails. With a minor twist, you may be able to use the clamp itself as a lever. It's a good idea to overcorrect slightly because the joist will likely slip back slightly. (See "Aligning Joists," page 138.)

FRAMING A CURVED SECTION

After installing the beams, let the joists run wild at the curved section. Mark them for cutting only after you've secured all of them in place. You'll need a laminated header for the curved section.

For V-pattern decking, lay out the joists, as shown below. Start in the middle. Establish the joist where the tip of the V-shape in the decking will fall. Next, measure 16 inches on center to either side of this joist. Install the joists using joist hangers secured to the ledger. Install the two short header joists, allowing them to run longer than needed. For the curve, splice the joists over the beam, and allow them to run wild past where they will be cut. Double the thickness of the center joist by scabbing on pieces of 2x4. Make sure that you attach the joists firmly in place.

If your deck will contain decking running in one direction only, there is no need to add the doubled-up center joist.

FRAMING FOR CURVES

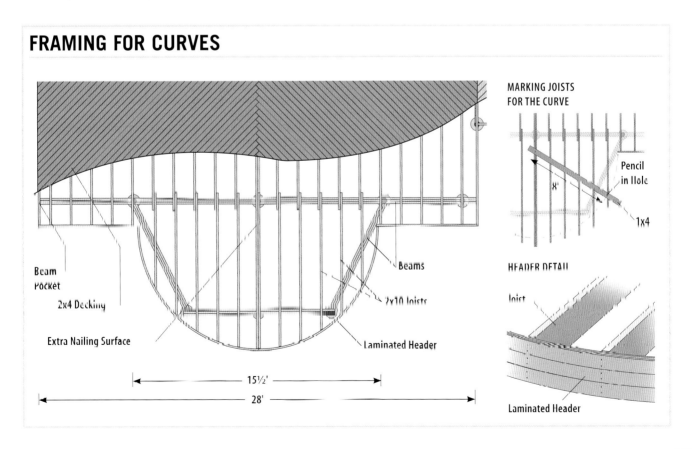

Beam Pocket

2x4 Decking

Extra Nailing Surface

Beams

2x10 Joists

Laminated Header

15½'

28'

MARKING JOISTS FOR THE CURVE

Pencil in Hole

1x4

HEADER DETAIL

Joist

Laminated Header

PROJECT: 🐁🐁🐁
ALIGNING JOISTS

... your brace, transfer them from the marks on your ledger.

TOOLS & MATERIALS
- Square
- Pencil
- 1x4 brace
- Hammer
- 10d nails
- Clamp

1 When you attach your brace, you will probably find some joists out of alignment.

2 Push or pull the offending joist into alignment. Use clamps or spreaders for this job.

Mark the Curve. To mark the joists for the curve, loop string around your pencil lead. For the dimensions shown here, set the string length at exactly 8 feet. To establish the centerpoint of the radius, set the other end of the string at the center of the doubled-up joist. Now swing your compass around the arc to mark the top of each joist. Adjust the size of the compass to the dimensions of your deck.

Use a square to mark plumb lines down from the compass marks, and cut each joist with a circular saw. Note: Adjust the bevel of the saw for each cut to make sure that it follows the compass mark on top of the joist.

Curved Fascia. To make a curved header/fascia, resaw 2x4s into 5/16 x 3 1/2 inch pieces using a table saw. But beware! A table saw is a very dangerous tool and re-sawing 2x4s on edge is a tricky, dangerous job. If you're a typical do-it-yourselfer, avoid this step. An alternative is to get an experienced carpenter's help. Then laminate five or six of these strips together. Cut the 2x4s longer than you'll need so that the fascia won't end up short.

To make a gluing form, cut pieces of plywood that match the curve of the deck. Then laminate the strips together using epoxy, clamping them to the curved form every 6 inches. You'll need to use lots of clamps. Cover every strip thoroughly with epoxy, or the slats may delaminate. Allow the assembly to dry for 24 hours, then belt-sand the edge to produce a finished appearance.

Set the pieces in place, and fasten them to the ends of the joists, driving two nails into the edge of each joist. Once you've stacked three of these assemblies on top of one another (for 2x10 joists), you'll have a strong laminated fascia.

DECKING OVER A SLAB

Concrete patios have two problems. Many slabs eventually develop so many cracks that they basically look broken. And after you patch the cracks, the repairs stand out, making the slab look even worse. You could keep patching, or jackhammer the slab into oblivion and start from scratch with more concrete. Here's another alternative: covering the cracked concrete with wood decking. This approach uses sleepers—supports that serve in place of conventional joists. If you plan to use composite decking over the sleepers, check with the manufacturer—some require more ventilation underneath than this design provides.

Design Advantages

You'll see many advantages to this approach. **First,** you don't have to remove the slab, which is quite a job physically, and can add considerably to the cost of the project. That's mainly because concrete is heavy, and carting costs are generally based on weight.

Second, even an old slab with an unsightly surface can serve as the foundation for the deck. It won't matter if the surface is pitted or cracked on the surface, because you won't see it under the new layer of wood.

Third, the deck boards, generally 2x4s in this kind of project, are more flexible than concrete. That makes them more comfortable to walk on and provides a little resilience that can absorb some seasonal heaving in the slab. With concrete, even slight movement can cause splitting. And once a crack opens, water can enter, freeze up, and expand in winter and make the split even wider, which lets in more water in a cycle of ever-increasing deterioration.

The basic plan is to install wooden nailers on the concrete and a finished deck surface on the nailers. To prevent rot, use preservative-treated wood on the slab.

 SMART TIP

AVOID RECESSING BOLTS

If you recess, or countersink, bolts, you weaken the connection between the two things that are being bolted together. That's because, when you recess for the bolt heads, the bolt is now applying force to a thinner piece of wood. (Think of a phone book: you can't tear the whole thing in half, but if you ripped out half the pages, you'd have a better chance. The same dynamic applies in construction.)

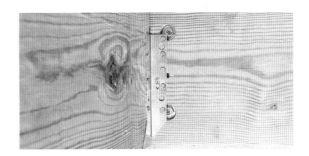

For more on laying out and cutting curves, see pages 82 and 83.

A curve adds an interesting design element. Finish with a curved fascia, or leave the end open for low-level decks.

To fasten the nailers, use (or allow a contractor to use) a nail gun that fires a small explosive charge to drive a hardened nail through the wood and into the concrete. You can get by without one and use a manual-powered hammer. The job may take a little longer, but it will be safer. Don't have to safely install sleepers to a concrete pad.

Nailing Sleepers

Once you establish your layout, including boards around the perimeter and interior boards spaced about 16 inches on center, determine the material you'll use. (If you're using angled, or V-shaped, decking, you must reduce your joist spacing to 12 inches on center.) You could use 1x4 nailers that would accommodate 2½-inch deck screws, but 2x4s provide more nailing substance for the surface boards. Thin nailers offer plenty of support but split too easily as you nail.

It's also wise to lay out the sleepers perpendicular to the main house wall. This will allow water to drain away from the house.

Remember that it's a good idea to use a respirator mask when cutting treated wood, particularly when you use a power saw. Even outdoors, this operation makes a lot of sawdust.

Also be sure to wear safety glasses while nailing. Because the concrete is so much harder than wood, nails sometimes can snap, and pieces of metal can fly up unexpectedly. You may not stick to safety glasses for odd jobs around the house, but this is one case where eye protection is essential. Unlike nailing in wood, where the force from a misdirected blow causes a bend, a hardened concrete nail can snap and ricochet off the slab into your face, packing quite a wallop.

It's best to use concrete anchors or fasteners to fasten the sleepers. Hand-nailing cut nails, or masonry nails, is difficult and ineffective. You'll also find that standard common nails used on wood framing will bend over before penetrating the slab. Using concrete anchors will also allow you to predrill holes using a concrete bit on a drill and avoid some of the hazards of nailing.

Be aware of another phenomenon peculiar to concrete nailing called hammer rebound. The hardened nail may hit a piece of stone in the slab, at which point all the force from your hammer blow comes right back off the nailhead and makes the hammer jump up in your hand. Try a few nails to get the feel of it—notice when the nail is penetrating and when you've hit an immovable object and are forced to move over an inch or so.

DECKING OVER A SLAB

Decking (parallel with house)

Sleeper (perpendicular to house)

House Wall

Drainage Gap

Concrete Slab

Gravel Base

Compacted Soil

With those caveats in mind, simply proceed to attach the nailers across the slab. Keep nails a few inches away from the edges of the concrete to avoid splitting off small chunks.

Here's one more reason for using 2x4s instead of 1x4s for your nailers. Although it may take more time to fasten the larger lumber (and cost a bit more, too), you can level out some irregularities in the slab. While thinner boards would bend up over the rises and dip a bit into the low spots as you nail, preservative-treated 2x4s will bridge most of the gaps.

If you have a few major depressions in the slab, nail the sleepers at the high spots and insert shims (wedge-shaped pieces of preservative-treated wood or cedar shingles) to keep the 2x4s level as they ride over the low spots.

Planning the Deck Surface

Now comes the nice part of the job—installing the surface decking. Because the surface 2x4 (or 2x6 if you like) decking doesn't sit directly on the concrete, air will circulate around the wood. That means you don't have to use preservative-treated wood, even though treated boards are likely to last longer than fir, redwood, or cedar out in the weather.

Some people just don't like the look of wood after it has undergone the chemical treatment. Most treated products lose their original look over time; others will keep their original look. You can use treated boards and coat them with a semitransparent wood stain to kill the tinge. Using standard construction framing timbers and applying a water-resistant surface sealer to protect the wood is not a substitute for using treated lumber.

Nailing the Deck

To make the surface look really nice, take care with the spacing between boards needed for drainage through the deck surface and nail placement through the surface timbers into the sleepers. The old-fashioned and reliable system is to use the shank of a common nail as a spacer between boards. Or you can insert any convenient spacer that will allow something like ⅛-inch clearance to start with. (Some products shrink considerably. Check product data sheets or with the manufacturer for specific nailing instructions.)

Each surface 2x4 or 2x6 should get two screws. Be sure to select a deck screw that reaches through the deck boards and most of the way into the sleeper but not into the concrete.

Ground-level decks transition easily to the yard.

Now comes one of the most rewarding parts of building a deck: adding the decking. This is the part of your project that will show the most, so take your time. Maintain even spacing between boards, and follow the manufacturer's directions if installing synthetic decking. If you haven't decided on material, see "Material Types and Estimating for Decks," beginning on page 26. To brush up on deck-building techniques, including cutting and attaching decking materials, see "Building Techniques," page 66.

MAXIMUM SPACING BETWEEN JOISTS

5⁄4x6 Southern pine or Douglas fir, perpendicular	16"
5⁄4x6 Southern pine or Douglas fir, diagonal	12"
5⁄4x6 redwood or cedar, perpendicular	16"
5⁄4x6 redwood or cedar, diagonal	12"
2x4 or 2x6 Southern pine or Douglas fir, perpendicular	24"
2x4 Southern pine or Douglas fir, diagonal	16"
2x6 Southern pine or Douglas fir, diagonal	24"
2x4 redwood or cedar, perpendicular	16"
2x4 or 2x6 redwood or cedar, diagonal	16"
2x6 redwood or cedar, perpendicular	24"

Note: Be sure to check allowable spans between supports and all lumber requirements with the local building department.

💡 SMART TIP

WHICH SIDE UP?

The United States Department of Agriculture has determined that it doesn't matter whether boards are laid bark side up or down, but installing deck boards bark side up is a well-known rule of thumb of deck building. The bark side is the side of the board that faced toward the outside of the tree. Because of the round shape of trees, the bark-side grain has a convex shape that would seem to be good for shedding rain.

The idea seems to make sense because if the nonbark or dry side gets wet, the reasoning goes, it will trap water. But there are some major problems with the rule.

First, if you install boards that are still wet, or green, they will shrink as they dry out. And a green board installed bark side up is likely to dry into a U-shape, which means water will be trapped on the boards.

Second, if you use good lumber—especially cedar, redwood, or Douglas fir—there is little chance of significant cupping. And a small cup is not really a problem because no end grain is exposed to the water. So, unless you are using very wet or very dry treated lumber for your decking, just pick the side that looks the best.

DECKING OPTIONS

Laying the decking is the most gratifying part of building a deck. The work proceeds quickly because most of the layout work is completed at this stage. With a helper or two, you can cover the framing on a deck in a day, even if it has some angles or finishing details at the edges.

These can take the form of trim that covers the rough end grain of deck boards, fascias that cover rough joists or girders, and skirting that conceals the area under the deck and makes the structure blend in with the yard.

You may be anxious to finish the project at this point, but it pays to take the time to carefully space the surface boards and to drive your nails or screws the same way (with the same edge margins) over the entire surface. Of course, you should also take the time to examine boards; discard lumber with excessive twisting, cracking, or other problems; and set the best side up.

Plan for the Railings

Before you start laying deck boards, make sure that the installation will work with the railings. Guard posts require a lot of internal blocking and/or hardware within the frame area to support the post connections. It is very common for these posts and their reinforcements to be installed before the decking. If the decking overhangs the frame, you'll need notches for the railing support posts to sit flush against the joist. However, in some designs, especially those that incorporate benches, you must install posts or other supports before the decking. But you can take another approach: installing the posts first and notching deck boards around them as needed.

Also take into account the location of the fascia boards and skirting panels if you're using these finishing details. Because these components are generally screwed onto the outer joist or header joist, you will need a generous overhang on the deck boards to cover their top edges.

There are several factors to consider when you think about how to deck over the joists. Some of the options are limited at this point, of course, because you need to use decking lumber and a surface layout that will work with the joist spacing. On most decks, that's 16 inches on center. But there are plenty of choices. You still need to select a species of wood, its width and thickness, the decking pattern, how the decking will be fastened, and, in some cases, where and how to install the fascia boards and skirting.

Types of Decking

As manufacturers improve the appearance and performance of their products, synthetic decking has become an increasingly popular alternative to wood. It's a durable product that doesn't need finishing or periodic refinishing like wood

DECKING PATTERNS

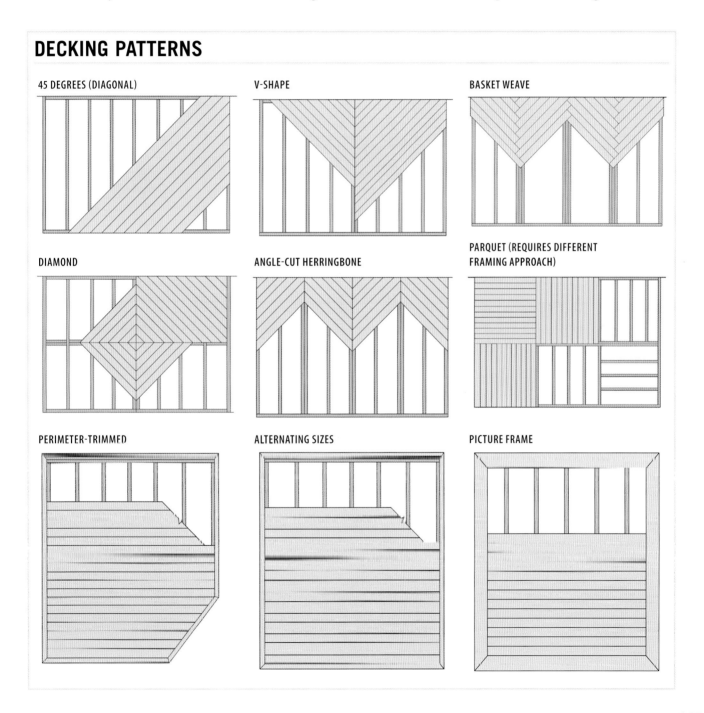

45 DEGREES (DIAGONAL)

V-SHAPE

BASKET WEAVE

DIAMOND

ANGLE-CUT HERRINGBONE

PARQUET (REQUIRES DIFFERENT FRAMING APPROACH)

PERIMETER-TRIMMED

ALTERNATING SIZES

PICTURE FRAME

does. Preservative-treated decking is another popular choice—it's rot resistant but made from southern yellow pine, which tends to twist, cup, and split. Cedar and redwood are naturally rot resistant and less prone to twisting, cupping, and splitting than treated wood. Cedar and redwood are also much more expensive. Synthetic decking can be far more expensive than cedar or redwood.

Lumber Dimensions

Most often, ⁵⁄₄x6 wood or synthetic decking is used. These materials are actually about 1 inch thick and 5½ inches wide. Whether wood or synthetic, ⁵⁄₄ comes with nicely rounded edges. You can also use wood 2x4s (actual dimensions 1½ inches by 3½ inches) or 2x6s (actual dimensions 1½ inches by 5½ inches). Boards that are wider than 2x6 will expand and contract more and have a greater tendency to cup.

Generally, 2x6s cover more ground and make the work go faster. They may be less prone to twisting than 2x4s, which are often cut from smaller, younger trees. When you run into a knot in a 2x4, you've got a nailing problem, whereas a 2x6 is wide enough to give you room to work around a knot.

Patterns

Most decks look best with boards running parallel with the longest house wall. Straight runs that cross the joists at right angles are also the easiest to install. There are many pattern options, but they often require extra framing and more cutting and predrilling on the deck boards. If there are a lot of angle cuts or a pattern of mixed sizes, count on ending up with extra waste lumber, too. Some herringbone and parquet designs can eliminate a lot of angle cuts. But bear in mind that

On most decks, the decking runs parallel with the house. But installing the decking on an angle to the house often creates an interesting design element.

1 Set a ½-in. strip of plywood against the house and set the first board in place. String a chalk line.

these patterns may run wild along the edges of your deck and make the overall pattern look incomplete. If your deck has different levels, you can create a basic pattern contrast by running the decking at a different angle for each level.

Fastening Systems

You can attach your decking with 10d or 12d galvanized threaded nails. Or you can use galvanized ring-shank or spiral nails, which have more holding power. However, for maximum holding power you can't beat deck screws—the best ones are ceramic-coated against rust. Today's deck screws use square or star-shaped bits that are much less likely to strip out the X-shaped Phillips bits. Using a power drill/driver, driving screws is easier than hammering nails, and screws are easy to withdraw if you make a mistake. There are also hidden fastening systems. (See "Fasteners," page 37.)

Fascias and Skirts

Both fascia boards and skirting tuck under the decking that overhangs the outer joists. This method is easy and is rot resistant because there are no places where water can be trapped against open grain.

With fascia boards, you might also cut the decking flush to the edges of the joists and cover both the joist and the decking with the trim boards. This detail calls for straight cut lines and high-quality lumber that won't twist or shrink over time. Even then, the seam where the butt ends of the decking meet the fascia can trap water and foster rot.

2 There are clearance requirements between different claddings and decking. Leaving a gap seems like it would have benefits, but ends up being a repository for leaf debris, etc. and allows water to collect.

3 Set out the boards and spacers if necessary. The end board should overhang the framing.

INSTALLING WOOD DECKING

Before you start fastening, it makes sense to sort through the boards, square-cut them, and seal all the surfaces. Then you can set the first board next to the house. Its position is important because it sets the starting point for the other boards. You can then lay down the decking, repeating your nailing patterns and spacing to make a uniform surface. Finally, you make the trim cuts and add the finishing touches, such as edging that covers exposed end grain, fascia boards, and skirting.

Preparing the Boards

Sort through the stack of lumber, and choose which side will be up for each piece. Weed out any boards with bad cracks, twists, or other damage. If you have a number of different lengths, stack them accordingly so it will be easy to find the boards you want.

If the boards are long enough, you can let them run over the outer joist and trim them later. Wherever a board end needs to be butted, you can make the cuts ahead of time or wait to see how the boards fall on the joists and make the cuts as you go. This is the way most carpenters do it. Cutting butts ahead of time seems to make sense, but it can get you into trouble if the on-center measurements are a bit off. You need to be sure that butted boards join in the center of a joist, which is only 1½ inches wide. If you find that boards are splitting because you have to nail them too close to the end, you can predrill those holes. Or an easier solution is to nail 2x4s along the length and flush to the top of joists where two decking boards will meet. Then you can nail one board to the joist and the other to the 2x4.

You should keep a can of preservative handy so that you can coat any freshly cut butt ends.

As you get ready to install the decking, lay out ten or so boards on the deck as they will go down—for example, with the lengths positioned to stagger butt joints. This keeps the work moving and provides a temporary surface to stand on.

Installing Starter Boards

Straight Runs. For decking that runs parallel with the house, pick a straight board and cut it to length, allowing for the overhang. Measure out from the house at both ends of the run, and mark the width of the decking board plus at least ¼ inch to leave a drainage gap. Snap a chalk line or string a line between your end marks, and check at several points along the wall with a block of decking to be sure you have enough room. (See "Laying Out Decking Boards," page 147.) If the house wall bows

in or out, you may need to increase the margin. Don't make the mistake of twisting the board to conform to the house wall. You want the deck boards to be straight. For decking butted to the house, you should follow the same basic procedure.

Diagonals. If you are installing a diagonal pattern, don't start with a short piece in a corner. Start with a straight board at least 6 feet long instead, and set it on a 45-degree angle by measuring equal distances from the starting corner. Before you fasten it, measure from the center of the board to the corner, and use blocks to check how the boards will fall. You don't want to end up with a tiny piece in the corner.

Herringbones. Generally, it looks best to use a pattern of full boards centered on the deck and equal-size partial lengths where the pattern meets the edges. Provide adequate nailing surfaces by doubling up deck joists where decking boards meet.

Fastening the Decking

It's best to use a pneumatic nailer for the obvious reason that nailing an entire deck by hand will cause your arm to tire out. But because a lot of deck work is best done on your knees, you may want to make the work easier by investing in knee pads.

Position and Cut the Boards. As you place each board in position, make sure the long end hangs over far enough to trim squarely and still cover fascias or skirts. For angled, herringbone, and parquet designs, you will need to measure and cut at least some of the boards as you go. When possible, hold the boards in place to mark them.

You may want to cut a few boards next to the house to length. But when you make trim cuts with a circular saw, you can get pretty close to the house wall and then finish the cut with a handsaw.

Fasten Nails and Screws. You can set all your fasteners as you go or set only a few to locate the boards and come back later to drive the rest. Many pros simply tack the decking down and then have a helper or less-experienced assistant complete the fastening. A pro is usually not going to spend hours sinking hundreds of screws, unless he or she is working alone. This can be an advantage if you discover mistakes later. But it's not hard to pick the best face of a board as you install it and take care of spacing and fastening in one shot. (See "Installing Decking," page 149.)

PROJECT: 🐿🐿🐿
INSTALLING DECKING

The house wall may bow in and out, but your first board should be straight. In severe cases, you can cut the first board from a larger timber and scribe it to conceal irregularities.

TOOLS & MATERIALS
- Decking
- Chalk-line box
- Measuring tape
- Fasteners
- Hammer

1 The decking should overhang the outer joist plus any fascia or skirting by 1 to 2 in. The first 6 decking boards installed against the house can be cut to the exact overhang at each end to eliminate being trimmed with a handsaw.

2 Set the first board on the chalk line drawn earlier. Maintain the gap between the board and house.

3 For professional results, keep fasteners (nails or screws) spaced evenly. Use the shank to locate each fastener from the edge.

4 Drive fasteners (nails or screws) an inch from each edge. Protect deck with scrap wood when pulling bent nails. Fasteners in composite decking should not be less than ½ of the material thickness from the outside edge to prevent bulging from the screw head.

5 Lay out 10 to 12 rows as you work. This will help you keep butt joints several rows apart and staggered as shown.

Use Nails as Spacers. You might try a thicker 16d nail if the wood is dry already, or a thinner 8d nail if it is still relatively wet. You can simply hold the spacer nail against the last nailed board. You should then be able to release the spacer by hand and tap it into place on the next spaced edge.

You drive a pair of fasteners (nails or screws) where each board crosses each joist, about ¾ to 1 inch in from each edge. Some people like to angle their nails slightly toward each other. The idea is that it provides increased holding power. But if you need more holding power you should use larger nails, or screws, instead of nailing incorrectly.

Pros generally drive nails or screws straight in to leave a flat head on the surface. An angled head can tear one side of the wood and create a small water trap. It's also difficult to seat an angled nail without digging your hammer into the surrounding wood.

You don't want to mar the deck boards with mishits, of course. Hit the nails hard, giving one final whack to set the heads flush with the surface. Don't tap lightly and use a nail set to seat the heads, or you will be there on your knees forever.

For appearance's sake, it's not much trouble to keep your nails evenly spaced on the boards and in a straight line across the deck. You can use a string line for a guide, draw a pencil line, or just look up to follow the line of set nails.

Predrilling to Prevent Splits. Even if you use screws, be sure to predrill near the ends of all deck boards to avoid splitting. Screws don't exert as much splitting force as nails because they have thinner shanks and turn their way through the wood, but within an inch or two of the end of a board, it helps to have a pilot hole. One rule of thumb is to use a pilot bit that is two-thirds to three-quarters as thick as the shank of your nail or screw.

If you see a crack start to open as you're working on a butt joint, back out the screw or nail and increase the hole size or move to another location. Any small split that appears now will only get larger with time.

Using Deck Board Hardware. Concealed fasteners allow you to fasten decking from below and leave the wood surface with no visible screw heads. They are a bit more expensive and take some extra time to install, but they may be worth it if you have beautiful decking boards that you want to show off to their full advantage. Check the manufacturer's recommendations about using the hardware with deck boards subject to substantial shrinkage. You may be required to work on the deck from below, but some concealed fasteners can be installed from above.

Straightening as You Go. Every third or fourth board, check the run for straightness. You can do this by holding a taut string line along one edge of the board, or by eye. But it's also wise to measure back to your starting row against the house at several points. This keeps the boards square to the frame.

STRAIGHTENING BOARDS

To bring a bowed board into line, you can use a specialized tool such as the Bowrench, **Photo 1** which locks onto the supporting joist for leverage.

Do not dig a pry bar into the top of the lumber on your deck. Since most pry bars aren't long enough to reach under the boards, pulling upwards will damage the wood. If you don't have a bowrench, you can use a scrap 2x4 to provide leverage as you straighten a bowed board.

PROJECT:
FITTING BOARDS AROUND INTERIOR POSTS

If your posts are attached to the inside of the rim joists, you'll need to notch deck boards to fit around them. This can be a little tricky if, as shown here, the boards meet the posts at an angle. Your cuts won't need to be perfectly accurate if you use bases that slip over composite posts. Start by cutting the board to approximate length and letting it run wild on the other end.

TOOLS & MATERIALS
- Decking
- Pencil
- Tape measure
- Angle square
- Post offcut
- Jigsaw

1 Measure from how deep the notch will be, then transfer the measurement to the board to be notched.

2 Use an angle square or combination square to draw a diagonal line from the post depth point to the edge of the board.

3 Place an offcut of the post material along the line, then scribe the other side of the notch.

4 Cut the notch with a saber saw or handsaw and check the fit. Let the board run wild past the notch, to be cut off later with the other boards.

5 With the notch fitted around the post, mark where the board meets decking on the other side, draw a line, and make the cut.

You can straighten most bends by pushing them into position. You may need to use a chisel or pry bar for the tougher ones, but be delicate. (See page 150.) Start at one end and fasten as you proceed down the board. Keep all your spacer nails in place until the whole board is straightened. Anchor the straightened parts of the board securely with two fasteners at each joist so that the straight part doesn't get bent while you work.

Making the Final Cuts

Measure out from the last joist to allow for an overhang of about an inch, and to account for a fascia board or skirting panel if you use one or the other. Measure the overhang at each end, snap a chalk line as a guide, and make the trim cut with a circular saw. Set your blade about ⅛ inch deeper than your decking thickness. (See "Edge Trimming," below.)

PROJECT:
EDGE TRIMMING

To get a smooth cut along the deck edge, use a sharp blade and set the saw depth slightly deeper than the thickness of the deck boards.

TOOLS & MATERIALS
- Measuring tape
- Pencil
- Chalk-line box
- Circular saw
- Handsaw

1 The overhang should cover the end joist and the fascia by about 1 in.

2 Snap a chalk line from one end of the deck to the other. This will be your cut line. Hook the chalk line on the last precut decking board at the house side if precut to eliminate using a handsaw to trim the last several decking boards.

3 Run the circular saw along the cut line with the saw's shoe resting on the deck. Make sure you set the depth properly. You will need to use a handsaw for any boards right up against the house.

PROJECT:
BREADBOARD EDGING

This detail is a favorite of furniture builders who use it to conceal and secure the end grain on wide planks that are fitted together to make a table. If you apply this technique, use appropriate fasteners to ensure they will hold up to the elements and won't corrode. This project uses untreated lumber for illustration purposes.

TOOLS & MATERIALS
- Decking
- Table saw
- Construction adhesive
- 8d finishing nails
- Hammer
- Drill & bits
- Belt sander

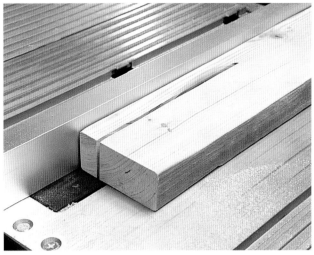

1 Rip ¾-in.-wide lengths of breadboard edging from decking material.

2 After trimming the deck boards, apply construction adhesive to the board edges.

3 Install the trim to the edges of the deck board using finishing nails.

4 Predrill nailholes at the ends of the breadboard trim to keep the wood from splitting.

5 Because some deck boards may be higher than others, trim the surface with a belt sander.

INSTALLING SYNTHETIC DECKING

Nothing quite matches the beauty of a wood deck, but synthetic materials are getting mighty close. And homeowners love the fact that synthetic decking doesn't warp, splinter, or require periodic refinishing. As you'll realize the first time you pick up a floppy piece of synthetic decking, it's not structural like wood decking is. It'll follow the contour of what it's fastened too, so it's extra important to get your joists straight and level. See "Synthetic Decking," page 36, to learn more about the different products available.

PROJECT: 🐾🐾🐾

INSTALLING COMPOSITE DECKING

If your deck will be a simple rectangle, lay it out as shown in "Laying Out Decking Boards," page 147. Here's how to lay out and install boards if your deck will include boards with angle cuts, as well as boards that overlap opposing rim joists.

TOOLS & MATERIALS
- Decking
- Tape measure
- Pencil
- Circular saw or power miter saw
- Drill/driver
- 2½-inch ceramic-coated screws for composite decking

COMPOSITE FASTENING SYSTEMS

In general the fastening systems for synthetic decking aren't much different that those used for wood. The main difference is that synthetic decking is never nailed. Whether screwed or attached with hidden fasteners, each product has its own fastener specifications. Often, composite decking is simply face-screwed to the joists, much in the same way as wood. (See "Installing Composite Decking," opposite.)

Some composite decking is tongue-and-groove. In this case the tongue is screwed at an angle into the joists and covered by the groove (1). In another system, capped composite is grooved on each side. The decking is secured by proprietary fasteners that are fitted into the grooves and then screwed to the joists (2).

Don't install synthetic decking with deck screws designed for wood. Screws for synthetic decking have two sets of threads—the bottom threads are designed to hold in the wooden joists and the upper threads hold well in synthetic materials. Also, the bugle-shaped heads of wood deck screws will cause the synthetic material to mushroom up when you sink the screws. Screws for synthetic decking have smaller heads that are flat on the bottom to prevent mushrooming.

1 Put each board that will be cut at an angle in position to measure the approximate length you'll need. Then cut a board to approximate length with a 45-degree cut on one end.

2 Lay out the deck boards that will run wild on both sides of the deck.

3 If a board needs to be notched squarely around a post, put it in place as shown so you can mark the edge where it meets the post. Then measure the depth of the notch and use a post offcut and a square to lay out the cut.

4 Install the first board. This typically will be the one against the house, but in this case it abuts an existing deck. Use two 2½-inch ceramic-coated screws into each joist. Here, a special driver with collated screws speeds the work (see "Quick Driving System," page 156), but you can use any drill/driver with a star bit.

5 Typically you want about ⅛ inch between deck boards. You can use 8d nails as spacers, or you can use spacers designed to fit conveniently over joists. Use spacers as needed—usually one on every other joist.

6 Finish screwing the boards to the joist. Then, as shown in "Edge Trimming," page 152, snap a line and cut off the boards that are running wild.

SMART TIP

QUICK DRIVING SYSTEM

If your deck is not large, you can use any corded power drill/driver to screw the decking in place. (A cordless drill will run out of power too quickly.) However, using a screw gun designed to accept screws that are collated like machine-gun belts will save you a huge amount of time and work. You insert the belt of collated screws and then just press the tip of the tool against the surface to shoot the screw. The tool comes with an extension so you can use it standing up—a great back saver. Your local rental center probably has one available.

SMART TIP

HIDING COMPOSITE ENDS

Composite boards have their color throughout, so you can leave the ends exposed if you like. However, there's no end grain, so the cut end of a composite board is not particularly attractive. For this reason it's common practice to cut the decking flush to the fascia boards and then run a 1½ inch or 2-inch wide rip of composite decking as trim board flush to the top of the decking as shown here.

This type of trim board is a must for capped composite because the plastic cap is a different color than the composite core. For capped composite, a solid PVC trim board is often used to match PVC fascia.

FASCIA BOARDS AND SKIRTING

If you select good-looking lumber for the most visible joists and install fasteners neatly in an even pattern, the deck frame may look fine. To improve the look of rougher framing, you can add a coat or two of stain or clad the exposed lumber with fascia boards.

Fascia boards consist of one-by boards tucked under the overhanging portion of the deck boards and are attached to the perimeter joists. They can be made of pine and stained or painted or they can be made of the same wood as a redwood or cedar deck. You can also use one-by polyvinyl chloride (PVC) boards—as is typically done with synthetic decking, which would clash with the treated framing below.

Installation is straightforward. First, cut the board to length and miter any corner joints. Then sand the boards as needed, predrill for screws or nails to avoid splits, and fasten the fascia in place. You may want to add construction adhesive. (See "Installing Fascia," opposite.)

Adding Skirting

There are several types of skirting material and a number of ways to close off the space between your deck framing and the ground. Lattice is the most common material, although you can use closely spaced 1x2s or fencing materials to create a similar effect.

One approach is to add a support frame near the ground and set the skirting along the outermost edge of the deck. This requires a fair amount of extra framing work because you have to hang the new supports from the joists. It's often easier to use the supports you already have: the row of piers and posts, and the beam that rests on them.

To avoid rot (even if you use preservative-treated lattice or 1x2s), it's best to keep the skirting an inch or two above the ground.

PROJECT:
INSTALLING FASCIA

Select a fascia board that is one size up from the joists—for example, a 1x10 to clad a 2x8.

TOOLS & MATERIALS
- Fascia
- Measuring tape
- Pencil
- Circular saw
- Sander
- Drill & bits
- Construction adhesive
- 8d finishing nails
- Nail set
- Hammer

1 Set your saw to cut 45-degree angles, and miter the ends of the fascia boards where they meet at corners. Keep in mind that in dry regions a mitered corner will shrink and open up. Use exterior wood glue applied to both sides of the miter joint to prevent this from occurring. Often, a butt joint will look better over time.

2 Before installing the boards, dress the exposed surface with a random-orbit or belt sander.

3 Predrill near the ends of the fascia to avoid splitting the wood. This will be a highly visible joint.

4 Apply construction adhesive to the end joists.

5 Finish the installation using nails. Use a nail set to seat the nails and avoid marks on the wood.

Assemble the Lattice. One good approach is to buy large sheets of prefab lattice and cut them to size. Then you can build simple frames around the panel sections to strengthen them and dress up the edges. Some lumberyards and home centers sell slotted trim designed to work with lattice, but any reasonably stiff frame will do the job.

To mount the panels, apply them to the front of your posts or add nailers on the sides of the posts so that the panels will tuck between them. (See "Installing Skirting," opposite.)

It's wise to do as much work as possible on the panels, including jobs such as staining and predrilling, before you have to crouch under the deck overhang and finish the installation.

Decking around a Tree

When you are installing decking at a framed opening in the deck for a tree, take the same approach as you do on the deck edges: let the boards run long, and make the final trim cuts all at one time. This is the best way to get a neat edge, and it saves the time of cutting each board to the exact length you need as you nail it down.

You may have to slice off the end of a board at an angle just to get it in place, but try to get all the boards close to the tree. Once they are fastened, it's time to figure how to make your final cuts. For most trees, you'll want to leave a gap of at least 2 or 3 inches between the tree and the decking. You can always leave more. Depending on the overall shape of your deck or the area of the tree, you may want to cut a square or a rectangle. Generally, a simple square shape with a roughly even margin around the tree looks best. But you also can use a saber saw and cut a contoured shape that mirrors the tree trunk. In all cases, cut the boards so that they overhang the box framing around the tree.

Cutting a Circle. If you prefer to cut a circle, use the framing that you can see around the tree for reference. (If the tree weren't there, of course, it would be easy to scribe a circle from a centerpoint.) If you want to be precise, establish four or eight equidistant points on the circumference of the circle. Or simply set a hose or extension cord around the tree.

Decking Curves

On most decks that have a curved corner, you lay the deck boards to overhang the framing, tack a nail at the radius of the circle, and mark the corner cut with a pencil and string that swings from the nail.

The easiest way to trim decking for a curve is by using a trammel to trace the curve on the ends of the decking. (See "Framing a Curved Section" on page 137 and "Laying Out and Cutting Curves" on page 82.)

SKIRTING SUBFRAME

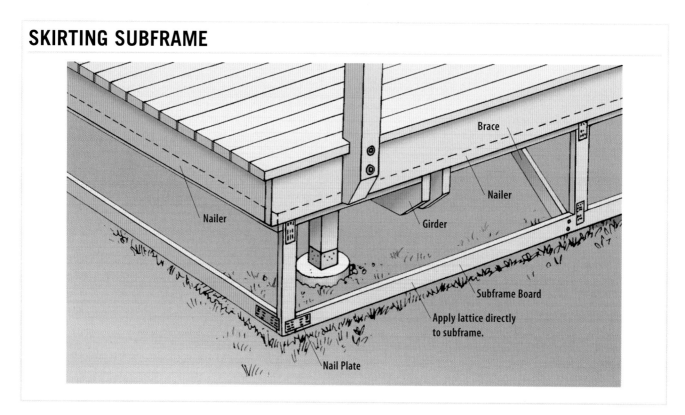

Brace

Nailer

Nailer

Girder

Subframe Board

Apply lattice directly to subframe.

Nail Plate

PROJECT: INSTALLING SKIRTING

Even on a relatively low deck, skirting can conceal the barren area beneath the framing.

TOOLS & MATERIALS

- Measuring tape
- Pencil
- Nailers
- Drill-driver & bits
- 2-in. screws
- Power miter saw
- Framing material
- Exterior glue
- Hammer
- 6d finishing nails
- Lattice panels

1 Measure between the posts to determine the length of the skirting panel.

2 To recess the panel, attach a nailer to the sides of the posts. Install the panel flush to the post edge.

3 Miter the corners of the frame material. The frame stiffens the lattice and hides its edges.

4 Join the frame sections at right angles using glue and nails. Some frames have slots for the lattice.

5 Attach the frames to the nailers on the posts. Use screws for easy removal.

PROJECT: 🐾🐾🐾
DECK BOARD SPACING

Spacing requirements vary with the material. Some will follow the directions shown here, but other products require no spacing between boards.

TOOLS & MATERIALS
- Common nails
- String
- Decking
- Measuring tape
- Fasteners

1 A common nail makes a good spacer for kiln-dried lumber, though it's best to avoid puncturing your joists from the top. You don't want to leave open untreated holes in the wood. Position the board, and remove the nail.

ESTIMATING MATERIALS

You could just figure out your square footage and then order enough lumber to cover it, plus 15 percent for waste. And the lumberyard would love it if you did because it could unload the lengths that are overstocked. To minimize waste and time-consuming butt joints on the deck surface, though, take the time to make a plan of your deck surface that shows every piece. Then you can determine the lengths that will work most efficiently and result in less waste.

To figure decking that will be cut at a right angle, start with the width of the deck to find out how many deck boards (or rows of deck boards, if the deck is longer than the longest deck boards you can buy) will be needed. Divide the total width of your deck by 5.6 (for 2x6 or ¾x6 decking) or 3.6 (for 2x4 decking). This figure adds about ⅒ inch for the space between boards. Once you know how many boards you will need, be sure to order the correct lengths to save money.

Estimating is more difficult for angled patterns. Start by calculating how many total linear feet of decking you will need. Divide the deck's square footage by 0.47 for 2x6 decking or 0.3 for 2x4. Add 5 to 10 percent for waste, and you will have a good general figure. Now look at your drawing, and estimate the most-efficient lengths you will need.

Sometimes it's possible to avoid making butt joints by buying extra-long pieces of decking—18 feet or longer. These may cost more per foot, but they're worth it: you'll have fewer rot-prone butt joints, and the installation will be easier and quicker. Where you do need butt joints, be sure to stagger them over different joists. It looks best to keep the joints at least two joists away from each other.

2 String a chalk line from one end of the deck to the other. Check for bulges and depressions.

3 Measure to the beam you are working toward rather than the house you are working away from, in order to keep things even until the end. This helps keep the courses square with the deck frame.

Better synthetic decking, such as the capped composite decking shown here, has color variations and texture that does a good job of imitating the look of wood.

EDGE DETAILS

No matter what kind of deck boards you use, there are three basic choices for fastening them along the edges of your deck. You can cut them flush, box them in with a fascia, or let them extend past the joists an inch or so. You can make a case that any one of them looks better than the others. But to build a durable deck, overhanging boards are best because they shed water and do not create water-trapping seams where wood can rot.

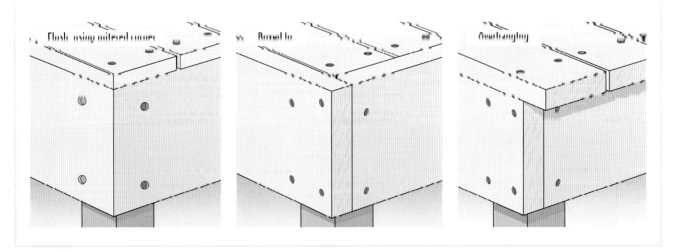

Any deck set above grade level will benefit from having stairs to provide a transition between the deck and the yard. Well-built stairs are comfortable and safe to use, and they add a distinctive design element to the deck.

STAIRWAY DESIGN OPTIONS AND LAYOUTS

Building a deck is one home improvement project that many homeowners can tackle, because construction is straightforward—until they come to the stairs. Even a drop of a few feet can present a confusing combination of dimensions that account for slope, tread size, and space between steps.

While stairs are an important part of most decks, they are usually left for last when the final details of the deck are in place. Then you can make a practical plan and do the calculations that account for any small changes made during construction. And, of course, local building code requirements will also figure into your plans.

Designing a stairway takes a bit of calculating, even though there are only a few parts. The stringers are the angled pieces along the sides of the stairs. They hold the treads, which are the boards you step on. The risers are the vertical pieces between the treads. Risers are not needed for strength, and rot-causing moisture and debris can collect where risers meet the treads below. For these reasons, many older deck stairs don't have risers. However, as discussed in "Building Code for Stairs," on page 167, the space between treads needs to be at least partially filled to comply with code. The rot problem can be mitigated by leaving a small space between the riser and tread.

Once the deck is built, you may find yourself changing your mind about the stairway—how it should look and how you will use it. If all you need is a way to get from the deck to the ground, a simple 36-inch-wide stairway with standard treads will do. And you can generally build it without much trouble using more than two stringers.

But whether you stick with a basic, straight-run design or combine your stairs with a landing, you must stay within the limits of building codes, which are stringent when it comes to stairs. Generally, you'll find that codes call for a tread depth of no less than 9¼ inches; a step up, or rise, between treads of no more than 7¾ inches per the code (however, local codes across the country amend

DECK STAIRWAY COMPONENTS

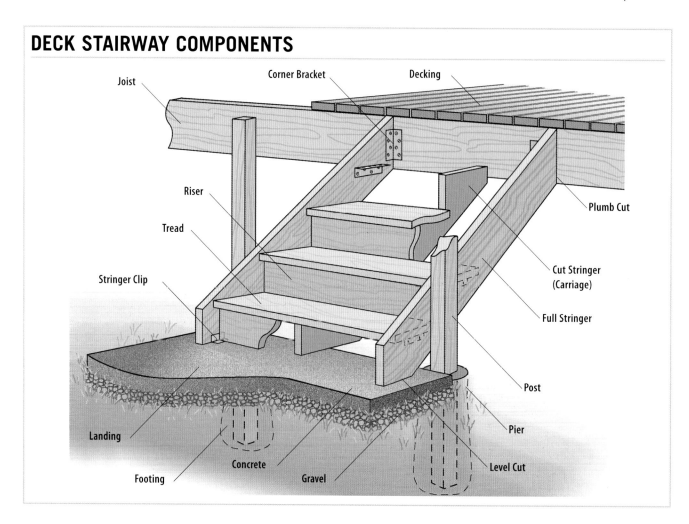

Joist · Corner Bracket · Decking · Riser · Tread · Stringer Clip · Plumb Cut · Cut Stringer (Carriage) · Full Stringer · Post · Pier · Level Cut · Landing · Concrete · Footing · Gravel

this; be sure to check yours first); and a stairway width of no less than 3 feet.

Treads and Risers

The horizontal distance each tread travels is called the unit run, while the vertical distance is the unit rise. It's convenient to plan a unit run of approximately 11 inches so each tread can be made from two 5/4x6s or 2x6s. You can leave a minimum of ¾ inch of drainage space between the boards to create a tread overhang called a nosing.

Because you usually have more horizontal space to work with outdoors than indoors, you might like to create a stair with shorter risers and longer treads. Many people find a shallower rise like this to be more comfortable to negotiate, and it helps a raised deck look more anchored to the ground.

You can use a large rise (generally up to 7¾ inches) to make the stairs as compact as possible. Or you can use a small rise (4 inches is generally considered the minimum) to stretch out the stairs with more treads. These variables are best investigated initially on paper. After that, you should clamp an uncut 2x12 stringer (one of the angled side supports for the treads) in various positions to see how different tread and riser proportions will work with your deck.

Another option is to create very deep steps that can double as seats. For instance, you might use three 2x6s with drainage spacing between for a total tread of about 16 inches (actually about 17 with an inch of overlap). But these low-angle designs may spread the stairs beyond the design capacity of standard 2x12 stringers.

Most important is to make the stairs uniform. As people approach stairs, going up or down, they generally find the handrail and take a look at the first step to make sure of their footing. But then they look away, assuming that the first stride will work the rest of the way.

It's also important to see where the last step falls. For example, shorter stairs on the side of a deck may fall within the boundary of the overall construction area, while longer stairs may project into the yard and get in the way. Remember, using fewer treads makes a steeper descent but a smaller footprint. Using more treads makes a more gradual descent but uses up more yard.

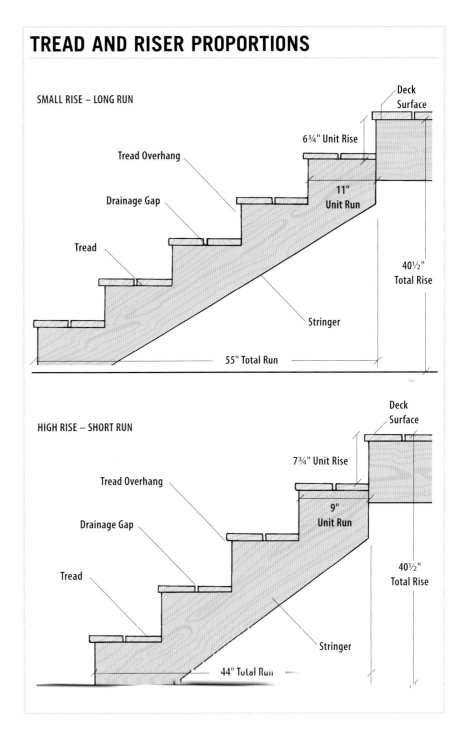

TREAD AND RISER PROPORTIONS

SMALL RISE – LONG RUN

Deck Surface

6¾" Unit Rise

Tread Overhang

11" Unit Run

Drainage Gap

Tread

40½" Total Rise

Stringer

55" Total Run

HIGH RISE – SHORT RUN

Deck Surface

7¾" Unit Rise

Tread Overhang

9" Unit Run

Drainage Gap

Tread

40½" Total Rise

Stringer

44" Total Run

Landing Design

A landing can break a long drop into two more manageable sections and serve as a landing beside the main deck. Landings should be framed like the deck itself, generally with the same-size joists. You can include a landing in your deck frame or build it separately and bolt it in position.

Stringer Design

Use 2x12 lumber for your stringers. Unless you are using 4x treads, you will need a middle stringer, or carriage, which will allow you to maintain the proper on center distance for your stair construction. The outer stringers can be notched to support the treads, or they can be solid with the treads supported by metal hardware or wooden cleats.

Notched Stringer. These are cut into a sawtooth pattern (be sure to treat the cuts with preservative) so that each tread has a flat support. You need to be sure of the layout because cuts can't be corrected. On older decks it was common to run the treads an inch or so over the outer stringers. In fact it is still common to see open-side stringers, as code does not prohibit them.

Notched stringers require careful cutting, but for some designs, especially when using synthetic decking and railing, the one-by fascia will look less clunky than exposed solid stringers. With careful work, you can build a stairway with notched stringers that will last for decades.

Precut Stringer. Many do-it-yourselfers will get the best results using precut notched stringers that are available at lumberyards and home centers. If the exact location of your bottom pad doesn't matter, you can adjust its position to accommodate store-bought stringers. Before buying, figure your Total Rise and Total Run and the number of treads required are correct. Be sure that the maximum variation between risers and runs in a stair is no more than 3/8 inch, total—code prohibits anything more. The last step to the landing should have the same rise as the wooden steps.

Solid Stringer. Also called a housed stringer because treads are contained within the angled framing, this type of stair support is used with metal hardware or wooden cleats that support the treads. You still have to make a layout with equally spaced steps, but you don't have to cut the pattern into the stringers.

And if you make a layout mistake, it's easy enough to shift tread hardware or cleats. The best hardware is L-shaped galvanized metal brackets that won't decay the way wood cleats can.

If your stairway is wider than 36 inches, one practical approach is to first cut a notched stringer (carriage), which will support the treads in the middle, and use it as a template for locating your tread brackets on the housed stringers. (Check your local codes about tread spans on stairs.) Just set it up against the housed stringers and mark the positions for the brackets, as well as the bottom plumb and level cuts.

STRINGER OPTIONS

Most do-it-yourselfers find it easiest to work with solid, or housed, stringers. You simply buy a few straight 2x12s, lay out the tread pattern on the sides, and screw on galvanized metal brackets to hold the treads. Notched stringers are more complicated to lay out, but many home centers and lumberyards sell precut stringers. The proportions are generally set to provide a 10- or 11-inch tread and a 7- to 7½-inch rise. The angle is fixed because the tread supports of the sawtooth pattern must be level; just cut the bottom edges to fit your site.

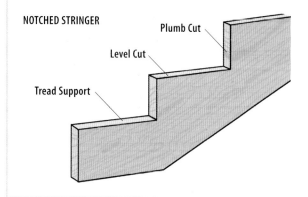

NOTCHED STRINGER
Plumb Cut
Level Cut
Tread Support

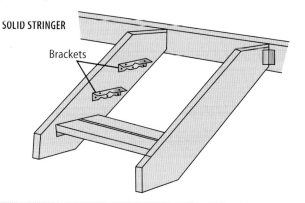

SOLID STRINGER
Brackets

BUILDING CODE FOR STAIRS

The International Residential Codes (IRC) has always made safety requirements for deck stairs the same as for interior stairs. Most municipalities follow the IRC, but not all, and the code does change. That's why it is always a good idea to check your local code before building. Here are three IRC stair requirements to be aware of:

Any stair that ascends more than 30 inches must have a guard. A rail is not required; only a construction feature to block you from falling. This could be a half wall, a planter box, etc.

On all guardrails—whether on the deck itself or on a staircase, the spaces between balusters must be small enough to prevent a 4-inch ball from passing through. The 4-inch-rule is designed to prevent children from getting their heads stuck.

The 4-inch-rule also applies to the space between a deck and the bottom of a guard. However, if you are planning an open stringer with a guard, the triangular opening formed by the bottom of the guard, the riser, and the tread must be small enough to prevent a 6-inch ball from passing through. For most stairs with guardrails, this means you'll need to use closed stringers or a fascia on the sides.

It once was common to use open risers. However, that space is now also covered by the 4-inch-rule. So, unless you have an unusually short rise of less than 4 inches, it also precludes risers that are completely open.

Any stairway with four or more "rises" must have a smooth graspable handrail. The top of the handrail must be between 34 inches and 38 inches above the nosing of the stair tread. It must run continuously and it must return on both ends so that nothing can get caught on it. The handrail must be no less than 1 ¼ inch in diameter and no more than 2 inches in diameter.

As you can see, the 2x4 or 2x6 top rail typically used to construct a deck stair guardrail does not qualify as a handrail. You can make your own handrail—some carpenters rout grooves in both sides of a 2x4 and round over the top to create a code-compliant profile. But the easiest way to get the job done right and meet code is to purchase a handrail kit that can be cut to fit and includes the returns and approved attachment screws.

Landing Design

Stringers must have something solid to support them at the bottom and protect them from ground contact. You can provide the support in several ways. On a small stairway, you can build two extra piers (one for each stringer). On a larger stairway, it's often more economical to build a concrete slab, which must be at least as wide as the stairs and at least 36 inches wide in the direction of travel. Of course, you also can combine piers with a landing made of bricks, gravel, or other material that does not have to support the stringer. Always check your local code to ensure that your landing meets any requirements.

STAIRWAY LAYOUT MATHEMATICS

Before you start figuring out the nitty-gritty details, here's the basic idea behind stair layout. To sort out the different possible dimensions and proportions, start by carefully recording two key measurements. One is the overall drop from the deck surface straight down to the level of the yard or landing. The other is the overall span from the edge of the deck to the end of the stairs.

To work out a preliminary plan, divide the drop into equal segments of *rise* (the vertical distance between tread surfaces), and divide the span into equal segments of *run* (the depth of each tread, including a 1-inch overlap).

If you use precut stringers, you have to set your bottom landing height to fit the precut riser height. You cannot cut the bottom riser more than ⅜ inch.

In stair terminology, the drop is split into increments called riser height, which is the total vertical distance between the top of one tread and the top of the next tread. Horizontal distance is split into increments called tread depth, which is the horizontal distance traveled by each step. The unit run consists of the width of the tread minus any overhang or nosing.

Most do-it-yourselfers have to experiment with rise and run ratios to find a design that will provide a safe, comfortable, and code-approved stairway. Here is the sequence you can use to come up with a final plan.

Find the Total Rise. If the ground below your deck is level, you can find the total rise simply by measuring straight down from the top of the deck. But the ground may slope away from the deck. In addition, the ground may slope across the width of the stairs. So you need to determine where the steps will land and calculate the total rise from that point. (See "Stair Stringer Layout," page 173.)

Find the Number of Steps. Let's say you would like a tread depth of 11 inches and a riser height of 7½ inches, and your deck is 36 inches off the ground. Divide the total rise of 36 inches by the unit rise of 7½ inches to get 4.8. Round up to find that you will need five steps if the ground is level. One of those steps is the deck itself, so subtract it from the equation when figuring total run. Because you are shooting to make each step 11 inches deep, multiply 11 times 4 to find that where your landing meets your first step should be 44 inches from the deck. However, you'll need to extend the landing 12 inches under the stairs, so you'll need to make the edge of the landing 12 inches closer to your deck.

Locate the Stair Width. Make two pencil marks on the edge of the deck to indicate the planned width of the stairway. Let's say you want to build steps that are 36 inches wide, including the thickness of the stringers but not including the overhang of the treads on either side of the stringers if you are using notched stringers. You'll probably want to make the landing a couple of inches wider on each side, so figure the pad will be 40 inches wide.

Locate the Landing Area. From the marks on the deck, measure out the proposed total run, making sure you are running your measuring tape square to the edge of the

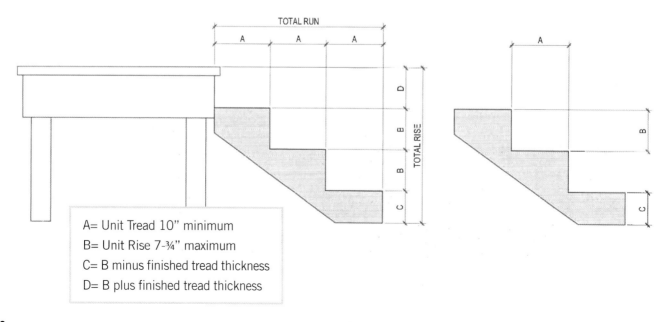

A= Unit Tread 10" minimum
B= Unit Rise 7-¾" maximum
C= B minus finished tread thickness
D= B plus finished tread thickness

deck. Drive a long stake into the ground at these points, making sure the stakes extend above the level of the deck. Plumb the stakes. (If these stakes are more than 60 or 72 inches tall, you will need to have a helper hold a level against them as you proceed, to be sure they are plumb.)

Have a helper hold one end of a string on one of the marks on the deck. Hang a line level on the string, and run the other end to the corresponding stake. When the line is level, mark the position on the stake. Repeat the process to make a mark on the other stake. Measure from the marks on the stake to the ground, or 1 inch above the ground if you want your landing to be an inch higher than your yard. If the two measurements differ, use the shorter measurement as the total rise.

Make the landing level so that it rises above grade on the low side to compensate for the difference. Let's say, for example, that the mark on the left stake as you face the deck is 40½ inches from the ground while the right stake is 42 inches from the ground. The ground slopes away from the deck and down from left to right. You take half the difference between the two total rises. This way the risers are uniform in the middle and only half the distance off on each end.

Figure the Unit Rise and Unit Run. Round the total rise off to the nearest whole number of inches, and divide by 7. If you know you want short rises, you can start by dividing by 6 inches instead of 7. In the example above, 40 divided by 7 equals 5.7. Round again to the nearest whole number. This tells you that to keep the unit rise and unit run you have in mind, you'll need six steps, including the one onto the deck, to cover the total rise.

You can adjust the unit rise or the unit run, or both, to accommodate your true total rise. In most cases, you will not want to change the planned unit run, because it is determined by the lumber you've chosen for stair treads.

The easiest thing to adjust is the unit rise. Divide the total rise (40½ inches) by six steps to get a unit rise of 6¾ inches. In our example, two times 6¾ inches plus 11 inches equals 24½ inches, which is close enough to the general guideline.

Now it's easy to determine exactly where your stairs will land. Again, because one of the steps is the deck surface, your stringers will have five steps, each traveling 11 inches for a total run of 55 inches. Of course, because you have added a step since figuring the tentative total run, that's 11 inches farther than the original total run of 44 inches.

That's fine, provided the ground is level where the stairs land; simply adjust the position of the landing. If the ground continues to slope, you are better off

increasing the unit rise so that you can stick with a four-step stringer. To do this, divide the total rise of 40½ inches by 5 (the rise includes the fifth step onto the deck). The calculator says that's 8.1, or for practical purposes, a unit rise of 8 inches, which is higher than what the national code allows, although some regional and local codes say it's okay. Two times 8 inches plus 11 inches equals 27 inches, which is also within the rule of thumb for proper stairway design.

Despite all the figuring, there is no substitute for marking up a stringer, clamping or bracing it in place, and seeing in this full-scale dry run exactly where the treads will fall.

Stair Construction Math and Formulas

TOTAL RISE is equal to the total vertical distance from the ground to the top of the decking board. (Include the lowest spot on the ground if the stairs end on a natural terrain rather than a concrete level surface)

TOTAL RUN is equal to the total horizontal surface the stairs will travel over. This is measured to the end of the cut stringer, NOT the face of the bottom tread.

UNIT RISE is calculated using the TOTAL RISE divided by the number of risers required to maintain the maximum allowable UNIT RISE by code.

UNIT RUN is the minimum tread cut in a cut stringer permitted by code which is 10".

NUMBER OF TREADS is the number of risers – 1.

TOTAL RUN of a stair is calculated by the number of treads times the UNIT RUN of each tread.

EXAMPLE:

Total rise from top of stair decking board to the top of a sidewalk below equals 84".

Each riser is desired to be 7".

84" total rise / 7" unit rise = 12 risers

12 risers – 1 = 11 treads

11 treads x 10" unit run = 110" total run

INSTALLING A PLATFORM

There are many ways to include a platform in your stairway. For example, you can support it with four posts and piers to stand away from the deck so that one run of stairs reaches from the deck to the platform and another reaches from the platform to the ground.

Another approach is to attach a platform to the deck to make a step-down landing. This works well if you want the stairs to tuck in next to the side of the deck instead of extending out into the yard. As you climb alongside the deck, you need a transition area, like a landing on indoor stairs, where you can turn and take the last step up onto the deck.

Incorporating a platform landing into your stairs is often easier (and better looking) than extending part of the deck to serve as a landing. This approach also allows you to build the frame independently, complete with joists and fasteners, and bolt the landing frame to the deck frame. However, it is not easy to bolt a dropped landing to the side of a deck, because there is very little overlap. In most cases, you will need at least one new pier to support a post at the outer corner of the platform. You may need two, but not if the side of the platform bolts to the deck and the back bolts to the house framing.

PROJECT: 🐾🐾🐾
FRAMING A PLATFORM

Use the same techniques on a stair platform that you use on a main deck, matching the joist size and spacing. Put aside good lumber for the exposed sides, and use screws for extra holding power.

TOOLS & MATERIALS
- 2x lumber
- Circular saw
- Square
- Clamps
- Drill-driver & bits
- 1¼-in. & 2-in. screws
- Brace
- Hammer
- Nails

1 For clean edges, make square cuts on the platform framing lumber. Allow for overlaps on the corners.

2 To assemble, check for square and then clamp the frame together. Use a brace if needed. Then use nails for framing.

3 Check the frame for square, and lock it into position using a diagonal brace.

PROJECT: 🐿🐿🐿
SETTING A PLATFORM

Attach the landing platform to both the deck and the house for support. Sink posts as you would for the main part of the deck.

TOOLS & MATERIALS

- Scrap lumber
- Clamps
- Level
- Flashing
- Bolts
- Wrenches
- Measuring tape
- Drill-driver & bits
- 3-in. screws
- 4x4 posts

1 Clamp the platform to a temporary post. Use clamps to hold the platform against the deck.

2 Check for level in all directions, and make adjustments as needed.

3 Install permanent posts as needed. Fasten the posts to the frame, and trim the tops of the posts.

Platform Framing

The platform needs to be as strong as the deck. You should plan to frame it with the same lumber you used for the main joists, but pick good-looking lumber for the exposed sides. Set the joists with the amount of deck spacing that your design and materials call for, and secure the connections with galvanized frame hardware. In addition to standard joist hangers, also use L-brackets to reinforce the outside corners of the platform frame. (See "Framing a Platform," opposite, and "Setting a Platform," below.)

INSTALLING A LANDING

Whatever design and material you choose for a landing, it's wise to build it somewhat oversized. This provides a margin of error of several inches in each direction when it comes time to install and bolt down the stringers. If you live in an area subject to frost, you may need to go below the frost line with your pad foundation. Be sure to check local codes for requirements. Here are some of the options.

Concrete. Use this material to make the strongest landing. The area is small, so there isn't too much work involved, though waiting for the concrete to set may slow down your job.

First, dig out enough sod and topsoil to accommodate at least 3 inches of gravel and 3 inches of concrete. Ideally, the pad should sit an inch or so above grade to help with drainage. It's also important to compact soil at the bottom of your small excavation (or leave it undisturbed), and to compact the gravel bed, as well.

One approach is to construct a frame of 2x4s laid on edge, reinforced with 2x4 or 1x4 stakes. This frame can be a permanent part of the pad (using treated lumber) or removed after the concrete has set. Make sure the frame is square and level. (See "Concrete Landing," below.)

Place the gravel in the hole, tamping firmly with a 4x4 or a hand tamper. If you will be using reinforcing wire mesh, cut it to fit loosely in the form (so you don't have any wire sticking out after you've poured) and place it in the form, using rocks to hold it up from the gravel.

Pour the concrete, and level it off with a 2x4 that spans across your frame. Finish using a concrete finishing trowel, and use an edging tool where the concrete meets the frame. If you like, give it a final brush stroke with a broom for a skid-free surface.

Brick. There are two main tricks to getting a nonconcrete landing surface that is strong enough. First, tamp the gravel and sand beds (if you're using sand instead of a concrete set). Second, set the landing material so that the load it carries from the stringers is spread over several bricks or pavers. Choose a solid edging to keep the bricks in place, such as preservative-treated landscape timbers or bricks set vertically.

Gravel. The most basic landing is a bed of gravel. This is not as stable or as strong as concrete, but it provides excellent drainage and if installed correctly can be surprisingly strong. Check with the building inspector before building a gravel landing.

Dig a hole 10 to 12 inches deep, fill partway with gravel, and install a frame made of treated 2x4s or 2x6s secured with stakes made of 2x4s or 1x4s. Lay 3 to 4 inches of gravel, compact it firm with a hand tamper or a piece of 4x4, then lay the next layer. Don't lay the final 1½ inches until the stringers are in place.

You might be able to use 2x4 blocks for a very small step to the yard, but generally the stair stringers should bear on concrete footings and then the gravel bed can act as the code-required landing in front for stepping on.

CONCRETE LANDING

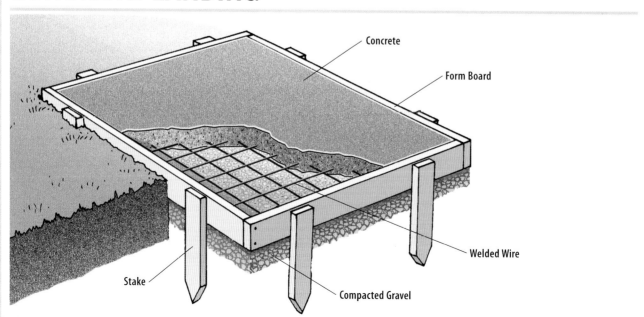

Concrete

Form Board

Welded Wire

Stake

Compacted Gravel

PROJECT: 🐾🐾🐾
STAIR STRINGER LAYOUT

You'll use a framing square to lay out stringers by "stepping off" each unit rise and each unit run. This can be done by simply aligning the rise and run measurements on the legs of the square to the edge of the board, but the work will go faster if you use stops as shown here.

TOOLS & MATERIALS
- Measuring tape
- 2x4 framing square
- Stops
- Horses
- Pencil
- 2x12 stringers

1 Extend a level 2x4 from the platform, and measure the distance down to a level landing area.

2 Set stops on a framing square, where numbers on opposite sides match your rise and unit run.

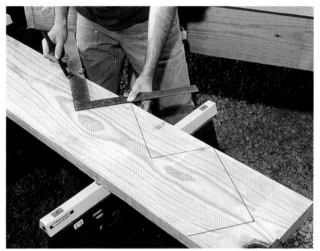

3 Mark the top of the stringer. Slide the stops along the stringer to repeat tread layout lines.

BUILDING THE STAIRS

Here is a look at the basic sequence of building a set of stairs. Of course, you may have to add some construction steps (or skip over a few) if you are building something more complicated or unusual than a relatively short, straight run.

Estimate Stringer Length. To buy the stock for your stringers, you'll need a rough estimate of their length. Here's a quick method. On a framing square, use the stair layout numbers on opposing sides as a guide. The idea is to measure on a diagonal between the number matching your unit rise on one side to the unit run on the other side. This will tell you how far the stringer has to travel per step. Multiply this number by the number of steps you will have, plus one (to be safe), and you will have a good rough estimate of how long your stringer needs to be. For example, a step with a unit rise of 7 inches and a unit run of 11 inches will travel 13 inches per step. If there are five steps, you should buy stringers about 6 feet 6 inches long.

Lay Out the First Stringer. Using a framing square, transfer the rise and run to a 2x12 with the crown side up. It helps to mark your square with tape if you can't find metal stops, sometimes called buttons. The stops are handy because they let you ride the square along the side of a stringer, maintaining the same angle for every tread. Mark the stringers in pencil. Don't be surprised if you get a bit mixed up and have to start over. (See "Stringer Layout," opposite.)

Start at the top of the stringer—the end that will meet the deck. When you come to the bottom step, shorten the rise by the thickness of the stock for the treads.

Make the Stringers. Cut the top and bottom of the stringer—you don't have to cut the notches yet—and hold it up to the deck in the position where it will be attached when you build the stairs. Rest the bottom end of the stringer on the landing, or a piece of lumber that simulates the height of your landing. Check that the layout lines for the treads are level.

To be safe (as long as you have some extra length in the stringer), you might want to sneak up on the plumb and level cuts at the ends of the stringer. For example, you might leave the mark plus ½ inch or so for the first dry run. You can always trim off the excess and use the margin to correct the angle one way or another.

To make the cuts for a notched stringer, use a circular saw. Because you are entering the board at an angle, you may need to retract the blade guard at the start of each cut to avoid cutting a wavy line. Rest the shoe of the saw solidly and evenly on the surface of the board as you cut. You can finish circular saw cuts with a handsaw.

It's generally neater to finish the sawtooth-pattern stringer cuts with a handsaw, holding the blade at 90 degrees to the board so you don't get overlapping cut lines on the other side of the board.

Treat all your cuts with preservatives, and let it sink into all of the end grain. Take care not to bump the projecting

STRINGER BASE ATTACHMENT OPTIONS

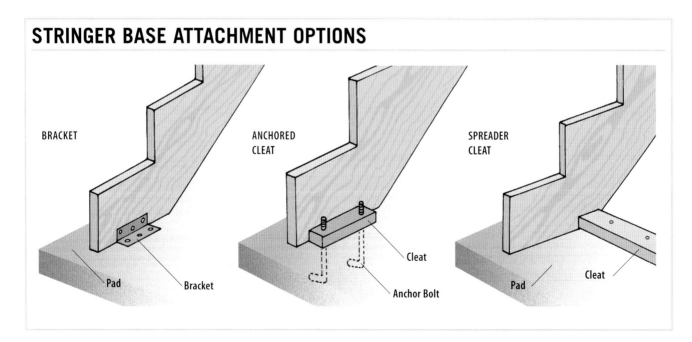

BRACKET

Pad

Bracket

ANCHORED CLEAT

Cleat

Anchor Bolt

SPREADER CLEAT

Pad

Cleat

When building a deck with a high rise, make sure to construct the proper sub-framing for the lattice. In the deck shown here, you can see the uprights that the lattice will attach to.

teeth of the stringer after they are cut and before treads are attached. The stringer teeth could split off.

After you have cut the first stringer, check it in position to be sure the cuts are correct. Then use it as a template for other stringers. If you are going to have two solid stringers and a notched center carriage, cut the notched piece first and use it to mark the housed stringers.

For a housed stringer, make the top and bottom cuts first. Then position the tread cleats; drill pilots; and fasten the cleats to the stringers with 1¼-inch lags or structural wood screws. If you're not sure of the tread layout, you can screw on the hardware after the stringers are installed. This gives you a chance to make corrections. (See "Installing Cut Stringers," page 176.)

Clamp a marked stringer in place to check pencil marks for treads before installing the stringer.

TOOLS & MATERIALS

- Level
- Measuring tape
- Combination square
- Stair stringers
- Drill & bits
- Stair brackets
- 1¼-in. structural wood screws
- Framing square
- Stair clip
- Lag screws
- Wrenches

1 Position the framing square and speed square on the stringer with the crown of the board facing you.

2 Use a sharp #2 pencil to mark the outside of the square for each tread and rise.

3 Repeat each required tread and riser and mark the line that creates the riser to mark the correct number required.

4 Reverse the framing square with the pre-set stair gauges and mark the top end of the stringer.

5 Remove the stair gauges and mark the starting riser square to the first tread.

6 Mark the starting riser as 1 and square a cut line to that. This represents a complete riser height minus the finished tread thickness. This should be a dashed line.

7 Marking the dashed line for the starting riser.

8 Starting riser and bottom level cut of the stringer created using a circular saw.

9 Circular saw used to cut each tread and riser line. Be sure not to overcut at the intersection of the layout lines.

10 Finish all inside saw kerfs from the circular saw with a sharp handsaw to prevent excessive vibrations of a jigsaw.

11 Finished cut stringer.

Design stairs to complement the overall look of the deck. Note: If you want to avoid having to use handrails, design no more than three risers between landings.

Locate the Posts. On some designs, you can install the stringers and treads completely, and then attach the main railing post. On stairs that project away from the deck with two railings, of course, you'll need two posts. If your 2x12 stringers are securely bolted into a concrete landing, you may gain enough strength for a railing post by bolting it to the pad and the stringer. It will be even stiffer once you add a substantial railing and balusters.

Another option is to set the stringers temporarily, mark the post locations, remove the stringers, and dig postholes. You might set the posts in concrete or build piers with hardware so that the porous post ends stay off the ground.

Attach the Tops of the Stringers. To attach a stringer to the face of a joist, you may be able to drive nails or screws through the back of the joist into the end of the stringer. In any case, be sure to secure the face of the connection with angled brackets or hardware specially designed for this job. You may see some parts of this hardware, but most will be concealed by the treads.

Attach the Stringers to the Pad. The stairway will be quite stable once the treads and railings are installed. But to lock the stringers in place, you can install a small

💡 SMART TIP

BOX STEPS

If your deck is only a step up from the yard, you might avoid stringers altogether and build box steps. These are easy-to-build rectangular frames, usually made of 2x6 treated lumber and covered with deck treads. For two or more steps, build a large box, placing progressively smaller ones on top.

galvanized bracket to the concrete pad. (See "Installing Cut Stringers," page 176.) Another option is to set J-bolts in the concrete while it is wet and attach a treated wood cleat to them. Or you can notch the bottom of the stringers and install a 2x4 cleat attached to the pad with masonry nails, or with lag screws and masonry shields. (See opposite and page 144.)

TREAD OPTIONS

On solid stringers, do not rely on nails driven into the treads through the stringers to support the step. This weak detail can cause splits and accidents.

Fasten treads by screwing through the flange into the bracket. On sawtooth stringers, the sawtooth pattern creates a ready-made support for the treads. **(Step 1)**

If treads extend beyond the stringers, finish treads with curved corners and beveled edges. **(Step 2)**

ATTACHING CLEATS

An alternative to attaching stringers to a pad with galvanized brackets is to attach a 2x4 cleat. Use wedge anchors for this purpose.

Screw stringers to the cleats.

Use wedge anchors to attach your 2x4 cleat to the concrete. Concrete anchors are an option or alternative.

Install Treads and Risers. Risers on open stringers are often installed flush to the outside of the stringers, but this design can lead to problems if your cuts are not perfect or if the boards shrink. If you let them overlap the stringers by ¾ inch or so, you will avoid these problems.

On notched stringers, you may like the floating effect that comes from extending the treads 3 or 4 inches beyond the edge of the stringer. If possible, the overlap should be equal on both sides of the tread.

If you're nailing, it's wise to predrill your treads. Driving screws is a better option and provides more holding power. Better yet, use concealed hardware, and drive screws up through brackets into the bottoms of the treads. There won't be any screw or nail heads on the surface of the tread. (See "Tread Options," above.)

Using concealed hardware for attaching treads to stringers is not the same thing as attaching decking to joists. Stairs require much more bracing when there is not a solid connection of the treads, and the treads alone cannot act as that bracing (as is the case with many concealed fasteners).

A railing provides a measure of safety, some privacy, and a place for displaying plants. Possible railing designs are endless, and the right design can enhance the look of your deck. Local building codes vary, but generally, decks built more than 30 inches aboveground will require a railing. The building code will specify minimum requirements for the design of the railing, including the railing height and the spacing of the balusters and posts.

RAILING DESIGN CHOICES

One approach to railing design is to work from two lists of dimensions: one that includes stock-size lumber, such as 2x4 and 4x4 posts, and another that includes code requirements, such as less than 4-inch spacing between balusters. You'll find there are many ways to put the pieces together.

Here is a quick look at some of the other factors that can affect your choice of materials and the overall design.

Matching Deck Overhangs. The first thing to think about in selecting a design is how you will attach the railings and posts to the deck. There are several possibilities. For example, if you have balusters but no bottom rail so that the balusters are attached to the joists or fascia boards, you may want to cut the decking flush to the joists. Otherwise you would have to make hundreds of little cutouts to make room for the balusters.

ATTACHING INTERIOR POSTS

Fastening a post to the inside of rim joists is one method of attachment. Always check your local code for the requirements for fastening a post. Here a composite 4x4 post is used, but the process is exactly the same for wood posts. Start by temporarily tack-screwing a block of wood under the joist to hold the post up while you install it. Then cut a block of joist material to fit snuggly between joists. Plumb the post, and then secure it with screws through the joists and the block. Also screw through the joists into the ends of the block.

Position and plumb the post. Secure the post with screws.

But if you are using several rails instead of balusters, or if you have a bottom rail to which you'll attach the balusters, then the decking can overhang the joist.

Choosing a Cap Width. If your top cap will butt between the posts, it should be the same width as the post—which usually means it will be a 2x4. If you want a wider cap (handy as a shelf), use a design that places the cap on top of the posts. This style looks best if the cap overhangs the posts by ¼ to 1½ inches on each side.

Most railing designs allow you to choose either a 2x6 or a 2x8 for a top cap. The 2x8 may look a little clunky, especially on a small deck, but has a lot of shelf space. Whatever design you choose, select the very best pieces of lumber for your top cap.

Attaching Posts. In general, notched railing posts are no longer allowed by most codes because they are too weak. However, your building inspector may allow shallow notches if the post spacing is close enough. This leaves you two options. One is to bolt full posts to the outside of the rim joists, but this can look clunky.

The best strategy is to attach the posts to the inside of the rim joists and cut decking to fit around them. The first step in doing this is calculating the length of your posts. For example, if your railing will be 36 inches high with a 1½-inch-thick cap rail, the post will extend 34½ inches above the deck. To this measurement add the thickness of the decking and the width of the joists. With 1-inch-thick decking and 7¼-inch-wide joists, the posts need to be 42¾ inches long.

Corner Posts. You can install a single corner post or two posts near one another on opposite sides of a corner. Single corner posts should be 4x4s or better.

RAILINGS: BASIC CHOICES

Whether you are standing on the deck or viewing it from the yard, the railing is the most visible part of the structure. The railing greatly influences the overall appearance of the deck, giving it either vertical or horizontal lines, an open or closed appearance, or a polished or rustic look. But railings must also be designed for safety.

Current codes typically call for a railing that is 36 inches high with balusters spaced so that a 4-inch ball can't fit through. If the railing incorporates a bottom rail, the space between rails and deck must also be less than 4 inches. (Be sure to check code requirements with the local building department.) But within these limits, you have lots of options, including building your own railing entirely from wood, incorporating manufactured components into your own railing design, or using a manufactured railing kit.

There's no heavy lifting and no messy digging at this stage. And with a few simple techniques, you can produce a structure that looks professional and handcrafted—something you can point to with pride for years to come.

RAILING MATERIALS

Some lumberyards and home centers carry prefabricated railing systems. They come with all the components ready for assembly, including railings and factory-milled balusters and newels in several different decorative patterns. You can also use cast metal, steel cables, plastic tubing, clear acrylic panels, and so on, as long as you get the approval of the local building department. If your decking is synthetic, you'll almost certainly want to use synthetic railings to match, either building your own of composite material or using a synthetic railing kit.

For wooden decks, the most popular and easiest-to-use railing materials are stock pieces of dimensional

This railing works well with the trim on the main part of the house.

lumber. You can cut and assemble one-by, two-by, and four-by materials in a variety of styles.

Lumber

It is usually best to have the railing materials match the decking and fascia, but this is not a hard-and-fast rule. Sometimes it works best to think in terms of matching the railing with the house, inasmuch as the railing is a vertical line that is seen with the house as a backdrop. For example, on a Colonial or Victorian house, turned spindles and fancy newels may look best, especially if they can mirror elements on the house.

And there's no rule that says you can't stain or paint all or part of the wooden railing to help it blend in. If you have an unpainted deck against a painted house, you already have wood and paint in combination, and there's no harm in continuing that pattern. In any case, paint or stain the top cap to protect it from the weather.

Selecting Lumber

The railing deserves the best lumber you can find. Not only do these pieces get handled, they also provide nooks and crannies through which water can be absorbed. And splinters on a rail can be downright dangerous. You must select railing material carefully. This particular component is important when it comes to appearance, and even more so when it comes to safety.

Cedar and redwood look best and splinter least. However, because they get handled and are exposed to the weather, plan on treating railings made of these materials with a UV-blocking oil at least every other year. Treated lumber of high quality can also work.

Precut Components. You can save time using precut components such as decorative 2x2 balusters. But don't change your railing design just to accommodate their size. It can sometimes be a problem to find good-looking 2x2s, because they often twist if not stacked well. Many DIYers select a larger stock and rip it into pieces to make balusters.

In some areas you can purchase lumber that has been milled to accept stock components. For example, you should be able to buy a top cap that has a 1½-inch-wide groove in the bottom to accommodate 2x2 balusters.

Fasteners

When things come loose on a deck, it is usually at the railing. There's a lot of exposed joinery, and the railing gets leaned on and bumped. So plan for a railing that is as strong as possible at all points.

CAP AND POST OPTIONS

Precut posts are available in many styles and sizes. You can cut them to length and combine them with stock sizes of railing caps and balusters. If you use stock posts, you can dress up the tops with flat or shaped caps. Many have a screw end, so you can drill a pilot hole and easily turn them onto the posts.

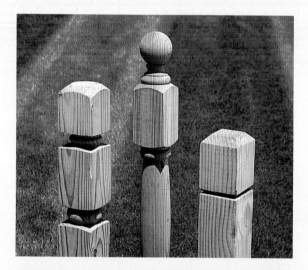

Unfortunately, there are few specialized railing hardware pieces, and they are not as effective as joist hangers for the framing. In general, the metal connectors for attaching rails to posts are unattractive and provide a place for moisture to collect. And unless they are galvanized, they can rust. There is a post-to-railing clip that is more helpful; it allows you to connect the top cap to the post while concealing the fasteners. Wood cleats that can add an extra nailing surface often look unprofessional and may be susceptible to water damage.

The upshot is the need to make the most of standard fasteners. Start off by attaching the support posts to the outermost joists with either lag screws or through-bolts. Through bolts offer maximum support. It's also wise to drill pilot holes for all nails or screws that are near the end of a board. Use 3-inch deck screws or 16d galvanized nails for plenty of holding power. Try to avoid driving nails or screws at an angle (toenailing), and driving more than two fasteners at railing connections. (For example, where you need to piece a horizontal rail over a 4x4.)

RAILING BASICS

All railings use some, but not necessarily all, of the following components. *Posts* are structural members, usually made of 4x4s. They keep the railing from wobbling and provide the main support that counteracts the weight of someone leaning or falling against the assembly.

Balusters are the numerous vertical pieces, often made of 2x2s, that fill in spaces between the posts and provide a sort of fence. *Bottom rail* and *top rail* pieces run horizontally between the posts, and are either flat or on end. On many designs, the balusters are attached to these rails. Some railings do not have vertical balusters, and use several horizontal rails instead. (Check local codes.)

Other designs use a *top cap,* a horizontal piece of lumber laid flat on top of the post and top rail. It covers the end grain of the post and can provide a flat surface that serves as a shelf.

Complying with Code

The railing is one part of your deck that an inspector will check closely. A deck more than 30 inches from the ground requires a railing that uses vertical components and must be at least 36 inches high.

If the deck is more than 8 feet high, you may want to build a 42-inch railing for extra security.

When you're planning the railing system, consider one of the most limiting codes: the minimum space between components. This dimension must be small enough so that a 4-inch ball can't fit through. This rule is designed to prevent children from getting their heads stuck between rails or balusters. Some codes may call for a smaller maximum opening at the bottom of the railing.

There also may be specific requirements about posts and fasteners to ensure that your railing is strong. But there are many design variations that you can use and still comply with code.

INSTALLING RAILINGS AND BALUSTERS

Construction methods vary with different railing designs, but usually you install the posts first, the top and bottom rails next, then the top cap (if you're adding one), and finally the balusters.

Putting up the Posts

Once you decide on the railing system, you'll know how to continue. Here is a basic sequence, which you may have to adjust somewhat, depending on the railing system you select.

Install the Posts. For many types of railings, you'll have installed the posts earlier in the process before you completed installing the decking (see page 112). If you haven't already installed posts, you'll need to determine the length of your posts, taking into account other railing members and the amount of end joist space the post will cover when it is installed.

Setting the Rails

Mark and Cut the Rails. When installing rails, measure it all at the base, so that the top and bottom rail are the same length and will pull and maintain the posts plumb. Ideally, of course, all of the rails will be single lengths, and you won't have joints except at the corners.

ALUMINUM BALUSTERS

An easy way to add elegance to your railing is to use aluminum balusters. Those shown here simply screw to top and bottom rails. Aluminum balusters cost more than wood, but they never warp and they never need painting.

Installing the Top Cap

Measure and Cut. Hold and mark the pieces in place whenever possible. The corners require precise, splinter-free cuts. Use a power miter saw or a guide for your circular saw. It's wise to leave boards long until you get a perfect miter at the corner. Then you can cut the caps to length.

Bevel-Cut the Splices. Avoid butt-end splices if you can, because if the wood shrinks they will look bad and invite moisture into end grain. When splices are necessary, place them on top of posts, and scarf-joint the boards with 45-degree cuts.

Install the Stair Railing Cap. You can use a bevel gauge (or sliding T-bevel) to mark the angle of the upper plumb cut on the stair railing. It's best to mark the cuts with the cap in place. Set your circular saw or power miter saw to cut both ends of the stair railing cap at this angle. Prevent waste by cutting the cap a bit long at first, so you can test fit the top end and adjust the angle if you need to. Some end grain will be exposed on both ends, so treat them with some preservative. Get the joint as tight as possible, and smooth the angle transition by sanding.

Setting Balusters

Estimate Materials and Spacing. You should be able to get a good lumber estimate based on how many balusters you will use per linear foot of deck. If you will be installing a lot of balusters in a long, uninterrupted run, pay attention to the spacing between each one, and try to let the odd-size spacing fall next to the house wall.

It is easier to plan spacing in units of balusters between posts. You can figure out the spacing mathematically, but it pays to clamp or tack a set of balusters in place to check your work.

Cut the Balusters. If you have a power miter saw, you can build a jig with a stop block so that you can mass-produce balusters. If you will be cutting with a circular saw, cut one baluster to the correct length, make the angle cuts on the ends if including that detail, and use it as a template for the other balusters. You'll probably cut the stair railing balusters at a different angle than the rest of the balusters, so don't cut them yet. (See "How to Install Balusters," opposite.)

Drill Pilot Holes. You can get away without predrilling on intermediate connections but not near the ends of boards. There you need pilot holes to ensure against splits and to

Spacing is easier to plan if you do the math based on how many balusters you need between posts.

make the joints stronger. And by laying the balusters side by side and drilling straight lines of holes (with a string line to guide you, if need be), you will add a touch of professionalism to your deck. Of course, you need to use a framing square to square-up your balusters before drilling.

Install the Balusters. Figure out the baluster spacing, and cut a spacer block as a guide so that you won't have to measure each installation. Use the spacer next to one of the posts and move on down the line of balusters. But double-check for plumb periodically. On long runs, you can make very small adjustments at each baluster (on the scale of $\frac{1}{16}$ inch) to adjust the spacing as needed.

Install Stair Railing Balusters. If you will have stair railing balusters that butt up against a rail cap, find the angle for the top cut by holding a baluster in a plumb position against the top rail and the top cap. Hold a 2x2 spacer on the baluster, and mark the angle. Then check an angle-cut piece in place.

If you are not using a top cap, you can simply attach balusters to the sides of the top and bottom rails. But you will have to increase the offset where the rails run at an angle, or duplicate the angle on the top and bottom cuts of the balusters so that they appear to step down the stairs.

PROJECT: 🐦🐦🐦
HOW TO INSTALL BALUSTERS

If you cut angled tops and bottoms on the main support posts, follow up with the same type treatment on the balusters.

TOOLS & MATERIALS
- 2x4s
- Table saw
- Circular saw
- Sliding T-bevel
- Clamps and horses
- Drill-driver and bits
- 2-in. screws
- Belt sander

1 Mark a sound 2x4 for cutting, and rip the balusters using a table saw.

2 Using the T-bevel, copy the angle on the support posts and transfer it to the balusters.

3 Clamp a group of balusters together, and remove imperfections using a belt sander.

4 Drill pilot holes for the screws in the balusters to avoid splitting the wood.

5 Work your way around the perimeter of the deck, fastening the balusters with screws.

BUILDING BALUSTRADES

An alternative method for building railings is to construct balustrades, which are complete sections of railings with balusters. You can assemble them flat on the deck as though you were making a ladder. Once these sections are built, you install them between the posts. This system does not have the margin of error provided when you install railings and balusters piece by piece.

Install balusters.

Attach the sections to posts.

DRAINAGE DETAILS

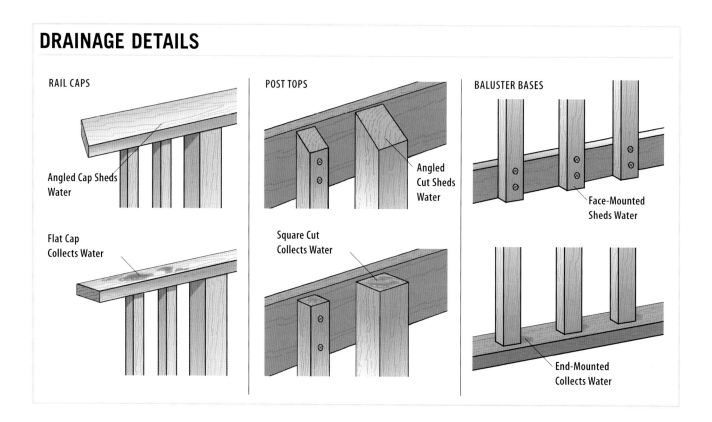

RAIL CAPS

Angled Cap Sheds Water

Flat Cap Collects Water

POST TOPS

Angled Cut Sheds Water

Square Cut Collects Water

BALUSTER BASES

Face-Mounted Sheds Water

End-Mounted Collects Water

BUILDING A COMPOSITE RAILING

Composite and vinyl systems must be installed per the manufacturer's installation instructions. There are many companies putting different products and materials on the market, and they all have their own unique installation instructions. The examples presented in this section may differ significantly from the installation steps you might have to take, depending on which synthetic decking system you choose.

If you are using synthetic decking, you'll most likely want synthetic railing to match. In this case, the deck was made of 1-inch-thick composite boards, so the railing is made of the same material. This railing could just as easily be made of ¾ lumber decking for a wooden deck. Essentially the railing consists of 1-inch by 1-inch balusters sandwiched between two bottom rails and two top rails with a 5½-inch-wide cap rail. The top and bottom rails are made by ripping 5½-inch pieces exactly in half. Doubled rails makes the railing stronger—a good idea because composite is not as stiff as wood. It also allows water to drain through between the rails. This railing is simple to build, but it will help to have a table saw to rip the

⚲ SMART TIP

GANG CUTTING & PREDRILLING

If you are cutting balusters on a miter saw, you can save time by measuring and cutting four balusters at a time (below left). And when you are predrilling for screws, it's always handy to have two drills—one fitted with the drill bit and one fitted with a driver bit. To speed the work even more, predrill all the balusters at once so you can just grab the drill with the driver bit and install all the balusters (below right).

A railing with sandwiched balusters is a design that is easy to execute with composite boards.

PROJECT: 🦫🦫🦫
MAKING A
SANDWICH RAILING

Although composite material is not as strong as wood, this system creates a strong railing that won't sag.

TOOLS & MATERIALS
- Composite decking boards
- Measuring tape
- Pencil
- Drill/driver
- Countersink bit
- Two-foot level
- Circular saw

1 Center the cleats across the width of the posts, make sure they are flush to the top of the post, then screw them in place.

2 Put the top and bottom rails in position against the posts, and scribe the layout line for the final length cut.

3 Toe-screw the outside top and bottom rails through the cleats into the posts.

4 About every 3 feet, install a baluster that extends to the decking. This will prevent the rail from sagging.

5 Screw the remaining balusters in place.

6 Scribe and cut the top and bottom inside rails and toe-screw them through the cleats into the posts. Then screw them to the top and bottom of every fourth baluster.

7 Use a circular saw to trim the protruding balusters flush to the top rails.

composite boards to the widths you need. You could also accomplish the task with a rip guide on a circular saw.

The railing is attached to 4x4 cleats that are attached to the inside of the joists. (See "Attaching Interior Posts," page 182.)

Installing Rails and Balusters

Attach the Outside Rails. The rails will be attached to 1x1 cleats screwed to the sides of the posts. Cut the cleats to reach from the top of the post to the bottom of the bottom rail. Predrill and countersink holes for three 2½-inch composite screws. Center the cleat across the width of the post and insert the screws. (**Step 1**)

Cut the rails to approximate length, then scribe the outside rails in position to fit between the posts. (**Step 2**) Cut these rails to final length, then predrill and toe-screw into the outside rails at an angle that will send the screws through the cleat and the post. (**Step 3**) Use two screws per connection.

Attach the Balusters. To prevent the railing from sagging, one baluster about every 3 feet will extend to the deck. Cut these balusters to reach from the deck to a couple of inches above the top rail—you'll cut them off in place later. Predrill, make sure they are plumb, then screw them to the rails with one screw at top and one at bottom. (**Step 4**) Secure them with one screw driven up through the decking into the bottom of the baluster.

Cut the rest of the balusters to ½ inch less than the distance from the top of the top rail to the bottom of the bottom rail. Predrill, plumb and screw them in place flush to the top of the top rail. (**Step 5**)

You can create unique designs with balusters and posts. But be careful—this beautiful railing violates most building codes because a 4-inch ball would fit through the space at the top center of each section.

191

1 With the meeting cap rails tacked in place, you can accurately mark where they meet before cutting a 45-degree miter on one board.

2 After mitering one cap rail, you can use it to scribe the cut on the cap that will meet it.

3 Untack the second board to make its miter cut.

Attach the Inside Rails. Put each of the inside rails in position against the posts to scribe and cut them to length as you did the outside rails. Put the bottom inside rail in place and make sure it is in the same plane as the outside bottom rail. Predrill and screw the bottom rail to every fourth baluster. Then install the inside top rail in the same way making sure it is flush to top of the balusters. **(Step 6)**

Trim the Protruding Balusters. You can use a handsaw or a reciprocating saw to trim the protruding balusters flush to the top rails, but the quickest and easiest way is to use a circular saw. **(Step 7)**

Installing the Cap Rail

In the sandwiched rail design, the cap rail is made of 1-inch-thick by 5½-inch-wide composite decking. The caps are mitered at the corners for a clean, professional look.

Miter the Corners. The key to creating a tight professional-looking mitered cap rail is to do the cutting in place so you can scribe the board lengths rather than measuring. Start by cutting the boards to a length that will overhang the corner posts by at least 7 inches. Then put a cap in place with approximately equal overhangs at each corner post and equal overhangs at the outside and inside of the top rails. Then temporarily secure the board with a couple of screws driven just far enough to keep

4 Retack the cap rails. Check the fit of the miter and that the overhangs are equal before permanently installing the cap.

5 Predrill and countersink for pairs of screws into the outside and inside rails, inserting screws in preparation for driving them in.

6 Drive in pairs of screws, spaced about four balusters apart.

the board from moving. In the same way, position and tack-screw the cap that will meet the first board, letting the boards overlap at the corner.

Now mark the point where the two boards meet at the inside of the railing. Extend the mark to the surface of the top board and use an angle square to lay out a 45-degree cut. Set your circular saw to cut about 1¼ inch deep. Place a block under the marked board to raise it up (unlike wood, the composite will flex enough to do this while still tacked in place). Make the cut. **(Step 1)**

Remove the block and use the cut on the top cap to scribe the miter cut on the cap it will meet. **(Step 2)** Remove the tack screws from the cap you just marked and make the miter cut. **(Step 3)**

Predrill and Fasten the Caps. Put the cap back in place and reinsert the tack screws, then check several places along both caps to make sure the overhang is equal on both sides. **(Step 4)** Predrill and countersink the caps for composite screws, spacing pairs of screws about four balusters apart. For each pair of screws, drive one into the outside top rail and one into the inside top rail. **(Step 5–Step 6)**

💡 SMART TIP

COUNTERSINKING

Composite screws are self-tapping, and in general you can drive them without predrilling. But in prominent spots, such as on a railing—especially when driving screws through the cap rail—it's a good idea to predrill and countersink screws for a neater appearance. Do this with a bit that combines a drill bit with a countersink. A #7 bit creates the perfect countersink for composite screws. However, #7 bits are not widely available. Every hardware store or home center carries #8 bits, which will work just fine.

INSTALLING A PLASTIC RAIL KIT

Plastic railings can actually have a more refined look than the typical homemade railing of composite or wood. The rails have molded profiles and there are no fasteners visible when installed. They blend beautifully with capped composite or PVC decking boards and can be purchased in matching or contrasting colors. There are various systems from different manufacturers, so be sure to read the instructions that come with your kit. This kit has sleeves that fit over 4x4 wooden posts. It employs round aluminum balusters with a powder-coated finish. In this kit all the fasteners are provided.

Preparing the Posts and Rails

Install the Sleeves. When you install the wooden 4x4 posts, plan them to be about an inch or so shorter than the plastic sleeves that come with the kit. The exception to posts at bottom of stair rails—it's a good idea to let those run longer than the sleeves in case you need to adjust the post lengths after the stairs are constructed. Slide the sleeves over the posts, **(Step 1)** then slip the post bases over the sleeves and slide them to the deck. **(Step 2)**

Install the Rail Support Brackets. The kit comes with a cardboard template to make it easy to locate the brackets that will be used to attach the rails. Secure the template

Continued on page 197

PROJECT:

HOW TO PREPARE THE POSTS AND RAILS

With the supplied template it's easy to get the rail support brackets in the right spots.

TOOLS & MATERIALS

- Post sleeves
- Post bases
- Rail brackets
- Rails
- Adapter strips
- Foot block
- Baluster spacers
- Balusters
- Post caps
- Provided screws
- Drill/driver
- ⅛-inch drill bit
- Measuring tape
- Miter saw
- PVC adhesive or silicone

1 Drop post sleeves over the 4x4 railing posts.

2 Slip the post base over the sleeve down to the deck.

3 Fold the supplied template around the post sleeve and secure it with a short bungee cord, rubber band, or tape.

4 Position the top and bottom rail brackets in the appropriate template holes and secure with screws provided.

5 Put one end of the bottom rail against the inside of one post and scribe a cut line against the inside of the other post.

6 Use a miter saw to cut the bottom rail to length, then use the bottom rail as a template to lay out a cut for the top rail.

7 Drill a ³/₁₆-inch hole for the foot block centered on the bottom rail. Screw the foot to the bottom of the bottom rail.

8 Cut the adapter strips to 2¼ inches shorter than the rails and center them so they won't interfere with the support brackets.

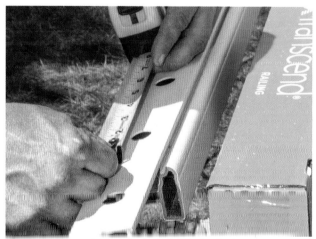

9 Measure and mark both ends of the baluster spacers so that balusters on each end will be equidistant from the posts.

PROJECT:
HOW TO INSTALL RAILS AND BALUSTERS

With all the parts cut to length, assembling the rails and balusters to the posts is a simple job.

TOOLS & MATERIALS
- Bottom and top rails
- Supplied screws
- Bottom and top spacers
- Support foot with cover
- Balusters
- Post caps
- Drill/driver
- ⅛-in. drill bit
- PVC adhesive

1 Attach the bottom rail to the posts with one provided screw driven down through the rail brackets.

2 Snap the bottom spacer into place.

3 Rotate the foot down to support the rail, predrill, and insert a provided screw.

4 Lower the foot cover.

5 Put the top baluster spacer over the lower spacer and fit the top rail over the top brackets.

6 Screw the top brackets to the bottom of the top rails.

7 Put the balusters in place through the holes in both spacers.

8 Pull the top baluster spacer up over the balusters and snap it in place under the top rail.

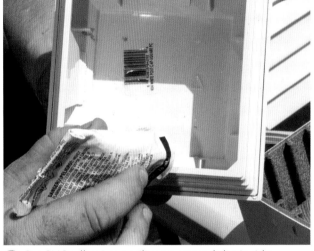

9 Put PVC adhesive or silicone around the inside perimeter of the post cap.

10 Press the post cap in place on the post sleeve.

to the post with a short bungee cord, a rubber band or tape. **(Step 3)** Two of the four holes in the template are marked Horizontal top and Horizontal bottom. Put a supplied bracket in these holes, being sure to orient it as shown on the template. Then secure the brackets with two screws each, using the screws provided for the purpose. **(Step 4)**

Cut the Rails. Place a bottom rail against the inside of one post and scribe for a cut where it meets the other post. **(Step 5)** Use a miter saw to cut the railing to length—bring the arm down slowly for a smooth cut. Then use the bottom rail as a template to mark and cut the top rail to length. **(Step 6)**

Install the Foot. The kit comes with an adjustable foot block to support the railing midway along its length. Find the center of the bottom rail and drill a 3/16-inch hole at that point. Attach the block to the bottom of the bottom rail with the screw provided. (**Step 7**)

Install the Adapter Strips. This same railing system can be used with square balusters, in which case no adapter strips are necessary. For the round balusters used here, cut the strips to 2½ inches shorter than the rails and then center them in the top and bottom rails. (**Step 8**)

Cut the Baluster Spacers. The baluster spacers are strips with holes in them that snap into the rails. They hold the balusters in place at the proper spacing. Position each strip in on its rail and measure so that the distance between each end of the rail and the closest baluster will be the same. (**Step 9**) Mark and cut both ends of the spacer strips.

Install the Rails and Balusters. Now that all the cutting is done, the rest of the job is easy. You just need to insert a few screws to connect the rails to the posts, put the spacers in place, and insert the balusters and install post caps.

Attach the Bottom Rail and Set the Foot. Fit the adapter strips into both rails. Put the bottom rail in place under the bottom rail bracket and secure each end with one screw that's provided with the kit. (**Step 1**) Snap the bottom spacer into place over the bottom rail. (**Step 2**) Raise the foot block cover to reveal the adjustable foot. Rotate the foot down until it is supporting the bottom rail, then put a ⅛-inch drill bit into the hole in the foot and predrill down into the deck. Secure the block with the screw provided and lower the cover. (**Step 3–Step 4**)

Attach the Top Rail. After you install the top rail, you'll be putting the balusters through the holes in the bottom and top spacers, then pulling the bottom spacer up the balusters to snap it into the bottom of the top rail. For now, lay the spacer strip for the top rail atop the bottom rail. Put the top rail in place over the top rail brackets and secure it by screwing through the brackets up into the rail. (**Step 5–Step 6**)

Install the Balusters and Caps. Put each baluster in place through both spacers. (**Step 7**) Work the top spacer up over the balusters and snap it in place under the top rail. (**Step 8**) Put a bead of silicone adhesive along the perimeter of the post caps and press them down onto the top of the post sleeves. (**Step 9–Step 10**)

INSTALLING THE STAIR RAILS

The system for installing plastic stair rails is similar to installing guardrails on the deck. There are a few minor differences because the rails meet the posts at an angle.

Cut the Parts. Slip the post sleeve over the post. Rest a bottom rail on the stair-tread nosings and mark the angled cut where it will meet the bottom post. (**Step 1**) Use the layout line to set the angle on a power miter saw and cut the rail. (**Step 2**) Keep this setting on the saw—you'll use it to make all the other cuts. But the cut you just made against the bottom post and scribe the cut to meet the upper post. (**Step 3**) Test fit the bottom rail. If it fits properly, cut the top rail to the same length at the same angle.

PROJECT: 🐾🐾🐾
HOW TO INSTALL STAIR RAILS

Mark the rail cuts in place for a perfect fit.

TOOLS & MATERIALS
- Top and bottom rails
- Rail brackets
- Stair baluster spacer strips
- Baluster adapter
- strips
- Supplied screws
- Pencil
- Power miter saw
- Drill/driver

1 Put a bottom rail along tread nosing and mark the angled cut.

2 Use a miter saw to cut the marked end of the first rail.

3 Put the cut end of the rail in position against the post and mark to cut the other end.

4 Cut the top rail to the same length and angle as the bottom rail, then cut the baluster adapters and spacers to fit.

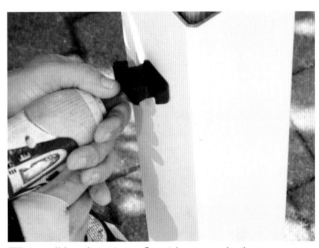

5 Install bracket pieces flat side up on the bottom posts as shown here. For the top posts, install the bracket pieces flat side down.

6 Clip another bracket piece to the installed one—the configuration shown here is on a top post.

7 Place the rails on the brackets as shown, and then drive a single screw through both bracket parts into the rail.

Railings can complement the look and feel of your deck.

The baluster spacers work in the same way as they do for the guardrails. However, they have oval holes because the balusters come through them at an angle. Cut the baluster spacers to fit the rails. As you did for the guardrails, cut both ends of the spacers so the end holes will be equidistant from the ends of the rails. Cut the baluster adapters to 2½ inches shorter than the inside of the rails to leave room for the brackets. (**Step 4**) The foot for stair rails is angled at the top to meet the bottom of the bottom rail. Center and install the foot as you did for deck guardrails.

Install the Rails. The stair rail uses the same bracket pieces as the guardrails. However, to follow the angle of the rails, two bracket pieces are used at each connection instead of one. Put the cardboard template in place as you did for the guardrails and attach one bracket piece at each of the two holes designated for stair brackets. For the posts at the bottom of the stairs, orient these pieces with the flat slide up. For the posts at the top of the stairs, orient these pieces with the flat side down. (**Step 5**) Then snap a second bracket piece onto each attached piece— for the bottom-of-stair posts it'll be beneath the attached bracket piece, (**Step 6**) while for the top-of-stair posts it will be on top of the attached piece.

Screw the rails in place through the brackets using one screw that goes through both bracket pieces into the rail. (**Step 7**)

Installing the Balusters and Handrail

Install the Balusters. Snap the bottom baluster spacer in place and put the top baluster spacer over it. Put the balusters through the spacers, pull the top spacer up, and snap it into the bottom of the top rail. (**Step 1**)

Cut the Bottom Posts and Install the Caps. Use a handsaw or a reciprocating saw to cut the bottom posts flush to the top of the post sleeves. Install the post caps as you did for the deck guardrail posts. (**Step 2**)

Install the Handrail. Most codes now require a graspable handrail on stair railing. (See "Building Code for Stairs," page 167.) The one shown here consists of a rail that you cut to length and two returns that get glued into the ends and screwed into posts. A cover hides the screws.

To determine the length of the railing, mark the center across the width of the posts and stick one return into the end of the railing. Have a helper hold the return and rail in place on one rail while you put the other return on it and mark the rail for a cut with a power miter saw. Slip the covers onto the returns. Put PVC adhesive on the returns and slip them into the rail. Before the adhesive sets, put the returns on a flat surface to ensure they are in the same plane. With a helper, hold the rail in position, keeping it flush with the baluster railing. Install with screws provided and slip the caps in place. (**Step 3–Step 4**)

PROJECT:
HOW TO INSTALL THE BALUSTERS AND HANDRAIL

This handrail is simple to install and will comply with any building code.

TOOLS & MATERIALS
- Balusters
- Handrail
- Supplied screws
- Rail end caps
- Drill/driver
- Reciprocating saw or handsaw

1 After putting the balusters in place, pull the spacer strip up to the bottom of the top rail and snap it in place.

2 Use a reciprocating saw or handsaw to cut the bottom posts flush to the post sleeves.

3 Position the handrail flush to the top of the stair rail.

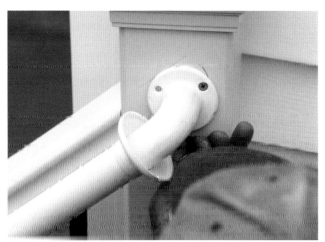

4 Screw the returns to the posts, then snap the covers in place.

MATERIAL LIST

LUMBER:

Note: All lumber must be pressure-treated.

- Two 12 ft. 4x4 cut for 9 posts
- One 8 ft. 4x4 cut for 4 posts
- Six 8 ft. 2x6s for lower deck girder
- Six 12 ft. 2x6s for upper deck girder
- Nine 10 ft. 2x6s for lower deck joists and rim joists
- Twelve 12 ft. 2x6s for upper deck joists and rim joists

- Twenty-five 12 ft. 2x6s for decking
- Twenty 8 ft. 2x6s for decking
- One 8 ft. 2x10 for stair stringer
- One 10 ft. 2x6 for stair riser
- One 12 ft. 2x12 for stair treads
- Four 12 ft. 2x8s for railing
- Twenty-six 14 ft. 2x2s for balusters

CONNECTORS:

- 30 post beam connectors with nails
- 109 joist anchors with nails
- 13 post base anchors with nails
- 6 staircase angles with nails
- 32 joist hangers with nails
- 12 lbs. 10d galvanized nails for decking

- 5 lbs. 8d galvanized nails for balusters
- 32 ⅜-inch dia. lag bolts with washers, ledger, and post
- 1 cubic yard concrete for piers and step pad
- 2 gallons staining material

Building this simple and functional deck design involves using many of the skills and tools covered in the previous chapters. Use this basic design as-is or let it inspire your own unique backyard retreat.

DESIGN AMERICA, INC.

St. Louis, Missouri

designamerica.com

Find this plan #002D-3016, along with other deck plans at houseplansandmore.com

9'-3" 10'-9"

8'-0"

14'-0"

12'-0"

INSTRUCTIONS

Before You Start

Before starting your deck, check with your utility companies to locate any underground utility or septic lines that may be in the way. If you find that you do have underground lines in the way you may wish to relocate your deck. In any case, be sure that the locations of any underground lines are properly staked.

Be sure to check with your local building department to determine the code requirements and obtain a building permit. When this has been accomplished you are ready to stake the position and outline of your deck.

Laying Out the Deck

The first step in laying out your deck is to mark the position of the lower deck on your house wall following the deck framing plan.

Measure out from the house the depth of your deck and drive a stake to mark each corner. Construct batter boards two feet each way past the outer corners using 2x4 stakes as shown in **Figure 1**. The top of the batter boards must be level.

Extend chalk lines across the batter boards to outline the deck. Each chalk line should be taut and level.

On the other line, ensure squareness, form a right triangle with the chalk lines:
- Mark the line 4 feet out from where the lines cross.
- Mark a line 3 feet from where the lines cross.
- Measure the distance diagonally between the marks on both chalk lines. When the distance measures 5 feet, your deck is square.
- Repeat the process at the other corner of the deck.

Locating Deck Posts

Now that you have your deck outlined with the chalk lines you must mark the location for each post.

Following the deck framing plan, locate the 4x4 posts and piers. Place a wood stake in the ground to mark each location.

Determining Deck Height

To determine the height of your deck you must first determine the height of your house floor from your grade line.

Once you have determined this height you should allow for a 2- to 4-inch step down from your house floor to the deck so water won't enter the house. The remaining dimension will be the height of your post from the bottom of the girder to the grade line.

Ledger

First, brace the ledger against the house wall at the desired height. For wooden walls, temporarily nail once at the board's approximate center, level the board with a carpenter's level, and temporarily nail both ends. Recheck for levelness. If you have stucco or masonry house walls, use makeshift braces for support. For stucco, drill lag screw holes through the ledger into the house floor frame header. For masonry, mark expansion shield holes on the wall and then drill using a masonry bit. Bolt or lag screw the ledger in place. Remove braces, if any, and recheck levelness.

Once the ledger is level, if you have wooden walls, you can secure it to the house wall by using washers and ⅜-inch lag bolts that are 2 inches longer than the thickness

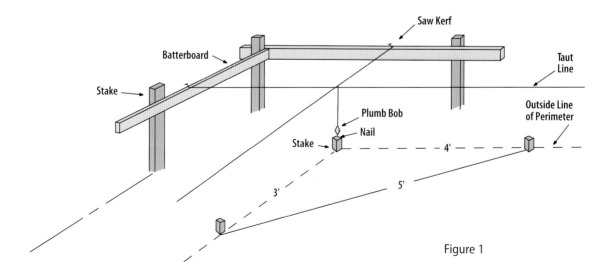

Figure 1

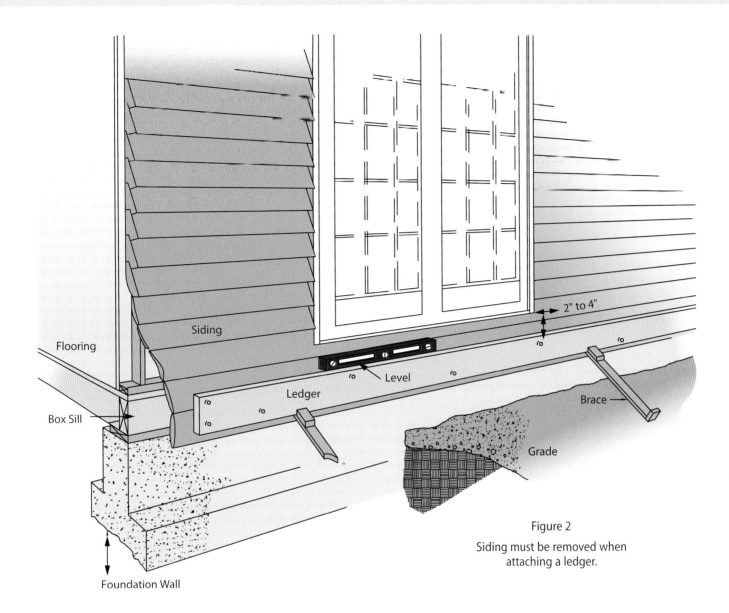

Figure 2

Siding must be removed when attaching a ledger.

of the ledger. Secure the ledger at a maximum of 2-foot intervals to the existing interior floor framing box joist. If you have masonry or concrete walls, you can secure it to the house wall by using ⅜-inch expansion bolts or lag screws that are 2 inches longer than the thickness of the ledger. Secure the ledger at a maximum of 2-foot intervals into the expansion shields. (See **Figure 2**.)

Piers and Posts

Dig post holes 10 inches in diameter. The depth of the hole should be half the height of the post above ground, but not less than 2 feet. (Check your local building code regulations. They may require that the pier extend to 6 inches below your local frost line.)

Fill each pier hole with concrete. When the concrete starts to set, position the post base anchor as shown in **Figure 3**.

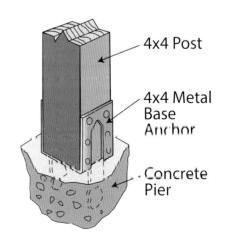

Figure 3

When setting the post, start with the lower-level post closest to the house. This will serve as the base post for setting the heights of all the other posts. Accurately measuring post heights is of utmost importance in building your deck.

Tie a string line to a nail set flush with the top of the ledger board. Extend the other end of the string over the top of the base post and extending over the tops of the other posts as they are set. Attach a line level and adjust the line at each post to the proper height. Cut off any excess post material.

Plumb and square the post with a level. When all the posts are square and level, nail them to the post base anchors.

Installing the Girder

Start with the lower level deck, cutting the 2x6s to be used for the girders to the proper lengths following the girder framing plan on page 209.

Place a metal joist hanger as shown on the girder framing plan on page 209 and nail it to the ledger board.

Join the 2x6 girders to the 4x4 posts using 16d galvanized nails. Nail one girder per side, then add post connectors as shown in **Figure 4**. Nail in place with the nails provided with the connectors.

Attaching Joists and Rim Joists

Cut the rim joists to their proper lengths as shown on the deck framing plan on page 210.

Attach a metal joist hanger to the rim joist as shown in **Figure 5**. This will enable you to set your joists in place and hold them level without any other help.

Repeat process for the remaining hangers, spacing them 16 inches apart on center.

Set the first joist from each end on the girder and connect to girder using a metal joist anchor and the nails provided. Then, set the rim joists in place and nail them to the two intermediate joists. Set the remaining joists in place and nail.

Nailing the Decking

Since this is the most visible part of your deck, care should be taken in nailing the decking in place. Start with the first board along the house wall. Since this first board will serve as a guide for the rest of your decking, try to place it as square as possible.

To avoid splitting the boards at the ends, we advise pre-drilling slightly undersized pilot holes for the nails.

Place the decking as shown in **Figure 6** with the bark side up in order to minimize cupping of the boards.

The decking should be nailed using 10d galvanized nails. Use three nails at the end of each board and two nails at the intermediate joists. Snap a chalk line to keep your nails in a straight line. Use 16d nails for spacers between the boards.

When all the decking is in place, snap a chalk line along the outside face of the end joists. Saw the deck boards at the chalk line so they are flush with the end joists.

Note: When securing the deck boards to the joists, you may want to substitute 3" long #10 coated decking screws instead of galvanized nails for a more finished appearance.

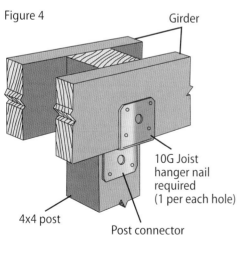

Figure 4

Girder

10G Joist hanger nail required (1 per each hole)

4x4 post

Post connector

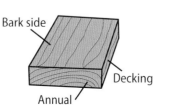

Bark side

Figure 6

Decking

Annual

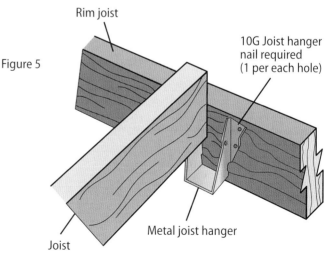

Rim joist

10G Joist hanger nail required (1 per each hole)

Figure 5

Metal joist hanger

Joist

Stair Construction

Metal step supports as shown in **Figures 7a** and **7b** are 10¼-inch long specially configured brackets made of 16-gauge galvanized structural grade steel. They make it easier to build stairs when it is necessary to adjust the angle of the stringers to span the distance between the deck and the ground.

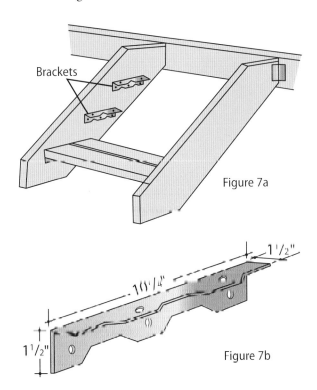

Figure 7a

Figure 7b

Measure the vertical height (rise) from grade to the top of deck. Divide the rise dimension by 7 inches or the stair rise you desire (7¾ inches is the maximum rise that should be used. It is also a good idea to check your local code requirements). This will tell you how many stair risers are required. In order to determine the total run of the stairs, multiply the number of steps required by 11¼ inches.

Cut the 2x10 stair stringers to size and fasten them to the deck framing with a 3-inch metal angle. Mark the step support position on both stringers. Step supports can be installed either from below the tread or from above it. Use ¼-inch diameter x 1½-inch long lag screws to fasten step supports to the stringers and treads.

If you have more than three steps up to your deck, a handrail must be added on each side of the stairs.

Adding a Railing

If your deck is more than 24 inches above the ground a railing will be required by most building codes. You may also want to add a railing to a low deck to enhance its appearance.

Finishing

You may want to let your preservative-treated wood weather naturally, but if you wish, you can apply a lightly pigmented stain that will offer protection without obscuring the grain of the wood.

Whether you stain or paint your deck, follow the manufacturer's instructions provided on the label.

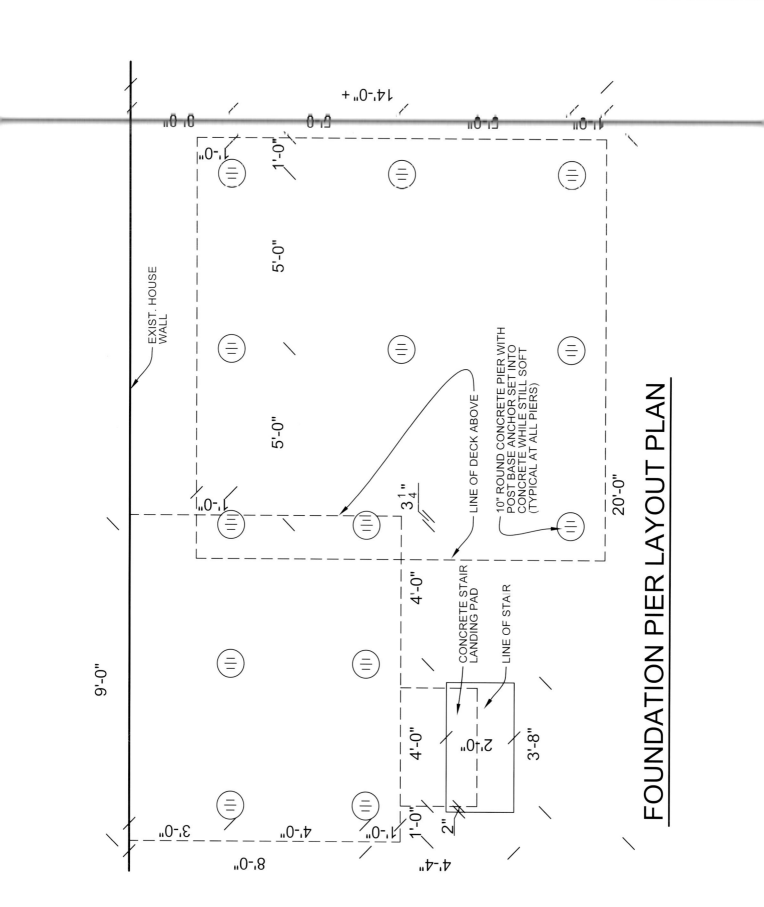

FOUNDATION PIER LAYOUT PLAN

EXIST. HOUSE WALL

LINE OF DECK ABOVE

10" ROUND CONCRETE PIER WITH POST BASE ANCHOR SET INTO CONCRETE WHILE STILL SOFT (TYPICAL AT ALL PIERS)

CONCRETE STAIR LANDING PAD

LINE OF STAIR

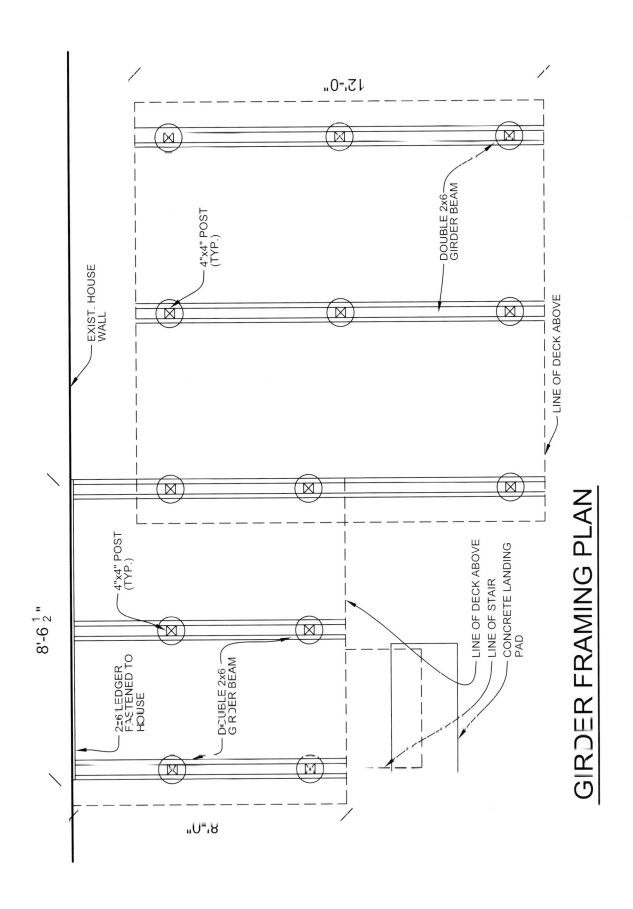

GIRDER FRAMING PLAN

12'-0"

8'-6 1/2"

8'-0"

EXIST. HOUSE WALL

4"x4" POST (TYP.)

DOUBLE 2x6 GIRDER BEAM

LINE OF DECK ABOVE

4"x4" POST (TYP.)

2x6 LEDGER FASTENED TO HOUSE

DOUBLE 2x6 GIRDER BEAM

LINE OF DECK ABOVE

LINE OF STAIR

CONCRETE LANDING PAD

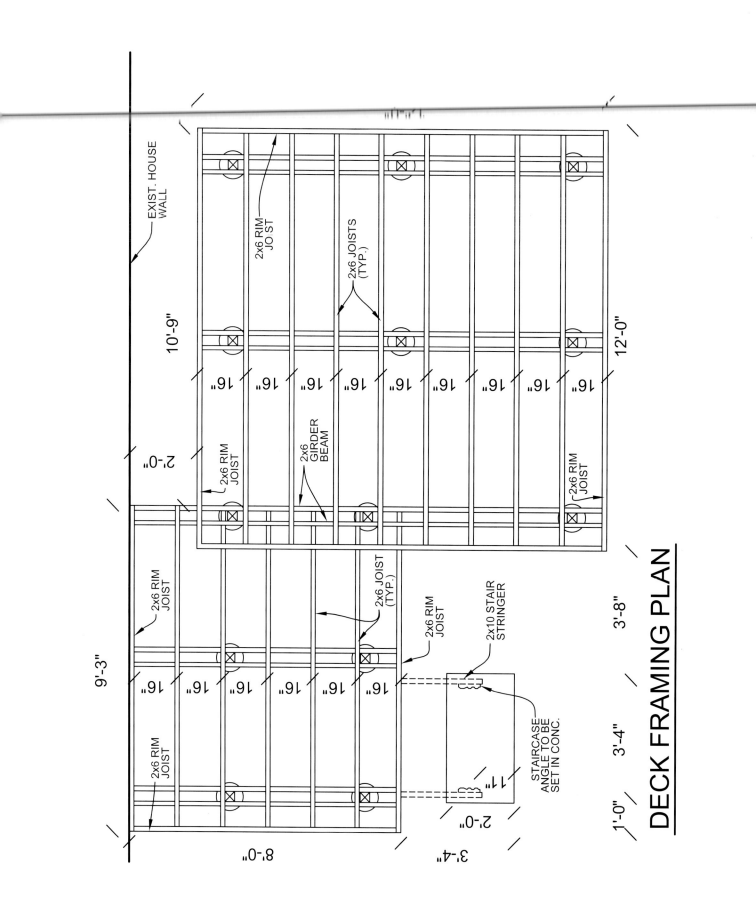

EXIST. HOUSE WALL

2x6 RIM JOIST

2x6 JOISTS (TYP.)

10'-9"

16" 16" 16" 16" 16" 16" 16" 16" 16"

12'-0"

2'-0"

2x6 RIM JOIST

2x6 GIRDER BEAM

2x6 RIM JOIST

2x6 RIM JOIST

2x6 JOIST (TYP.)

2x6 RIM JOIST

2x10 STAIR STRINGER

9'-3"

16" 16" 16" 16" 16" 16"

2x6 RIM JOIST

STAIRCASE ANGLE TO BE SET IN CONC.

8'-0"

3'-4"

2'-0"

11"

3'-8"

1'-0" 3'-4"

DECK FRAMING PLAN

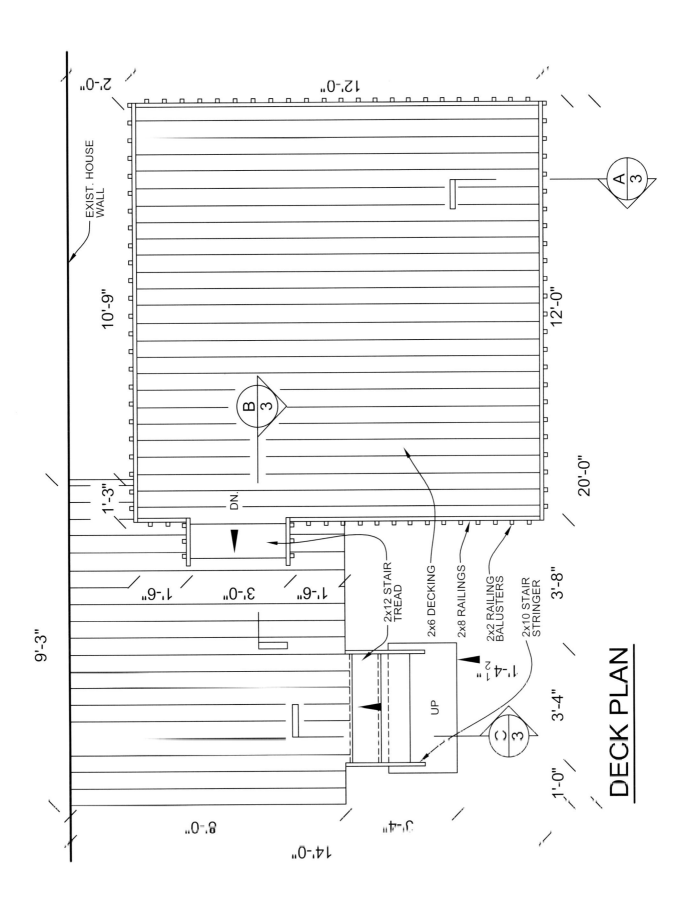

DECK PLAN

EXIST. HOUSE WALL

2'-0"

12'-0"

10'-9"

12'-0"

20'-0"

1'-3"

9'-3"

1'-6"

3'-0"

1'-6"

DN.

2x12 STAIR TREAD

2x6 DECKING

2x8 RAILINGS

2x2 RAILING BALUSTERS

2x10 STAIR STRINGER

3'-8"

1'-4 1/2"

UP

3'-4"

1'-0"

8'-0"

3'-4"

14'-0"

A / 3

B / 3

C / 3

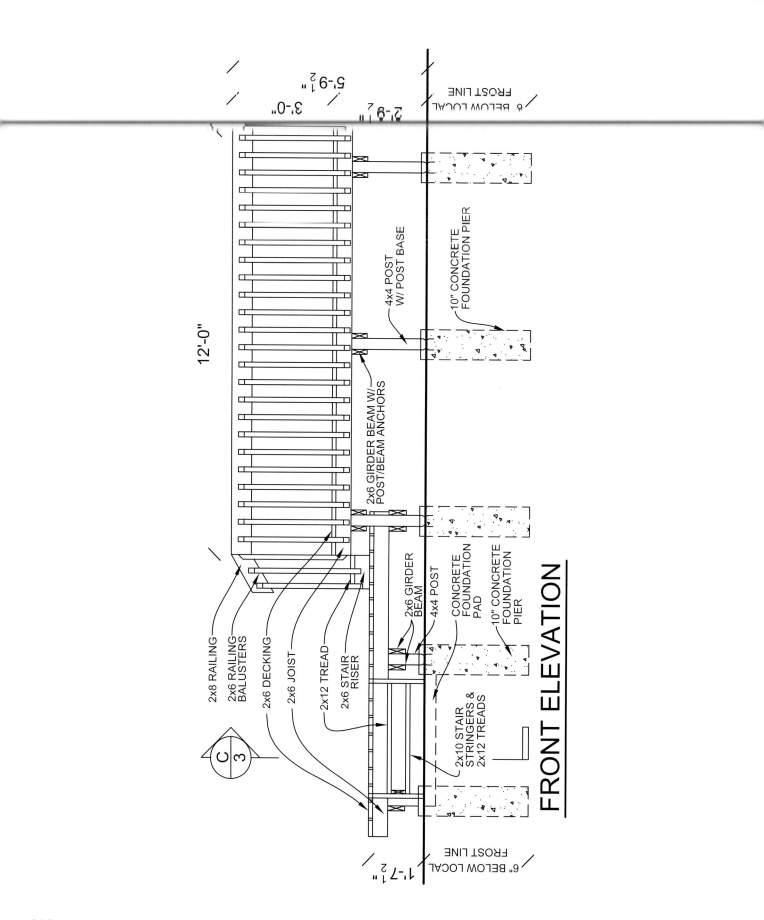

FRONT ELEVATION

12'-0"

3'-0"

5'-9 1/2"

2'-9 1/2"

1'-7 1/2"

2x8 RAILING

2x6 RAILING BALUSTERS

2x6 DECKING

2x6 JOIST

2x12 TREAD

2x6 STAIR RISER

2x10 STAIR STRINGERS & 2x12 TREADS

2x6 GIRDER BEAM

4x4 POST

CONCRETE FOUNDATION PAD

10" CONCRETE FOUNDATION PIER

6" BELOW LOCAL FROST LINE

2x6 GIRDER BEAM W/ POST/BEAM ANCHORS

4x4 POST W/ POST BASE

10" CONCRETE FOUNDATION PIER

6" BELOW LOCAL FROST LINE

C/3

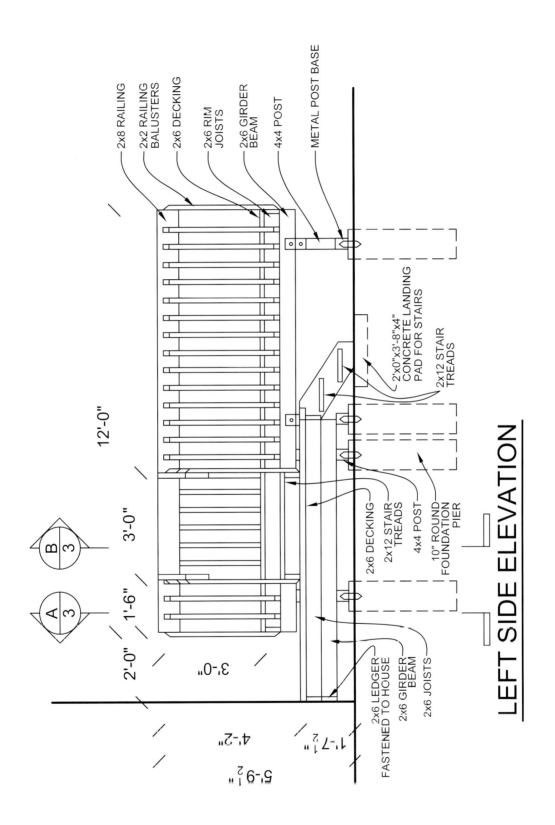

LEFT SIDE ELEVATION

2x8 RAILING
2x2 RAILING BALUSTERS
2x6 DECKING
2x6 RIM JOISTS
2x6 GIRDER BEAM
4x4 POST
METAL POST BASE

2'x0"x3'-8"x4" CONCRETE LANDING PAD FOR STAIRS
2x12 STAIR TREADS

2x6 DECKING
2x12 STAIR TREADS
4x4 POST
10" ROUND FOUNDATION PIER

2x6 LEDGER FASTENED TO HOUSE
2x6 GIRDER BEAM
2x6 JOISTS

12'-0"
3'-0"
1'-6"
2'-0"
3'-0"

5'-9½"
4'-2"
1'-7½"

A/3
B/3

213

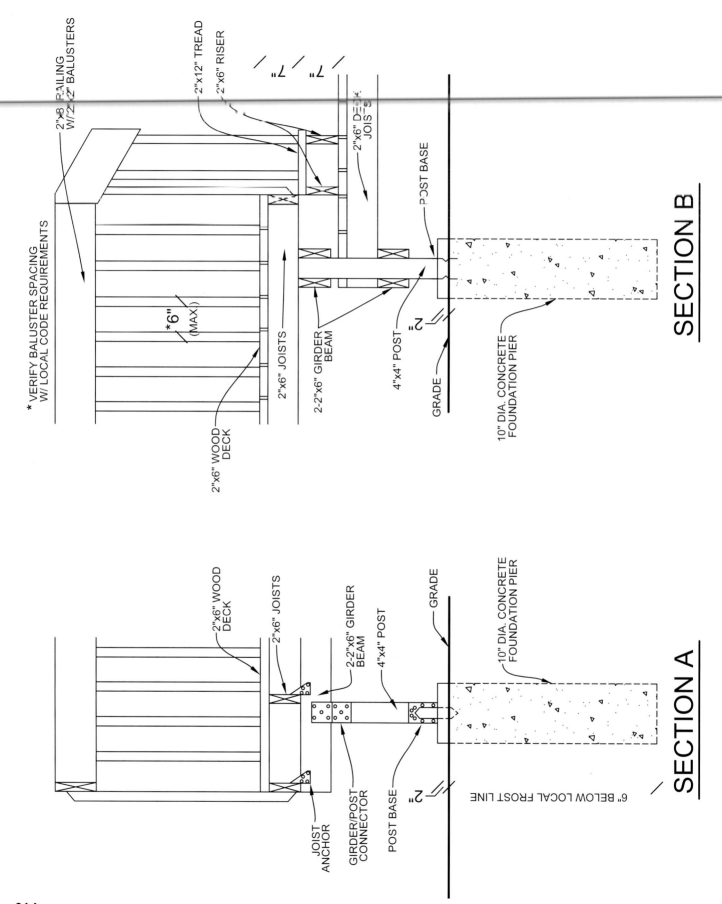

2"x8" RAILING
W/ 2"x2" BALUSTERS

2"x12" TREAD

2"x6" RISER

7" / 7"

2"x6" DECK
JOISTS

POST BASE

* VERIFY BALUSTER SPACING
W/ LOCAL CODE REQUIREMENTS

*6"
(MAX)

2"x6" JOISTS

2-2"x6" GIRDER
BEAM

4"x4" POST

GRADE

2"

2"x6" WOOD
DECK

10" DIA. CONCRETE
FOUNDATION PIER

SECTION B

2"x6" WOOD
DECK

2"x6" JOISTS

2-2"x6" GIRDER
BEAM

4"x4" POST

GRADE

JOIST
ANCHOR

GIRDER/POST
CONNECTOR

POST BASE

2"

10" DIA. CONCRETE
FOUNDATION PIER

6" BELOW LOCAL FROST LINE

SECTION A

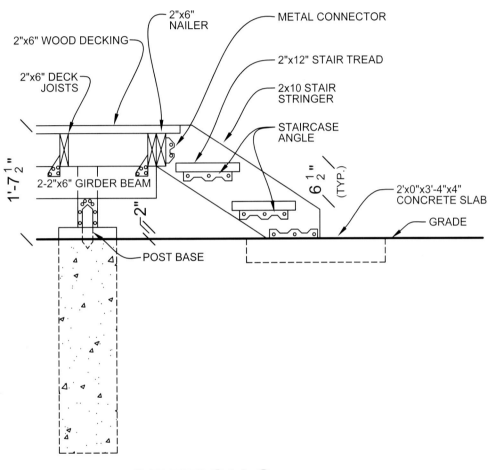

2"x6" NAILER

METAL CONNECTOR

2"x6" WOOD DECKING

2"x12" STAIR TREAD

2"x6" DECK JOISTS

2x10 STAIR STRINGER

STAIRCASE ANGLE

1'-7 1/2"

2'x0"x3'-4"x4" CONCRETE SLAB

6 1/2" (TYP.)

2-2"x6" GIRDER BEAM

2"

GRADE

POST BASE

SECTION C

THE DESIGNERS' WORK

Creative Homeowner selected six of the country's premier deck designer-builders and asked them to present some of their best designs to our readers. They represent a broad regional sampling: George Drummond lives in Virginia; Bob Kiefer and Gus de la Cruz in New Jersey; Gary Marsh in California; Barry Streett in Colorado and Rick Parish in Texas. Their decks, many of them design award-winners, appear on the following pages.

These professionals don't just design decks—they build them as well. They recognize that a superior design addresses questions of engineering and craftsmanship as well as aesthetics. They know that a structurally sound deck requires good footings and strong framing, and careful joinery and attention to detail.

For each of the designer-builders, you'll find a section called "Techniques, Tips, and Tricks," which summarizes what each has learned through years of practice and experience. Even if you never build decks like these, you'll find ideas here that you can use.

We hope you enjoy leafing through this impressive collection of designs and ideas. We also wish you luck in achieving your dream deck. The designer-builders welcome consultation by telephone, should you want to purchase plans for one of their designs.

Note: The decks shown in this section predate the most current code. Always check to make sure that your deck design and plans meet your local code.

Bob Kiefer

Gary Marsh

Samples of the builders' work show their high degree of craftsmanship.

George Drummond

Gus de la Cruz

Rick Parish

Barry Streett

217

CHAPTER 12
DECKS BY KIEFER

Bob Kiefer, owner of Decks by Kiefer in Martinsville, New Jersey, designs and builds custom decks for a demanding clientele. He begins each design by interviewing his clients about their likes and dislikes, and how they plan on using the outdoor living area.

DECKS BY KIEFER

Martinsville, New Jersey

www.decksbykiefer.com

TECHNIQUES, TIPS, AND TRICKS

For his well-to-do clients, Kiefer usually spares no expense to ensure that a deck will withstand warping and cracking for decades. Although economy may factor into your project, you can still use Kiefer's ideas and techniques to add strength and elegance to your deck.

- Kiefer prefers 2x4 redwood (or 1x4 ipé) for decking, whereas most builders use (nominal) 6-inch-wide stock. The narrow boards account in part for the distinctive appearance of his decks. However, if you use a grade of lumber that contains knots, 2x4s can present a problem. If you end up with a large knot in a location that requires a nail, you won't have room to work around it as you would with 2x6 decking. By using lumber that has virtually no knots, you can eliminate this problem.

- Wherever possible, Kiefer avoids miter cuts in decking and rail caps. He's found that any slight imperfection or shrinkage will mar the appearance of a mitered joint. Instead he uses square cuts, staggering them in the decking to create a pleasing herringbone pattern.

- Kiefer steers clear of end-to-end butt joints along the length of the decking. These joints often crack because the boards must be nailed so close to their ends. If shrinkage occurs, unsightly gaps can result. Where feasible, he uses 20-foot-long decking runs (or 18-foot if 20-footers are not available). To avoid overly long decking on larger areas, he usually chooses to install boards in a herringbone pattern.

- To install structural posts, Kiefer uses an unconventional approach. By waiting until the deck is nearly completed before pouring concrete, he avoids errors in footings that can make building the rest of the deck a nightmare.

- For structural support, he uses lumber no larger than 2x10. Larger pieces tend to shrink and crack. Kiefer's beam design is simplicity itself: he gang-nails three 2x10s to form a support that is considerably stronger and much less likely to crack than a 4x10.

- He usually builds rail posts out of 2x4s and 1x4s. They assemble easily, resist cracking, and look more elegant than a 4x4. (See photo, oppposite.)

- To achieve the distinctive banded appearance of his fascias, Kiefer stacks several 2x4s rather than using a single 1x8 as most builders would. The 2x4s don't crack as readily as the wider, thinner boards, and the round milled edges on the 2x4s accent the horizontal lines between the boards. To economize, you can use 1x4s and round the edges with a sanding block or a router equipped with a roundover bit.

- Kiefer makes curved fascia under the decking using a technique that is feasible for anyone who owns a decent table saw. However, his laminated curved benches and railings may prove too difficult for the average do-it-yourselfer.

To avoid butt joints and miter cuts, Kiefer often uses shorter decking boards and herringbone patterns, left. Also note the distinctive banded design of the fascia, repeated on many of his decks.

By fastening 2x4s and 1x4s together, Kiefer crafts handsome, unusual-looking posts.

SLEEK RETREAT

With its sinuous curves, this handsome deck may remind you of an appliance or car from the 1950s. The natural softness of the wood makes it a relaxing place to withdraw from the world, however briefly.

DESIGN CONSIDERATIONS

The deck's smooth lines emphasize the curved, banded fascia. The overall effect contrasts markedly with most (rectangular) houses in style and materials, yet the horizontal lines harmonize well with the siding found commonly on today's homes.

From the house, you step onto an upper level designed as a barbecue area that will accommodate a table and chairs. This 13 x 20-foot space provides generously for traffic flow. An overhead trellis offers support for hanging flower baskets or climbing vines and provides shade for a table and chairs that you might set up for dining.

A wide, curved step leads to the lower level, which projects farther into the yard. Ample space allows for plenty of general seating and entertaining. Three large planters bring foliage onto the deck. Curved benches tie into the planters and follow the deck's contours.

Instead of simply stepping the deck down to the yard, Kiefer includes a small landing as part of the stairway. This extends the deck farther outward, making a smoother transition from deck to yard. The elevated landing makes a pleasant place to sit and sip a drink. A second, standard-size stairway next to the house allows more convenient daily traffic flow to and from the yard.

Ground View

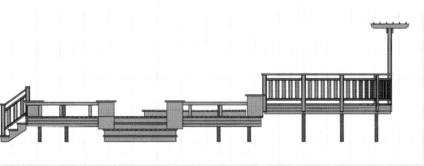

RAISED DECK WITH SWEEPING OVERLOOK

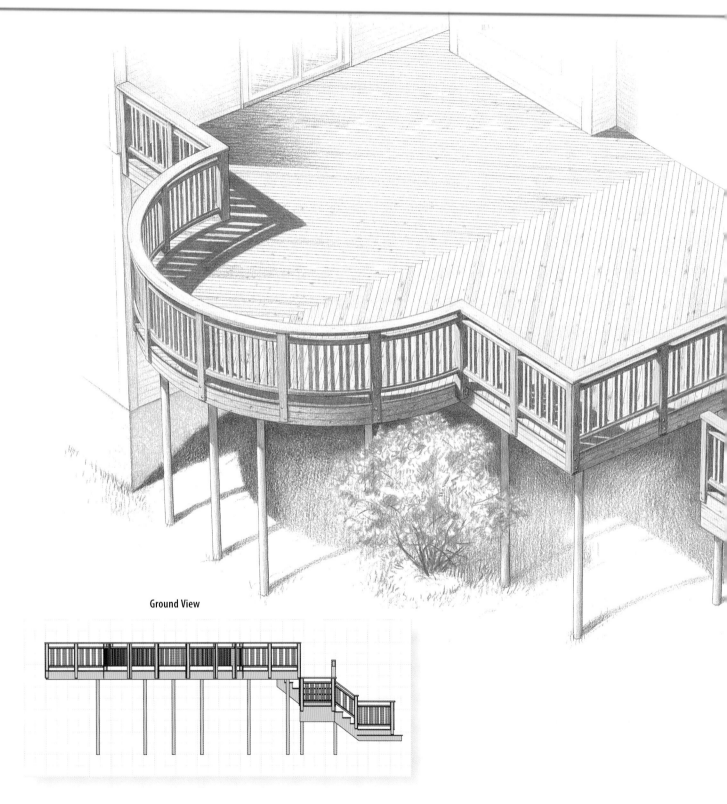

Ground View

The backyard of this house slopes steeply down to a lovely pond. The homeowners needed a stairway down to the pool in the side yard and wanted a clear view of the pond. To accommodate them, Kiefer built a set of stairs off to the side and a round balcony that overlooks the pond.

DESIGN CONSIDERATIONS

When the homeowners met with Kiefer, they requested a generously sized deck but not a particularly expansive one. For large parties, they intended to entertain below by the pool. The deck design had to provide room for a standard patio table with four chairs as well as a barbecue area, without impeding the traffic down to the poolside. The central, offset semicircular area measures about 8 feet in diameter—room enough for the out-of-the-way dining area. It also makes a nice vantage point from which to lean on the rail and admire the pond below.

At 12 steps down, a simple, straight stairway would have jutted far out into the yard. Even a stairway with one landing would have protruded too far to suit the homeowners' tastes. Building two upper landings took extra work but proved well worth the effort, keeping the steps close to the deck. The third landing at the bottom provides a small conversation area or a space for potted plants.

One small vertical area just above the middle landing is covered with skirting, while the rest of the deck's underside is left exposed. Although it may seem desirable to have concealed some of the framing, a skirt that large would have made the deck appear box-like and would have added considerably to the expense.

A curved balcony like this one creates a dramatic effect, especially when elevated high in the air. The combination of circles and rectangles looks almost Victorian.

FRONT PORCH/DECK FOR A CORNER LOT

These homeowners wanted a deck with a spa, but they had a corner lot with no true backyard. Kiefer designed a structure that serves as an entry porch on one side and a deck on the other. A striking curved overhead structure adds elegance.

DESIGN CONSIDERATIONS

Those who own corner lots can feel like second-class citizens because they often have little or no private yard space to call their own. One solution is to build a tall fence, but that can seem unfriendly to the neighbors and make the owners feel claustrophobic. A deck with a substantial railing or trellis can provide some privacy without making it look as though you're trying to shut out the world.

As part of his solution for these homeowners, Kiefer simply treated the rear of the house as a backyard by placing a spa there. A railing with an attention-grabbing overhead structure provides a subtle barrier. The wide expanse of deck space, with its lawn furniture and potted plants, further screens off the spa area and makes it feel more like a deck than a front porch.

Part of the deck serves as an entryway. Just outside the sliding glass doors, a curved landing one step up from the main surface mirrors the larger curve of the deck. A short section of railing, two planters, and an angled bench form an ensemble that nicely frames the entrance into the house.

Two sets of steps that provide access to the lawn incorporate substantial landings. These set off the deck as a private space belonging to the house much more effectively than simple stairways would.

The overhead structure, made of laminated curved pieces and winglike rafters, is a stunning achievement. It contributes more visual appeal than it does shade, and it looks even more inviting with clematis or wisteria climbing up it.

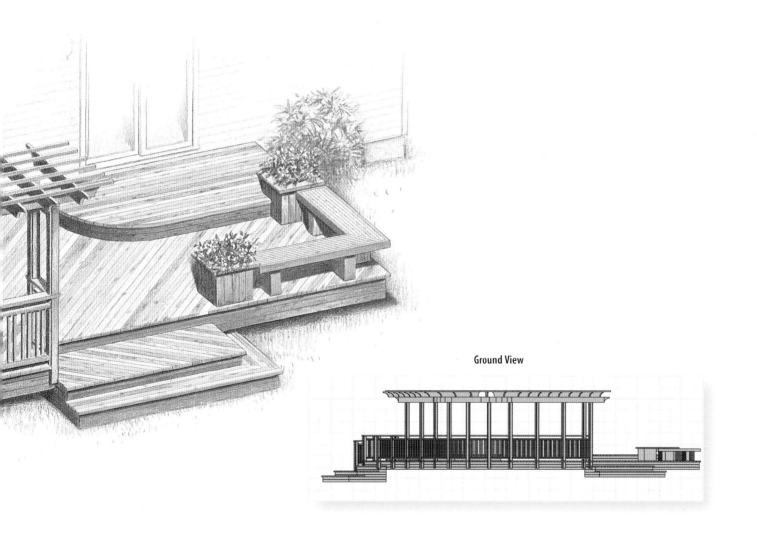

Ground View

VERANDA WITH TURNED BALUSTERS

The homeowners needed a front porch, but they wanted more than just a structure for entering and exiting the house. By making the porch fairly large and adding a couple of distinctive flourishes, they ended up with a cheery yet classic-looking veranda.

DESIGN CONSIDERATIONS

A backyard makes a good place for a showy deck with interesting curves, angles, and levels, but a complicated structure on the front of the house looks out of place. This more public area calls for a more subdued design.

On the other hand, the standard front porch, with its small landing and set of stairs, can look pretty drab. And though you probably wouldn't want to sunbathe, dine, or lounge on a front porch, you might want to sit in a chair and read the paper, pausing to wave to the neighbors from time to time.

This combination porch-deck recalls verandas of the Old South. It can make your neighborhood a slightly friendlier place without putting you entirely on display. The railing partially screens a person sitting in a chair.

The design, which could hardly be simpler, consists of a rectangle with a set of stairs. Several details, however, give it a distinctive look. Kiefer designed and built one-of-a-kind newels for the post tops, but the store-bought turned balusters add classic elegance without requiring custom work. The fascia, made from two 2x4s and one 1x4, adds depth to Kiefer's usual banded look.

Ground View

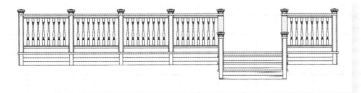

MULTI-RETREATS ON MULTILEVELS

The owners of this deck wanted to be able to reach the deck from different rooms of the house. They also specified clear sight lines from the house to the swimming pool in the yard.

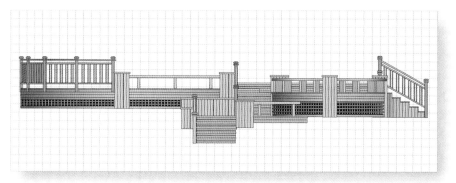

Ground View

DESIGN CONSIDERATIONS

Sometimes too much of a good thing can turn into a problem. For this deck, the homeowners had a long wish list and a yard large enough to accommodate just about any design Kiefer developed. Building a big deck is not the problem, but creating a large deck that is full of interesting design details can be difficult.

Kiefer began by planning access from the house. A door leads from the kitchen to the deck. Two groups of French doors that make up a corner of a family room connect that room to the outdoors.

To break up the large space, Kiefer used two techniques. The deck surface descends a series of levels from the high point near the kitchen to the pool area. Some levels are only a step down from the one above, but in some areas there is a longer drop. Kiefer designed stairs for these sections, but he did it in such a way that no one group of stairs has more than five steps, which helps him accomplish a number of design goals.

A large landing separates the two groups of stairs in the front of the deck, creating an additional area for

entertaining that includes a built-in bench. Lowering the deck by levels means the pool is visible from the house. There are also spaces for built-in benches and planters.

The planters are a necessity here. Because property surrounding the deck is extensively landscaped, the planters and what they hold help the deck blend in with the surroundings.

ELEVATED DECK WITH A SWEEPING STAIRCASE

The owners wanted a grand outdoor living space, but they also wanted a deck that looked as if it was conceived as an integral part of the house—not an afterthought.

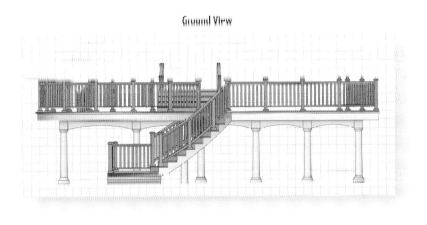

Ground View

DESIGN CONSIDERATIONS

People whose only knowledge of New Jersey is of the flat southern part of the state are often surprised to learn how hilly the northern end can be. And it is in the central and north areas that Bob Kiefer designs and builds decks. Yards that slope toward the rear of the property line, such as the yard that holds the deck shown here, are quite common in Kiefer's area, and it's evident in his portfolio.

As is the case with most of his clients who own swimming pools, these homeowners wanted a large dining and entertaining area, but they did not want the deck or its railing to block the view of the pool from the house. Kiefer met this objective by building a landing one step down from the sliders that lead into the interior of the house. The landing is connected to the main part of the deck by a short flight of stairs. This drops the main area of the deck enough to allow a clear sight line from the house to the pool.

The lines of the deck follow the contour of the house. There is a rectangular area that serves as a dining space and a large circular area for entertaining, sun bathing, and other outdoor activities.

Sites like this require the designer to think of how the bottom of the deck will look from the ground, especially when there is a pool or patio area in the yard. Kiefer answers this challenge in a couple of ways. Rather than install the typical deck stairs, Kiefer likes to add on curving staircases. These dramatic features are often focal points in their own right. For this deck, he encased steel columns in decorative columns to add design interest.

CHAPTER

13 BARRETT OUTDOORS

Gus de la Cruz operates Barrett Outdoors in New Jersey, a fairly large business that keeps three or four crews busy much of the time. The company—named after Syd Barrett of Pink Floyd, a favorite of de la Cruz's—has won numerous building and designing awards.

BARRETT OUTDOORS

Allentown, New Jersey

barrettoutdoors.com

TECHNIQUES, TIPS, AND TRICKS

More and more of de la Cruz's decks are built using metal framing. He uses metal joists and beams, manufactured by a decking company, which are galvanized and powder-coated. Metal framing is stronger than same-size wood framing, which means it can run for longer spans—requiring fewer posts—with the result that there is more usable space below the deck. Because metal joists are perfectly straight, they make for wonderfully flat deck surfaces. (Wood joists typically are at least slightly crowned, and composite decking shows these imperfections more clearly than wood decking.) Metal decking is approved in most areas of the country, but not in wet climates.

- He designs to avoid any butt joints in the decking. To accomplish this and to add design detail, de la Cruz often frames decking sections with divider strips (or "breaker boards") running across the middle of the deck surface. He also often frames the deck's perimeter with decking boards that frame the deck for a more finished look.

- He often runs decking in two or more directions. This not only makes the deck more interesting to look at, but also helps define use areas and reduce tripping hazards. The overall look is more distinctive when use areas are on different levels.

- He usually uses composite decking boards that have grooves on the side edges to accept hidden fasteners, so no fastener heads are visible. This material is more expensive but results in a deck surface that is neater in appearance and easier to clean because dirt cannot collect at the fasteners. When installing ipé or other wood, he uses different hidden fastener hardware.

- He builds extra strong. Where most codes require a deck to be strong enough to support a 40-pound "live load," his decks are engineered for 60 pounds or more. The result is a deck that feels solid and without any bounce.

- When installing in-ground posts, de la Cruz uses 6x6s (15cmx15cm) rated for "permanent foundation" use, which are more resistant to rot than boards rated for "ground contact." Permanent-foundation boards may have to be special-ordered and cost a bit more, but they ensure that the deck's structure will not rot.

- He often uses plastic footing "feet" rather than pouring concrete footings. These units install quickly, saving money, and have been engineered to provide more-than-adequate support.

- For upper-level decks with living space below, he offers an under-deck drainage system that funnels rainwater dripping between deck boards to a gutter and downspout, keeping the lower patio or deck dry.

(Above) The stairway and landing leading to the yard offer an opportunity to showcase de la Cruz's conscientious craftsmanship.

(Opposite bottom) This medium-size deck adds plenty of outdoor living space: a generous dining area, an outdoor kitchen, and a sheltered living room. With natural ipé wood decking, stone pillars, and an artfully rounded front, it is also stunning to look at.

CURVY PARTY DECK

The customers wanted a large space for entertaining, with a varied mix of spacious rooms for sit-down dining, relaxed conversation, barroom tippling, grilling, and sitting around a firepit.

DESIGN CONSIDERATIONS

A long site like this provides space for multiple "rooms." The trick is to make it flow easily while clearly defining different use areas. Two doors lead to the deck. The sliding door on the left (as you look at the deck from the yard) emerges from the house's living room, so it is natural to make this portion of the deck an extension of that living space, with a large semicircular sofa and a small table for snacks and reading matter. This living room is raised one step above the rest of the deck.

Walking one step down from the living room, you meet the stairway to the yard, which is positioned within easy reach from the living room or the dining area. The dining area has plenty of space for a large table, as well as wider-than-usual traffic paths—which are important when hosting large groups.

Moving on from the dining room, you encounter an outdoor kitchen with two counters; the eating counter with stools is perfect for socializing with the chef(s). The roof overhead makes it possible to cook even during rain. And moving on from there, you walk a step down to a patio with lounge furniture and a firepit. All in all, there are at least four distinct rooms, with four different ways to meet and greet family and friends.

RELAXATION STATION

This modest-sized deck satisfies the owners' unpretentious goal: to provide a gracious space for enjoying the peace and quiet of the backyard.

DESIGN CONSIDERATIONS

The owners were not interested in heavy-duty grilling or formal outdoor dining, and they already had a good-size paver patio for gatherings. They pretty much just wanted a place that felt like a comfortable seating area.

Shape and Size. Sometimes a small, simple change can make all the difference. The existing, narrow rectangular deck lacked "flow" in two ways: moving around on it was often awkward because of a bottleneck when people sat on chairs; and it just felt boxy. Gus de la Cruz solved these problems by bumping it out an additional 5 feet (1.5m) away from the house at one end, and he did this with a 45-degree angle.

The change eliminated traffic flow problems and gave the deck a spacious, open feel with plenty of legroom for people in lounge chairs and plenty of space for potted plants. The bumped-out area is also just wide enough for a six-person dining table, should they choose to add one in the future.

In some ways this deck feels like a larger-than-average front porch. It has a narrow section that functions simply as a walkway to the driveway. But because it is 6 feet (1.8m) wide rather than the more common 4 feet (1.2m), it feels like a usable space; the grill comfortably resides here, or it can be wheeled out to the wider area when needed.

Materials. The decking and the railing are similar in color, forming a soothing monochromatic palette agreeable with the landscape. Lighter tones in the lattice skirting, which is only about 2 feet (61cm) tall, perk up the view from the yard or patio.

All visible parts of the deck and rail are made of high-quality composite for easy maintenance. This is especially welcome in a woodsy setting; organic matter like seeds and leaves accumulate and would be a cleaning headache for other surfaces.

George Drummond of Casa Decks in Virginia Beach, Virginia, has a knack for building modestly priced decks that have plenty of flair and tailored features. Though the majority of Drummond's decks are on the small side, they never seem to feel cramped. He manages to use space efficiently and eliminate traffic bottlenecks by allotting just the right amount of room for all the things people usually do on a deck.

CASA DECKS

Virginia Beach, Virginia

casadecks.com

14 CASA DECKS

TECHNIQUES, TIPS, AND TRICKS

Whenever a deck calls for steps, Drummond likes to make them at least 14 inches deep. Although 11 to 12 inches is considered the standard tread depth for a stairway, this dimension, in his view, doesn't "feel right" on a deck. Drummond believes that standard-depth treads pose a tripping hazard because people expect deck dimensions to be more relaxed and expansive than those on a regular stairway.

- Although preservative-treated pine is generally held to be of lower quality than redwood or cedar, it offers superior resistance to rot, dents, and scratches. And, of course, it costs less. As Drummond's decks show, if you choose the boards carefully and stain them, treated lumber can rival redwood for comfort and appearance.

- For the decking, railing, and other visible elements, Drummond pays extra to get No. 1 lumber. This grade is less likely to shrink and crack, which ensures a better-looking deck over the long term and fewer splinters. It also has fewer knots and tends to be straighter.

- Drummond's approach—planning for functional areas and traffic paths—makes it easier to maximize your possibilities with limited resources. But even if you're building a large deck with expensive materials, make sure you allot space carefully for each functional area, or you may end up with lots of unusable space.

- For the structural members, Drummond pays less but still chooses carefully. He uses "No. 2 or better," which most building departments require, but he selects old-growth lumber. In most parts of the country, pine will offer better quality than "hem-fir," a general designation that includes wood that sometimes shrinks and warps severely. (In some regions, hem-fir may perform well, but check with people who have used it.)

- Drummond allows his lumber more ground contact than most builders—many of his skirts extend below lawn level—but he takes precautions to ensure that it can handle the moisture. He is very careful about the treated lumber he chooses for these applications, going with the highest preservative retention levels possible. Lumberyards don't generally carry the products he wants, but they can be special ordered.

- New composite decking and railing materials have gained some acceptance in Drummond's area, and he uses them quite often.

- Note the counter design. Instead of mitering the corners of the countertop and bench pieces on the deck, Drummond carries them through, giving the structures a great deal more strength as well as a more interesting appearance. And as most experienced deck builders have discovered, mitered joints tend to pull apart as wood shrinks, leaving unsightly gaps.

- When building low to the ground, Drummond places landscape fabric on top of the joists before installing the decking. If you live in an area with lush vegetation as he does, the fabric ensures that you won't have grass growing up through the cracks in the decking.

- When building a deck that sits less than 5 feet off the ground, Drummond usually does not attach it to the house with a ledger board. This may add a bit to the up-front materials and labor cost because it requires more footings and posts. But on most decks, Drummond believes that even a flashed ledger may allow moisture to collect, which over the long term can damage both the deck and the house.

- Most of Drummond's decks have "solid" skirts that hide the framing and concrete footings. (Actually, there are ⅛- to 1-inch gaps between the vertical or herringbone-patterned skirt pieces.) Although a skirt gives a deck a finished look, some people are reluctant to install one, either because it adds labor and expense or because they worry about cutting off air circulation beneath the deck. However, Drummond has found that a skirt adds little to the overall cost and effort, and that the gaps between the skirt and decking pieces allow adequate circulation, even during the hot, humid summers in Virginia.

Drummond creates decks that contain defined activity areas—note the ground-level seating area off of the main part of the deck.

244

FLOATING OCTAGONS WITH WALKWAYS

Rather than build a small rectangular deck just off the house for barbecuing and lounging, Drummond and the homeowners came up with this solution, which extends the outdoor living areas farther into the yard. Wooden pathways lead to octagonal platforms that sit among flower beds and overhanging trees. One octagon serves as a small dining area, and the other contains a bar and refrigerator.

DESIGN CONSIDERATION3

The surface of this treated-pine complex rises only slightly above ground level, making it more a part of the surroundings than a promontory from which to view the yard. In fact, the octagons and walkways seem almost to "float" in the yard.

That sensation is modified, however, by the built-in bench and counter, which emphasize that this structure is a dining and entertaining center. The smaller octagon offers just enough space for preparing and barbecuing food. The larger octagon easily accommodates a large table and chairs for dining.

Planter Boxes. The benches and counter both incorporate generously sized planter boxes. The boxes contain large pots rather than loose dirt, which allows the homeowners to change plants as they flower. The planters that adjoin the counter house small cabinets underneath.

Drummond routed wiring to one of these to provide power for a small refrigerator. This keeps food and drinks cool for when the clients entertain on hot summer days.

Building a deck this close to the ground (especially one with no ledger) requires a lot of digging. If the soil in your yard is difficult to excavate, you may want to choose a design that doesn't protrude so far into the ground.

Ground View

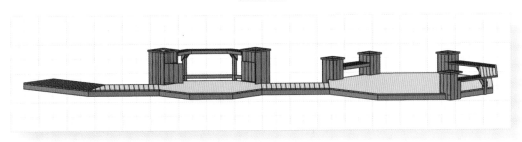

ABOVEGROUND POOL SURROUND

As Drummond's clients discovered, this is a handsome way to dress up an inexpensive aboveground swimming pool. However, be aware that materials and labor for a structure like this can run up some serious expense. If you don't already own an aboveground model, you may find that a standard in-ground pool wouldn't cost appreciably more.

Ground View

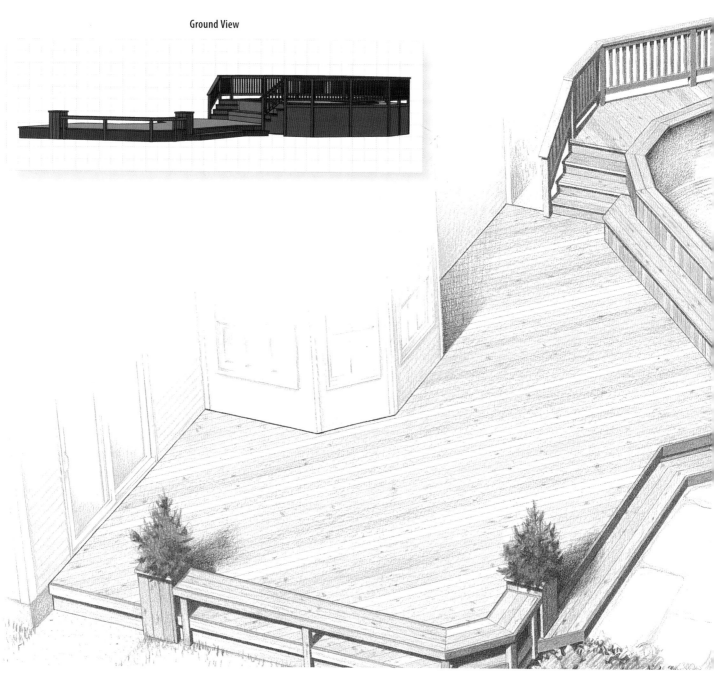

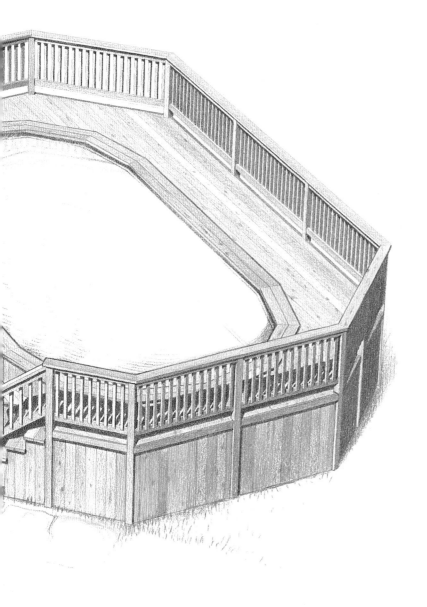

DESIGN CONSIDERATIONS

The homeowners primarily wanted a smooth transition to the pool. The house occupies a corner lot, which means that setback requirements limited the area that they could use. Still, they wanted something of a rambling feel. Drummond's design allows them to step from a breakfast nook onto a lower deck that provides ample room for dining and lounging, and to move easily from there up to pool level.

Pool Surround. A 4-foot-wide walkway runs around two-thirds of the pool, allowing enough room for swimmers to pull themselves out of the water and sit with their feet dangling in it. This also provides enough width for a lounge chair, provided there isn't much traffic. (If you prefer a full-scale lounging area next to the pool, allow at least 6 feet.) Because there are two walkways leading to this area, traffic rarely poses a problem.

Along the other one-third of the pool, a fixed bench on the lower deck provides a place for buffet eating. The skirting that covers the pool serves as the back for the bench. Around the perimeter of the pool, solid skirting alternates with lattice panels, some of which are hinged to allow access to pool machinery and to provide usable storage space.

TWIN DECKS
SURROUNDING A PORCH

The homeowners' house had a rectangular screened back porch with a simple set of steps leading down to the yard. Because traffic flowed right through the middle of the porch, there was no good place to dine or lounge. The homeowners do a lot of entertaining, so they wanted more usable space as well as clearly defined areas. Drummond's solution called for rebuilding the porch as well as installing twin decks.

DESIGN CONSIDERATIONS

A screened porch provides welcome refuge during those nights when the mosquitoes are swarming, but it doesn't offer the outdoor feel of a genuine deck. The ideal situation for many people is to have both.

The existing screened porch was one of the "stick-'em-on" types often added by home builders as an afterthought. A simple rectangle, it

had little visual appeal. Worse than that, it had a major design flaw: the locations of the entry door and the screened door leading outside created a traffic problem, which rendered the porch useless for entertaining.

Drummond thus decided to reroute traffic through the porch. He tore out the existing screening and installed two doors, one on each side and close to the house. This freed

up most of the porch for dining and lounging.

Deck Wings. Each of the doors leads to a separate deck area: a sun deck with benches to the right and a dining/cooking deck to the left. Although smaller, the sun deck has a more spacious and relaxed feel because it usually contains less furniture. The dining/cooking deck has ample room for a table with chairs as well as a barbecue.

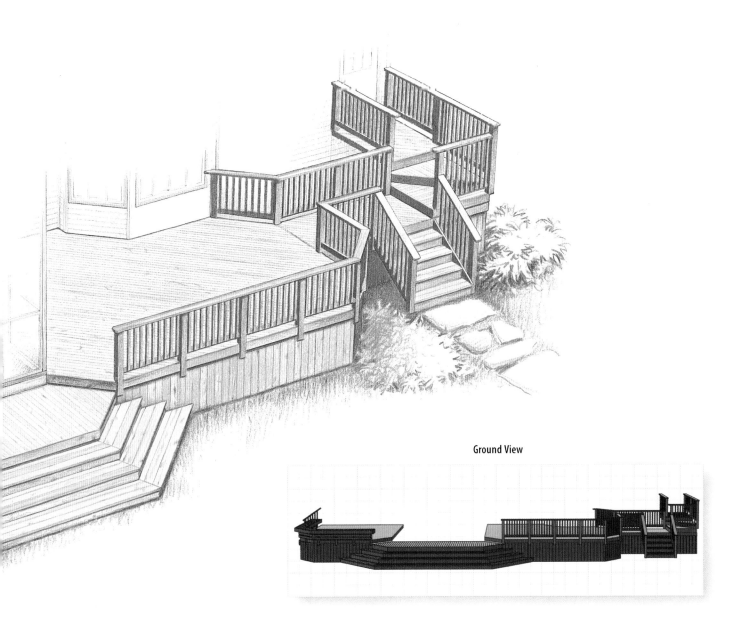

Ground View

This house has vinyl siding, which can easily be damaged by heat. Drummond cautioned the owners about this, so they located their grill 6 feet away from the house. Keep this in mind if your siding is made of vinyl or other flammable material.

Like many homes in warm climates, this one has heat-pump units (which also provide air-conditioning) that are situated outdoors. Homes in other areas may have air-conditioning units located outside. A walkway leads around the outdoor units and into the house via a utility room that is near a bathroom. This allows guests who are on the deck easy access to the bathroom; it also leaves the pump units accessible but not visually exposed.

To the east of the house, a park provides a fine view, and the owners wanted to give guests ample opportunity to gaze in that direction. They also wanted to connect the two decks. Drummond addressed both problems gracefully by adding a small deck to the east of the porch with three spacious stairs that lead down to the lawn. The two larger deck areas remain clearly separate, but the steps allow easy movement between them and provide a perfect place from which to admire the view.

COZY DECK WITH BENCHES AND PLANTERS

The homeowners wanted a deck that would provide a smooth transition from the house to the pool and help to focus attention on the pool. They wanted plenty of planter space for flowers as well. Drummond came up with an unusual bench/planter to take care of these latter two requirements. He positioned it so that people sitting on it would face the pool.

DESIGN CONSIDERATIONS

Perfect symmetry generally makes for an uninteresting deck, but the design should have balance. This one illustrates that principle well. The bench/planter, which is fairly massive, anchors one end of the deck, but it faces toward the homeowners' pool, helping to establish it as the focal point of the yard. The other two smaller planters on the yard side of the deck balance the barbecue area on the house side.

Bench/Planter. With its 3-foot height (plus the height of the flowers) the bench/planter helps to enclose the deck. Guests can easily ignore the neighbors and focus on the deck area and pool just beyond. The two other planters step down one level toward the pool, contributing to the sense of privacy without imposing a walled-in effect.

The bench/planter does triple duty: it offers comfortable seating, generous planting space, and easily accessible storage beneath the lift-up seat panels. The entire bench sits on top of the decking, which forms the floor of the storage compartments.

The Finer Points. The multiple levels of this deck seem to cascade gently toward the pool. A landing at the entry door provides just enough room for a couple of chairs and a small table. From there, a single step drops down to the main deck. As you approach the pool, another step down to the patio surface is gracefully emphasized by the planters, one of which sits on the main deck, the other on the patio.

Against the house, there's room for a modest-size barbecue. At about 4½ by 6 feet, it falls short of Drummond's recommended 5 x 8-foot minimum for a cooking area. But because it sits slightly above the patio surface, it works well enough.

At the homeowners' request, Drummond rounded off the edges of all decking boards. This subtle touch emphasizes the joints between the boards, creating a distinctive effect. If the boards cup slightly, which is common, it also lessens the likelihood that water will collect in the small valleys. The same effect can be achieved by using specially milled grooved-and-beveled decking.

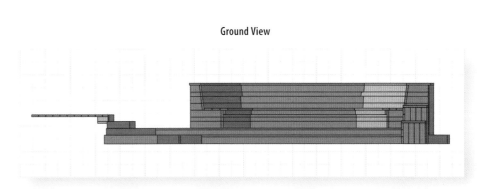

Ground View

MAKING A SQUARE DECK LIVELIER

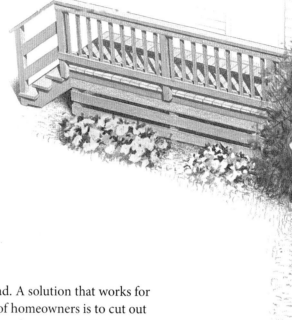

DESIGN CONSIDERATIONS

This design departs from Drummond's usual precepts about functional areas. He calls it an "impact deck," intended as a visual statement that would make a dull deck exciting. It provides room for a table with chairs, but a great deal of space could be considered wasted because it has no clearly assigned use. Sometimes, however, "wasted" space can lend an air of expansiveness and luxury.

The circular addition provides a graceful transition to the yard. Because this area sprawls expansively, a person walking on it does not feel funneled in a particular direction. The wooden surface fans out and seems more a part of the lawn and landscape than a stairway toward it.

Adding On. If you have a squarish deck that lacks style, resist the temptation to tear it down and start over from scratch. You can probably save some money as well as labor by adding on to the structure instead. A solution that works for a lot of homeowners is to cut out a triangular area and attach a new section of decking that runs at an angle to the existing deck. If you then add a distinctive curve or some unusual angles and put in a bench or a new style of railing, you'll hardly remember the ho-hum structure that stood there before.

Chances are that you won't be able to match the existing decking exactly. The old surface will have weathered or may have been built from material that is now hard to find at the local lumberyard or mill. However, most of Drummond's add-on clients find that a difference in color or texture is not displeasing to the eye, especially if the new surface begins one step up or down, as with this deck. For extremely different wood colors, a deck stain—either semitransparent or solid-color depending on the severity of the problem—will hide any discrepancy.

Years ago, a previous owner had added a sturdy, rectangular deck onto the homeowners' house. When the homeowners called in Drummond, they had no complaints about the deck's usefulness, and it provided ample room for everything they needed to do. But they still felt that they had outgrown it: their yard had developed into a thing of beauty, which left the deck looking like a poor relation. The homeowners' purpose in modifying the deck was strictly to spruce up its appearance. Drummond proposed that they cut off two corners and add a large circular section.

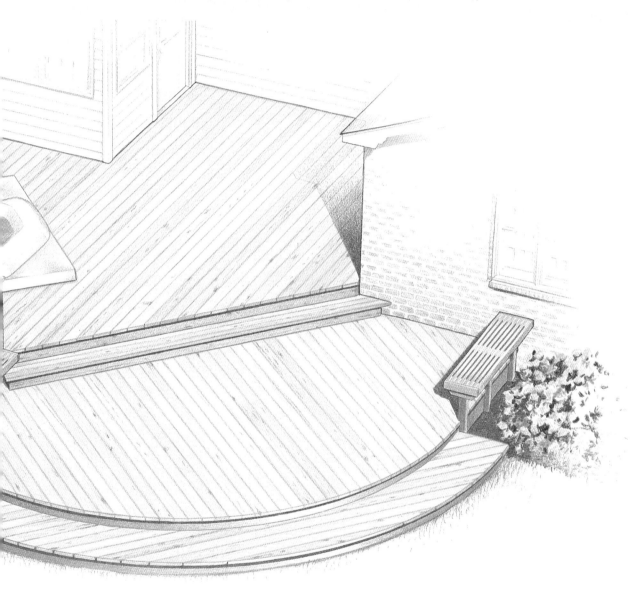

Ground View

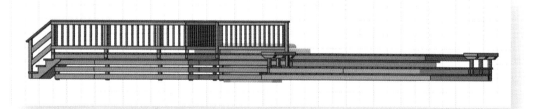

A DECK BUILT
FOR ENTERTAINING

The owners wanted a large deck, but they also wanted style, and they
didn't want to disturb the large, stately trees growing in the yard.

DESIGN CONSIDERATIONS

Every deck design involves juggling a number of variables, but this deck seemed to have more than most. Drummond had to consider the size and shape of the building lot, the way the house was situated on the lot, and the location of a number of mature trees that the owners wanted to preserve. They also wanted an open space for entertaining a large crowd that would have an unobstructed view of the backyard and the landscaped area beyond.

Drummond responded by designing a deck made up of three areas. The first is a cooking area that connects to the kitchen. This deck meets the threshold of the kitchen door. The space is large enough for a grill and is enclosed by a railing system.

The midsection of the deck is considered a transition space. It is one step down from the cooking area, and it follows the shape of a bay area of the house. The area also contains stairs that lead down to the yard. This area is only 5 feet wide at its narrowest point. Providing stairs to the transition area means that traffic can reach the kitchen or the cooking area of the deck without cutting across the large open section of the deck. The open section measures about 24 x 22 feet.

Ground View

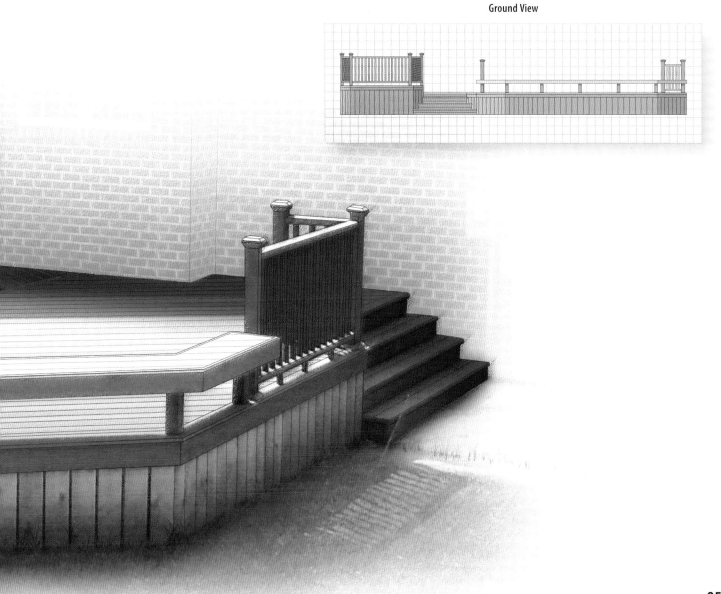

POOLSIDE DECK

This deck has two distinct areas. The upper portion is used for dining and relaxing, while the lower section serves as a continuation of the pool deck.

Ground View

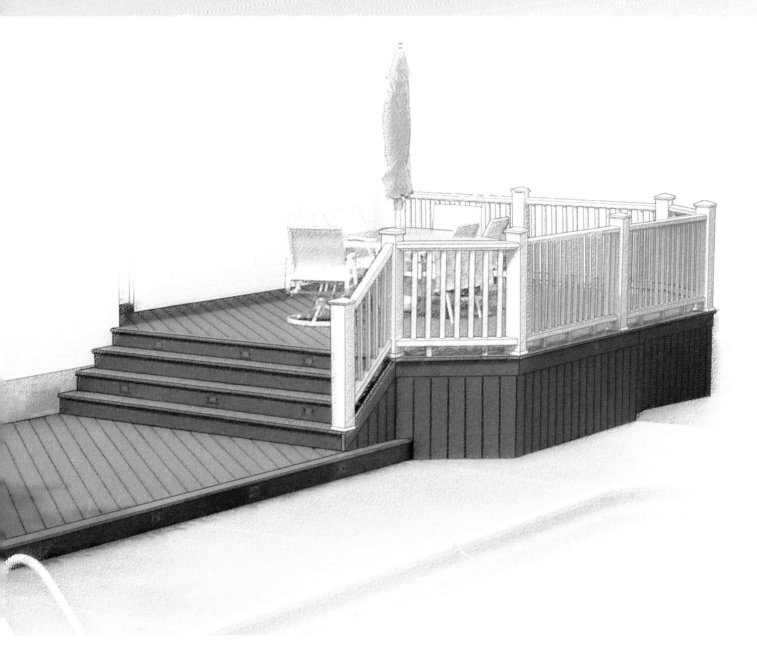

DESIGN CONSIDERATIONS

The 550 square feet of this deck are divided between two levels—each with a specific function. The top level contains enough space for a table, chairs, and a cooking center. It is where the family does most of its outdoor dining and relaxing. The deck extends out beyond the edge of the lower level to provide some design interest. And it is enclosed within a distinctive railing system.

The lower level is located four steps below the upper area. It is part of the same structure as the upper portion, but it has a closer relationship to the in-ground pool than it does to the elevated dining area. This ground-hugging platform is only 7 inches off of the concrete pool deck. Swimmers use this part of the deck as a staging space for the pool and pool activities. Built-in benches at the far end of the deck are used for seating and to hold towels for swimmers. It is also a good spot for adults to supervise small children in the pool. The benches also serve the design function of balancing the weight of the elevated portion of the deck. Benches closest to the house shield an air-conditioning unit located near the deck.

The steps between the two areas span the entire depth of the deck. This opens up the space, facilitates traffic flow, and does not block the views from the upper deck. The steps serve as emergency seating when needed.

A SHADED AREA TO ENJOY THE VIEWS

Space was tight for this deck, and the homeowners wanted a combination sitting/eating area that would not interfere with the views of a nearby golf course.

Ground View

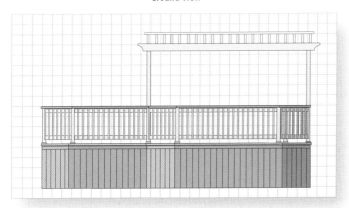

DESIGN CONSIDERATIONS

At first, the design parameters spelled out by the homeowners seemed a little daunting. They wanted a combination sitting, dining, cooking area; a shaded retreat; and an unobstructed view of a nearby golf course.

They also wanted the deck to be level with the main living area of the house so that the new deck would function as an outdoor extension of the interior living area. However, local covenants concerning limits on the size of decks and other structures limited Casa Decks in the design approach it could take.

The limits on space did not prevent Drummond from coming up with an interesting design that projects only about 12 feet from the house at its widest point—well within the established space limitations. This area is covered by a wood pergola system that matches the trim of the house. The railing is a standard wood railing system that is topped with a gray composite material.

This design shows how plans can change during construction or after the homeowners gain some experience living with their new deck. In their original discussion, the homeowners wanted room for a cooking area on the deck just outside the kitchen. The final design provided enough room for a grill and cooking area, but the homeowners decided to move the grill off of the deck. This provided more room for dining, and it opened up the views from the deck and interior of the house.

SMALL DETAILS
ENHANCE GREAT VIEWS

The homeowners wanted a large outdoor living area, but they also wanted a deck that would not obstruct the view from the house. The result was a multilevel design with distinctive details.

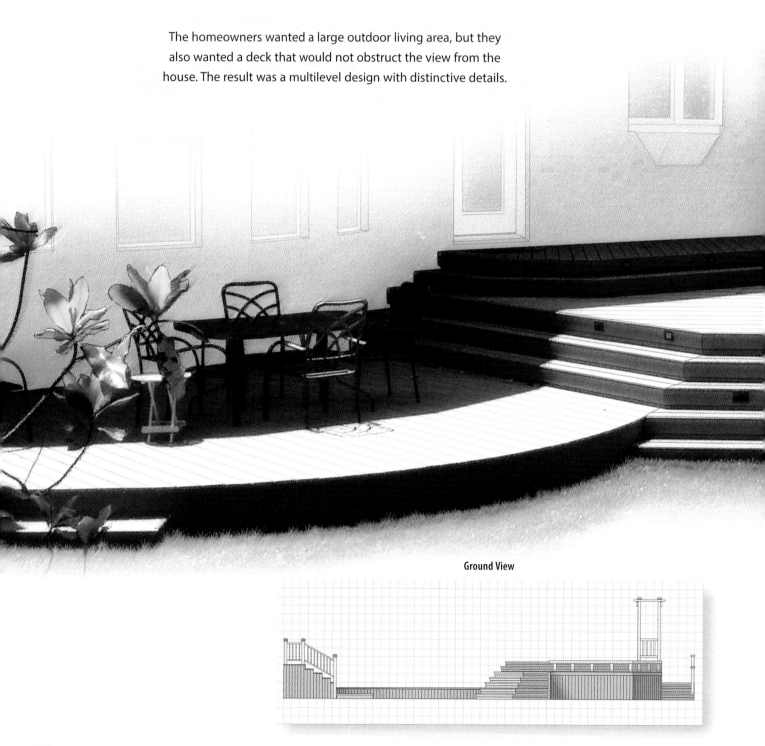

Ground View

DESIGN CONSIDERATIONS

The owners of this deck had definite requirements in mind when they began discussion with Drummond. They wanted the deck to fit with the overall design of the house; they wanted defined areas within the design; and they wanted to preserve the view.

Drummond's first goal was to create a design where the leading edge of the deck was no more than 30 inches high. Anything above that height would have required a railing system that would obstruct the view. He was able to meet the height requirement by building a 7-foot-wide level off of the back door of the house. This level steps down to a middle area whose height is within local building code height limits.

The top platform extends to the end of the house where it serves as a cooking center. The far edge is covered by a small vinyl arbor. The arbor is wired for lighting, making it possible to cook and serve food into the evening hours.

The cooking area can be reached directly from the yard by a set of utility stairs on that side of the deck. The stairs consist of a step-down platform with steps running from the front and back of the platform. Drummond always tries to manage traffic flow in his designs. These stairs provide access to the deck and the back door of the house from both the driveway and the yard without the need of crossing the main deck areas. Such an arrangement helps ease congestion on the deck when the owners are entertaining. Children playing in the yard can reach the house without disturbing adults on the deck.

The lower level of the deck not only provides a large eating or entertaining area, it also connects the kitchen to a screened room at that end of the deck, tying together the main outdoor living areas.

Barry Streett has been building decks for about 25 years, starting in Maryland and then moving to Colorado in 1995. Many homes in his part of Colorado are on steep sites, which means that they do not have usable backyards. So his decks often effectively take the place of a backyard. Streett long ago decided to work at the high end of the design and skill scale. He prides himself in doing work that other builders cannot do, and feels that he can meet the needs and fulfill the desires of the most exacting customers.

ROLLING RIDGE DECK AND OUTDOOR LIVING COMPANY

Evergreen, Colorado

www.rollingridgedeck.com

TECHNIQUES, TIPS, AND TRICKS

Streett enjoys difficult engineering challenges—feats like building on severe slopes, creating elaborate curves, and building decks elevated more than 20 feet (6.1m).

- To create custom metal railings, he first designs them himself and then has a metalworking partner make the railings to fit. A strong powder coating is applied for great protection against rust. It is important to use a reputable and experienced fabricator and powder-coater to ensure that the rails are solid and last a very long time.

- Streett often uses large engineered beams—cedar exterior glue-laminated beams, for instance—which span longer distances because they are stronger than the usual doubled two-bys (5cm-bys). This enables him to be a minimalist below the deck. The fewer the posts, the more pristine the deck looks from the outside. (Cedar glue-laminated beams might not be approved in wetter climates; there, preservative-treated beams are often required.)

- For joists and beams, he uses the best lumber: No. 1 southern yellow pine kiln-dried after treatment (KDAT). It is worth the extra cost because it is so stable and straight.

- He also sometimes builds with steel framing, which produces perfectly flat deck surfaces with fewer beams. He prefers to use "G90" galvanized joists rather than the usual "G60" because they are stronger. In his dry climate, powder-coating the joists is not needed.

- Streett's footings are often extra heavy duty, especially when supporting high decks with few posts. This means digging to below the frost line or, better yet, to bedrock and pouring steel-reinforced concrete columns that rise 8 inches (20.3cm) or so above grade. In his dry climate, he can install non-treated Douglas fir posts. In looser soil, he often installs massive helical piers, which are actually screwed into the ground with special equipment.

- Streett does not like the look of exposed decking ends; he prefers a cleaner appearance. So he usually cuts decking flush with outside joists, then installs the fascia so that its top edge is flush with the top of the decking. This method works well for high-quality composite materials but is not recommended for wood decking or lesser-quality composites, which may warp, leading to unsightly gaps between decking and fascia.

- Although Streett's decks are by no means inexpensive, he is opposed to wasteful spending. He tends to "value engineer" when designing, meaning that he may change the size or shape of a deck to save a significant amount of money. A 16-foot (4.9m) framing expanse may cost a great deal more than a 14-foot (4.3m) one, for example, so he may encourage the customer to go with a slightly narrower deck.

(Above) Sun shining through a pergola creates partial shade with a playful pattern of light for this spa and lounging area.

(Opposite bottom) Many of Streett's decks include covered porch areas. Here, a vaulting bead-board-and-timber ceiling provides cover for a full-service outdoor kitchen.

LOG CABIN CHIC

This deck packs a lot of outdoor living options into a comparatively modest space—and it all fits beautifully, with no wasted space.

DESIGN CONSIDERATIONS

The homeowner had a long wish list: an outdoor kitchen with lots of features, a dining area, and a fireplace with wide-open seating facing it. A larger deck could have been built, but it would have looked out of scale with the medium-size house. So Streett designed carefully.

The outdoor kitchen is just out the door from the house's kitchen. The dining area, off to the side on its own lower level (barely visible at left in the photo on page 266), has room for a round table for four or six plus some potted plants.

Logs

The log railing system, produced by a local fabricator, is a sentimental favorite in Colorado. It is made of lodgepole pine, which has a natural honey color and is prone to rustic cracks and splits. Less-expensive log structures have the bark peeled by machine, resulting in a mostly smooth surface that has been called "semi-rustic." The more expensive method, used here, removes the bark by hand with an old-fashioned drawknife. The result is a more authentic pioneer look. Rails and balusters are hand-cut to fit into holes, and the resulting imperfections are all part of the charm.

Streett normally discourages buyers from purchasing log railings because they typically last only about 10 years and then need to be replaced. He builds in such a way that replacement can be done without dismantling the whole deck, but it is still an expensive proposition. Some homeowners love the logs so much, though, that they are willing to pay for replacement down the line.

Fitting In

The house itself is standard horizontal siding with plain trim and no rustic features. To help tie things together so that the new rough-hewn railings would fit with the house, Streett made a couple of alterations. He framed the house's door with poles in a simple post-and-lintel arrangement. This framing is simply ornamental; the door's original trim is left in place and simply covered by logs. And when building the deck, he applied cedar trim to match the color of the house trim; it can be seen on the deck's fascia and the fireplace roof. Small complements like this go a long way toward pulling together two different styles.

Fireplace and Outdoor Kitchen

The outdoor living room faces the fireplace, which is the deck's focal point. Because the fireplace is gas-fired, it does not need a chimney, stays clean looking, and does not produce smoke. It is housed in a structure that is covered with natural "thin stone."

The spacious L-shape kitchen features a large high-end grill, together with a refrigerator and matching stainless-steel doors for access to storage underneath. The counter siding incorporates the same stone as the fireplace. The two-level countertop, made of small slate tiles, has a decorative diamond pattern along the edging. The work surface is 36 inches (91cm) tall, while a snacking/bar surface is 42 inches (1.1m) tall with an overhang to accommodate bar stools.

SCALLOPS AND CURVES

This soaring deck nimbly wraps around the house on three sides, with nary a straight line on its outer perimeter, and no curve like another.

DESIGN CONSIDERATIONS

The owners were tired and bored with their existing quadrilateral deck and wanted something special. Streett came through with flying colors, crafting a one-of-a-kind deck with unique crescent contours.

High Deck

The deck is about 12 feet (3.7m) aboveground. Streett installed an under-deck drainage system, with a gutter and downspout tucked away behind the beam. This keeps the space below dry, so it can be used as a sheltered porch/patio.

The tall structural posts are made of treated Douglas fir, a material that is extremely stable but exhibits a pattern of incisions required for the treatment process. To make the space below more attractive, Streett stained the posts. He also clad the beams with fascia boards and covered the undersides of the joists with plywood panels to create a ceiling. After the patio was installed, he clad the bottom 4 feet (1.2m) of the support posts with stonework.

The Curves

The deck is made with multiple curves. Looking from right to left (as you view the deck from the outside), there are two scallops reminiscent of the top of a heart shape. Continuing on, the curve becomes progressively flatter, until it forms an S-shape and turns the other way at the house's corner.

A bench snugs up to the railing at the second scallop. Recent code changes in some areas no longer allow you to put a bench next to a railing because children might stand on the bench and climb over the rail; check your local building codes to be sure.

Curved railings like this, which follow the contours of the deck precisely, call for first-rate workmanship and professional-level tools

The Stairway

It is common for an upper deck to have an all-metal spiral stairway, which can be purchased as a kit. This stairway is much more ambitious because it is made of decking material and follows the curve of the deck. Streett had to build the stair stringers in place, a painstaking process (left).

Layout

The homeowners can get access to the deck from inside the house via two sliding doors. The grill area is near the kitchen door in the first scallop, for convenience. A firepit area, suitable for buffet dining or just creating a convivial atmosphere, occupies the second scallop, and the dining table fits nicely in the large area to the left. There is room for a lounge chair near the dining table. Tucked away at the end of the deck, around the corner, is a private area for relaxing or sunning, big enough to accommodate several recliners and a small table.

PRIVATE FAMILY ROOM

Like a large fresh-air great room, this space serves several functions: it includes a spa, a luxury outdoor kitchen, and a cozy area for buffet dining and campfires.

DESIGN CONSIDERATIONS

Though they had only a small space with which to work, the family wanted an outdoor kitchen with plenty of amenities, room for a firepit and living room, and a roof to cover about two-thirds the deck, so they would be able to enjoy it when weather was bad. A spa was also on the wish list; a dining table was less important. Streett built a beautiful deck that suits their lifestyle to a T.

Size and Shape

The space for the deck is a 27-foot-long (8.2m) alcove at the back of the house. The family did not want the deck to protrude outward too far into the yard, and Streett agreed; a larger deck would overpower the house and seem out of place.

The deck design features his signature curves. On a deck this small there was no need to throw in an S-curve for visual interest. A single standard-radius bump-out, with straight lines on each side, looks complex enough. An added patio made of stamped and stained concrete offers its own curves and creates a fun transition to the yard.

Instead of a dining room there is a sort of all-purpose area that includes stuffed chairs, a firepit, and occasional tables. Food can be brought directly from the indoor kitchen to this area, or it can be served buffet style in the outdoor kitchen on the other end.

Spas are often placed in a destination area well away from dining and cooking areas, but this deck design integrates it for a cozy effect. Placed just in front of the deck and unsheltered by a roof, spa bathers are safely out of range of grilling smoke and can enjoy the starlight once the sun goes down. Given the size of the deck, the spa feels remarkably like its own space.

Outdoor Kitchen

The outdoor kitchen is on the far side of the deck from the kitchen door. Because of the overhead, it was necessary to put the grill on the periphery with open space on three sides so that cooking smoke can dissipate. (If a grill is placed near walls and is covered by a roof, you would need to install a commercial-grade exhaust fan, or diners would

find themselves choking from the smoke.) A spacious traffic path makes the indoor kitchen easily accessible.

The outdoor kitchen counter is faced with thin stone and topped by a granite counter with colors to match the hues in the facing stones. It includes a large gas grill, a refrigerator, storage doors and drawers, and a double side-burner. (Like many builders in areas with freezing winters, Streett tries to talk homeowners out of a sink with running water because if they forget to shut off and drain the supply and drain lines prior to winter [easily done!], the pipes will freeze—with disastrous results.)

The Roof

A roof overhead was high on the list of priorities, but a number of builders had said it could not be done. Sometimes you have to keep looking for the right builder: Streett carefully installed a watertight roof that blends well with the house.

He built the roofline at an angle that fits naturally with the house's architecture—and with no visible sections of unsightly metal flashing. For the front roof beam, Streett used a glue-laminated lumber, which can span a long distance. That means that there is only one post near the middle of the span; a second post would have made the deck feel more constrained.

A pair of skylights brings in natural light while sealing out rain, and recessed canister lights brighten the space at night.

To make the deck usable most of the year, a ceiling fan provides a pleasant breeze during the summer, and electric infrared heating units keep things comfortable on frosty nights. These heating units are popular because they provide ample directed heat for a small energy cost. Homeowners claim that they extend the outdoor season by as much as two or three months.

ROCKY MOUNTAIN HIGH LIFE

Because of the steep slope at the back of the house,
this high-end deck takes the place of a backyard.

DESIGN CONSIDERATIONS

The customers wanted a large, interesting-looking space to emphasize the treetop view. Their backyard is flat for 4 to 5 feet (1.2m to 1.5m) near the house, then drops off steeply. There is a lovely view of the Colorado Rockies out the back of the house on the second floor; building a deck that extends out at that level makes it even better.

Shapes and Sizes

A major theme here is simply "big." In each of its use areas, the deck is a large blank canvas where people can relax and enjoy a feeling of space and openness. Walkways are wider than they need to be, and seating areas have extra room.

As with most of Streett's decks, there are plenty of curves. The upper level offers two sections defined by outward curves; the inward curve in the middle coincides with a bump-out at the house to clearly mark the areas as separate. As you leave the house, a dining area is to the left, and the outdoor kitchen is to the right. So both spaces have easy access to the indoor kitchen and to each other, yet cooking smoke blows away. (The upper level is mostly covered by a third-level deck, which we will not discuss here.)

If you walk from the outdoor kitchen to the lowest level, you pass through a series of cascading landings; walking directly from the house kitchen, you reach the lower level via wide, arcing steps.

The lower level features a large outcropping deck area that juts heroically into the landscape. Even though it drops four steps down from the upper level at its most forward point, this area sits about 18 feet (5.5m) above grade. It captures a panoramic view of surrounding scenery, including a nearby manmade waterfall.

Bench, Planters, and Railing

An unusual curved bench, located in the middle of the deck on the house side, provides couch-like seating. The back and seat are made of decking with capstones topping off the bench

and thin stones providing stylish cover for the area under the seating. Built-in planters covered with the same thin stones flank the bench on each side.

Several large wooden planters covered with thin stones help tie the design together while adding splashes of color. The planters are made of treated plywood and have galvanized liners, which prevent rust and lengthen the life of the wood.

The railing, made of natural cedar with a dark stain, follows the curved and straight lines of the deck. Massive 6x6 (15cmx15cm) posts suit the character of the spacious setting, and thin, dark metal balusters barely inhibit the view.

Bar-Style Outdoor Kitchen

This outdoor kitchen is not very close to the indoor kitchen, which is the usual arrangement, and has enough amenities to function on its own. The large gas grill can handle just about any barbecue challenge. Most of the time, however, the homeowners use the kitchen like a bar in a finished basement. For that reason, it has a sink with running water, an ice-filled cooler, a refrigerator, and an overhanging counter where you can pull up bar stools.

Materials

The decking is a composite material that looks and feels a lot like natural wood. This is partly because it has a matte rather than shiny finish and partly because there is greater-than-usual variation in color and pattern. Materials like this cost more but make a deck feel more natural while retaining the low-maintenance advantage of composites. The decking runs in several directions, helping to define various areas.

The thin stone used for the outdoor kitchen, planters, and bench siding is "chopped," meaning it is hand cut. It is installed dry stacked, without mortar in the joints. This is a more challenging installation because the pieces have to fit together tightly, but the results look more like solid stone.

16 ALL DECKED OUT

When not visiting with clients or designing and building decks, Gary Marsh, owner of All Decked Out in Novato, California, spends a good part of his time sculpting in a variety of media. Auto-body putty and clay are two of his favorites. He keeps his workshop surprisingly tidy and organized, despite a profusion of objects that tell of his interests: four or five sculptures in various stages of completion, a professional drafting table, and a serious collection of woodworking tools.

ALL DECKED OUT

Novato, California

garymarshdesign.com

TECHNIQUES, TIPS, AND TRICKS

As long as you're not building on a steep hillside, you won't have to take the sometimes extreme steps that Marsh does to support his decks. You can use standard footings and posts. The upper portions of most of Marsh's designs contain a number of stylish features and finishing touches that you can incorporate into your deck if you work with care.

- Marsh approaches each job with an open mind. Rather than limit himself to conventional formulas, he spends some time dreaming about the possibilities. As you plan your deck, you'll naturally think in terms of mimicking those you see in your area. But compared with house building, it's usually (but not always—especially in Marsh's unique situations) fairly easy and inexpensive to build a deck that incorporates unusual twists and turns. Don't be afraid to use your imagination.

- Because of the tremendous views that many of his clients enjoy, Marsh thinks hard about which way people will face. Whenever possible, he orients a bench so that a person sitting on it won't have to twist around to take in the scenery. This sometimes requires altering the shape of the deck so that occupants won't be forced to stare at the house.

- Though Marsh speaks jokingly of being "at one with the wood," he takes lumber selection very seriously. He spends plenty of time both choosing material at the lumberyard and deciding at the job site which pieces will go where. For every part that will be touched when the deck is finished, such as handrails, he reserves the best-quality stock. For pieces that need to remain stable—railing caps, for instance—he uses only certified kiln-dried material. Pieces that will be bent into curves, on the other hand, call for green lumber with a vertical grain. If you're unsure about selecting the right lumber for a particular application, ask for help at the lumberyard.

- Although you probably won't need to resort to Marsh's more serious engineering efforts, note how he reinforces some portions of his decks for specific purposes. For example, he avoids the conventional approach of screwing or bolting rail posts to the side of the deck. These will fail over time, especially in situations where extra strength is needed. In almost every deck that Marsh designs and builds, he uses posts that are bolted within the framing for a strong connection.

- Marsh uses a variation of an unusual technique for making caps on a curved railing. He cuts the curves out of a piece of 2x12 (or two 1x12s) but doesn't throw away the waste. Instead, he uses the offcuts from one section as parts for others. This requires serious laminating: you must use glue that will stand up to the weather and join the pieces tightly to avoid ending up with a sloppy-looking cap. This will save you a good deal of expensive material.

- To enhance the appearance of moldings, Marsh often finishes them using a router equipped with a roundover or chamfer bit. He'll often stop the roundover or chamfer short of the edge of the board to add a distinctive look. (See "Soaking and Dining Areas with Shingled Siding," page 294.)

- To bend curved horizontal rail members and fascia pieces, Marsh uses another unconventional technique. Because some boards, for one reason or another, bend more readily than others and some curves are tighter than others, he treats each piece individually. He starts with a green piece of one-by lumber and planes it down until it bends enough for the curve in question. This means that some pieces will be a bit thicker than others, but because several pieces will be joined to make laminated rail or fascia members, the total thicknesses of the members end up identical.

- Marsh's planter design is more elaborate than most. It calls for a galvanized metal liner with a downspout. He orders the liners from a sheet-metal shop and builds simple boxes around them. He then positions them carefully so that no structural members will be regularly soaked by the runoff from rainfall or overwatering.

Well-thought-out design and attention to detail are hallmarks of Marsh's decks.

SWEEPING ELEGANCE
IN A SMALL SPACE

A stunning pool with a waterfall was located only 10 feet from the house. But in this setting, the beauty of the surroundings called for a deck that conveyed a sense of spaciousness. By using curved lines throughout and incorporating a stairway that appears much grander than its actual size, Marsh created a sense of open-ended luxury in a limited space.

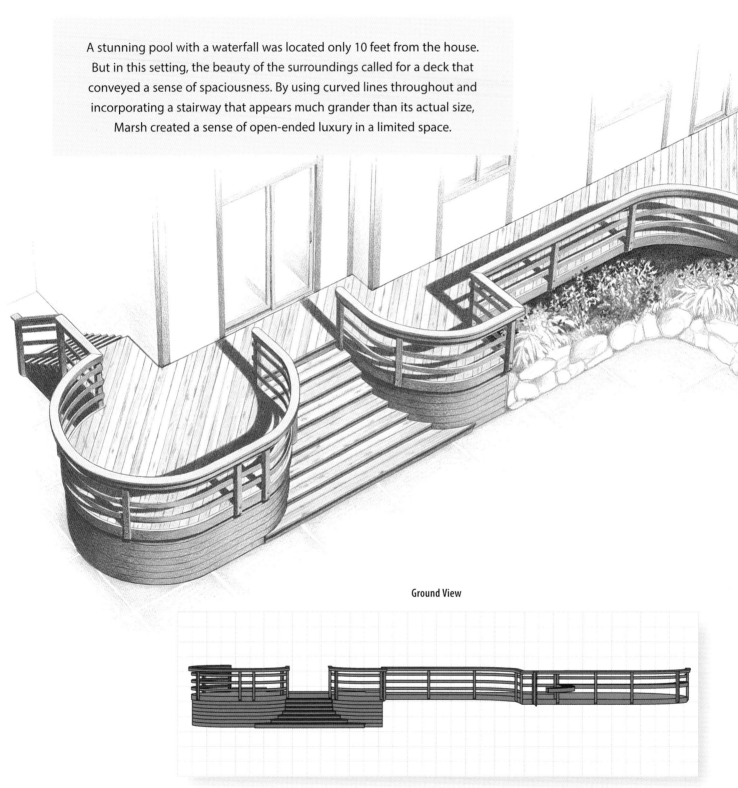

Ground View

DESIGN CONSIDERATIONS

The homeowners wanted a convenient means of descending to the pool (outside the sliding doors of the house) that wouldn't obstruct the expanse of the deck. In addition, they requested separate areas for sunning and dining.

Marsh met both challenges by incorporating an unusually shaped stairway near one end. It helps to define the circular sunning area next to it without taking up much space. Yet despite the stairway's small footprint, its sides curve away from each other, creating a sense of grandeur. You hardly notice that its steps have only 7½-inch risers and 11-inch treads—dimensions that are usually found only on standard porch or interior stairways.

Aside from the point where the deck meets the house, there's hardly a straight line to be found. The deck jogs and snakes around, partly to follow the contours of the pool, spa, and gardening areas below and partly for aesthetic reasons. Looking out onto a steep backyard filled with a wild profusion of foliage, an angular deck would seem out of place. This one blends nicely with the yard's natural curves and slopes.

Functionality with Style

The deck was planned to be functional as well as aesthetically pleasing. The curved walls that enhance the stairway also hide pool equipment. The center walkway measures only 5 feet wide to accommodate the plantings below. This leaves enough room for guests to lean on the railing and gaze out while traffic flows through comfortably behind them. Between the walkway and the stairway is a barbecue area just large enough for a small charcoal grill and a food-preparation cart. (You could also build a wide shelf into the straight section of railing in this part of the deck as a permanent food-preparation area.)

The main deck provides ample room for dining. A bench with a back follows the circular contours of its perimeter partway around, giving those who sit facing the house a sense of enclosure. For those who'd rather look outward over the lawn, a backless bench extends out into the decorative rockwork area that surrounds the spa.

The elegant railing features a curved cap and three horizontal rails. (The local building codes may not permit such a railing. Check with the building department in your area.) Marsh routed a detail into the caps that gives them a furniture-like appearance.

For the skirting that covers the rounded sections on each side of the steps, he used horizontal bands that mimic the railings above. From ground level, this gives the whole ensemble—steps, skirt, and railing—the appearance of a unified structure rather than that of a basic deck with a few features tacked on.

SHELTERED BUT OPEN

The homeowners already had a simple deck in place when they called Marsh. What it needed most urgently was shelter from the elements. The deck sat above the treetops near the rim of a valley, which left it exposed to gusty winds that often made eating or lounging unpleasant. They also wanted some relief from the sun, as well as a few design strokes that would relieve the deck's rectangular plainness.

On the other hand, the homeowners didn't want to give up their spectacular views. Marsh responded with a tempered-glass windbreak that surrounds about half of the deck's perimeter, a pergola that covers a third of its area, and some generously sized planters that bring color on board. Here, Marsh uses a basic shape to create a deck that feels not the least bit squarish yet still satisfies the eye with its clean, uncluttered lines.

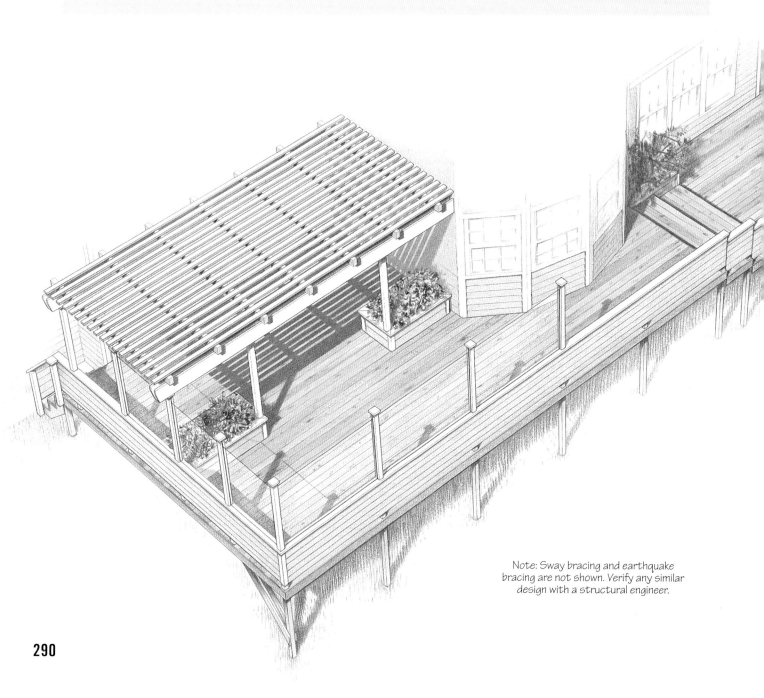

Note: Sway bracing and earthquake bracing are not shown. Verify any similar design with a structural engineer.

DESIGN CONSIDERATIONS

The existing deck on this site provided more than ample space for lounging and dining. In fact, it felt too roomy, and the lack of interesting angles or curves heightened the sense of bare expanse. A quick and obvious solution would have been to buy a large collection of patio furniture and add a few flowerpots. However, it's much easier to achieve a sense of harmony if you can build in elements that express themes and variations.

Blending Design

The house was covered with painted, rough-textured siding, and Marsh decided to continue that look throughout the deck. He covered the railings and planters with rough beveled siding and used rough-sawn material for the posts and beams of the pergola. In keeping with the straightforward design, Marsh used simple squares for the post caps. The closest thing to a flourish is the routed detail he added to the pergola's rafters.

Coping with Wind and Sun

As for the wind problem mentioned earlier, a simple solution proved best. On part of the deck, large panels of tempered glass span the distance from post to post. During times of high wind, this area provides comfort as well as unobstructed views. To enclose the entire deck with glass, however, would have transformed it into a room. This way, when the wind settles down, the rest of the deck still has the wide-open feel of an outdoor space.

With no tree cover, the deck sometimes got so hot that it radiated heat into the house itself, making it uncomfortably warm as well. The pergola covers the section of the deck that gets the most sun. By spacing 2x4s across the top at 7 inches on center (resulting in an interval that equals their width), Marsh achieved a pleasing symmetry as well as the right amount of shade.

The rough-hewn look of the planters complements that of the railings. Marsh equips the planters with galvanized sheet-metal liners and drain spouts that eliminate the possibility of overwatering.

Ground View

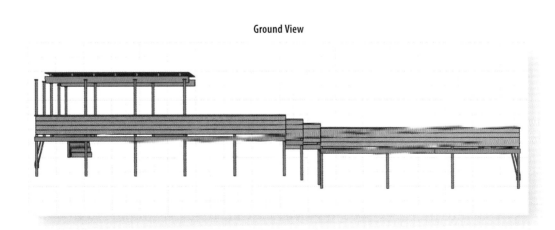

SHADY GARDEN SPOT

Besides an unobstructed view, the homeowners wanted a cozy getaway that would surround them with foliage. Oversize planters and an extensive overhead structure help make this deck a snug nest from which to view the world.

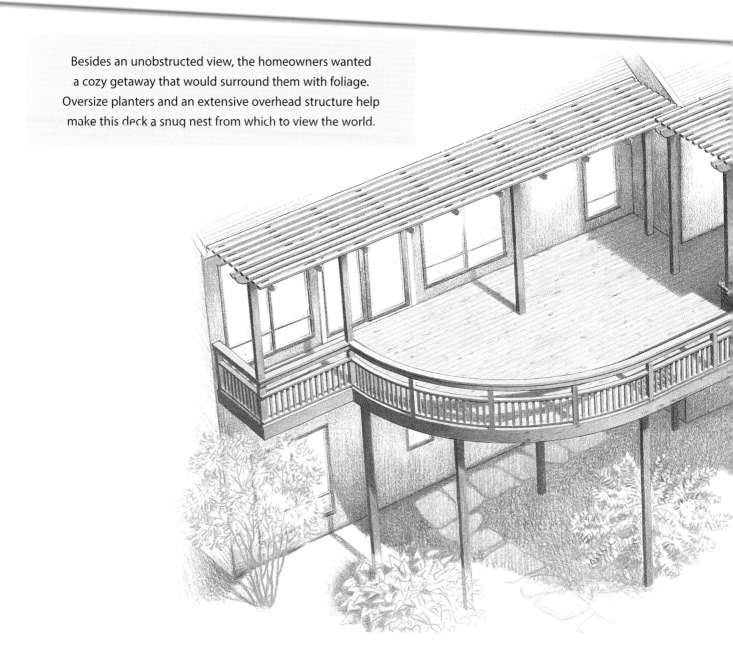

DESIGN CONSIDERATIONS

Although the overhead structure shelters much of this deck, plenty of sunshine still gets through to keep plantings healthy. Because the deck faces south, its perimeter receives full sun for most of the day, making it a good location for flowerpots. Two gigantic planters are set back a bit, which gives them partial shade. Other areas get various amounts of sun, allowing the owners to choose a range of shade- and sun-loving plants.

A Gardener's Deck and More. This makes an ideal deck for a serious gardener who still enjoys comfort. A simple potting table located beneath the pergola features a sink with faucet and plenty of counter space. You can work in the heat of the day without breaking a sweat. If gardening is not your forte, the counter can be put to other uses or omitted.

The planters sit 2 feet above the deck surface, which saves the

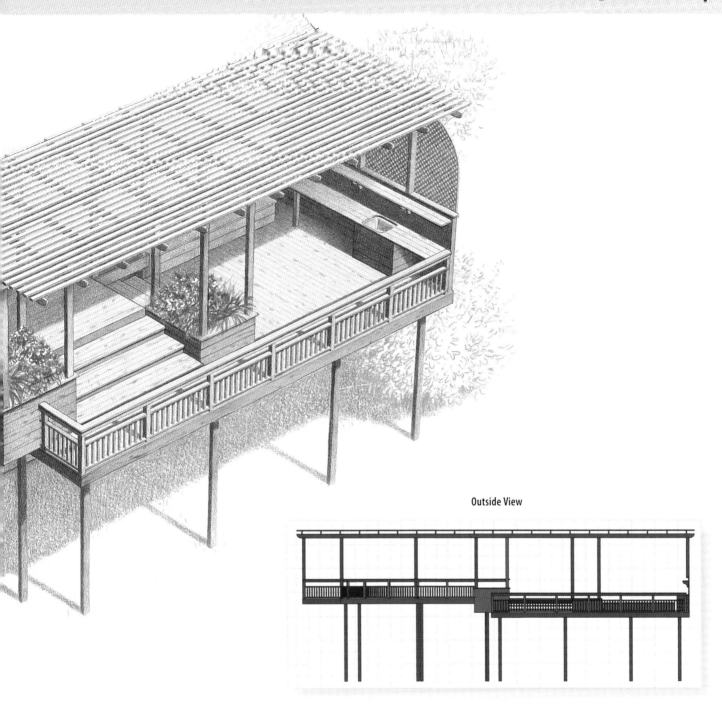

Outside View

homeowners a good deal of back strain. At 4 feet square, they resemble small gardens that allow easy access from several sides.

Because dining usually takes place after the sun has sunk low, the eating area remains uncovered. The deck's only curved line helps to set this space apart, and the wide arc encourages diners to give the view a sweeping gaze.

From the eating area, you pass between large planters and down wide steps. One stairway descends toward the view, and a second, smaller set of steps leads to the work area and potting table. Benches set against the house also make this a pleasant place for a rest or chat.

SOAKING AND DINING AREAS
WITH SHINGLED SIDING

A small deck with a hot tub already existed, but it didn't provide adequate room for dining and relaxing. The homeowners liked having the tub near the house, but the railing obstructed the view from tub level. Marsh solved this problem by building a new deck area three steps down from the tub and incorporating a glass panel into the railing.

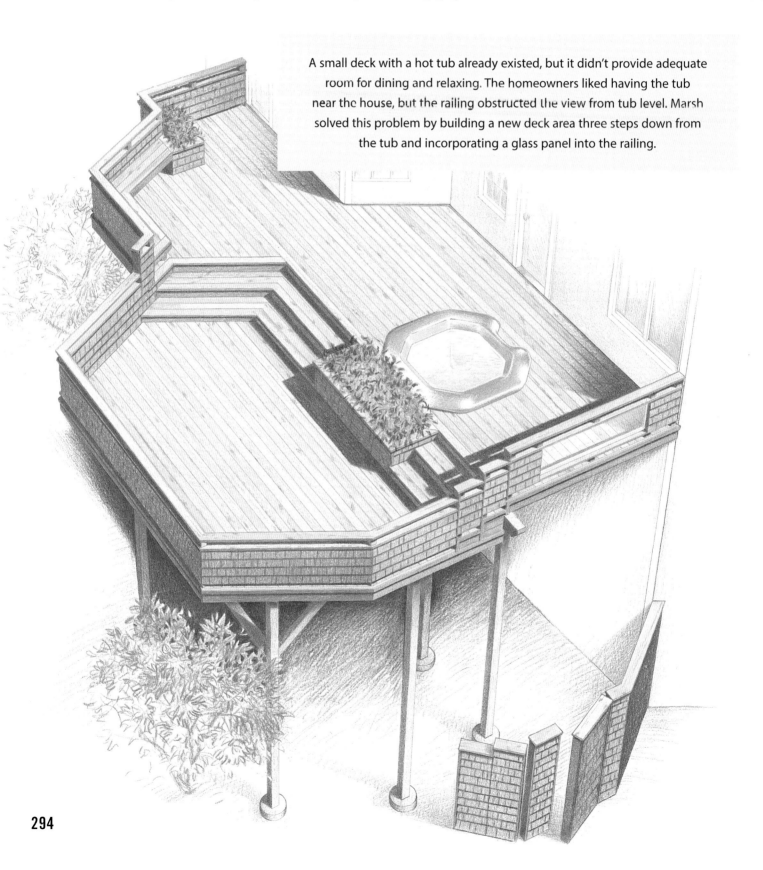

DESIGN CONSIDERATIONS

The old deck's railing measured less than 2 feet from the hot tub, cramping guests as well as blocking their view. Because the tub is supported by a massive structure, moving it was out of the question. In addition, the homeowners liked having the tub nearer to the house than the dining area, simply because they did more soaking than outdoor dining.

Improving the View. On every deck that involves a railing, Marsh designs with the view in mind. In most cases, he has to consider several vantage points. Whether people are sitting on benches, looking out a kitchen or living-room window, or lounging in chairs, they prefer to look at the surroundings rather than the railings. To clear an obstructed view, Marsh often lowers all or part of the deck, as he did in this case. By dropping the deck area down three

steps, Marsh was able to increase its size as well as improve the view from the hot tub.

To further enhance the view, Marsh installed a tempered-glass panel in the railing where it comes closest to the tub level, allowing soakers to gaze at the countryside and some greenery. This panel opens up the view from the nearby bedroom window as well.

Other Considerations. Marsh also placed a large planter next to the tub on the panoramic view side, dropping it down a step so as not to create an obstruction. When filled with plants, it frames the view of the trees beyond with a foreground of foliage.

The lower deck is large enough that a table with chairs can be set off to one side where they won't hinder the view from the tub. Dropping this level down three steps from the tub's lofty height also served to nestle the

dining area pleasantly among the tops of the trees.

The railing and benches are sided with cedar shingles, the same material that covers the house. Lightly stained rather than painted, the shingles give the deck a warm, homey feel. However, too large an expanse of solid siding would make the railing seem massive, so Marsh added a 4-inch gap below the cap to open up the design.

As with most of his decks, Marsh installed low-voltage lighting at various points, especially on the step risers. Unless you have security concerns, bright floodlights usually detract from a deck's atmosphere. Multiple soft lights provide adequate illumination without the glare. Marsh finds that his clients often like to set the lights on timers so that the deck automatically becomes a part of their house at night.

Outside View

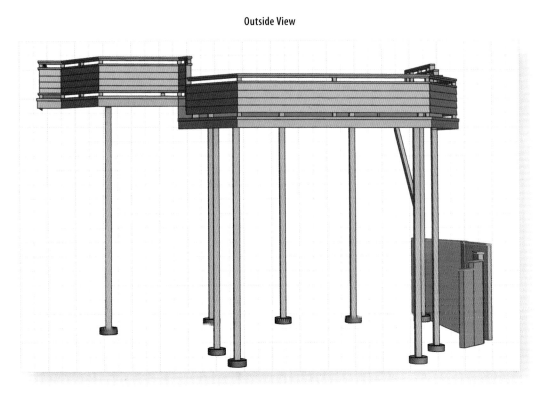

Note: Sway bracing and earthquake bracing are not shown.
Verify any similar design with a structural engineer.

STATELY AND SYMMETRICAL

The homeowners wanted a deck that would run along the entire 60-foot length of their house but wouldn't appear monstrous. They also wanted something a bit more formal than the usual deck. To create a stately but not massive look, Marsh designed a curved structure that evokes the shape of a grand piano and used turned and painted balusters in the railing to lighten its effect.

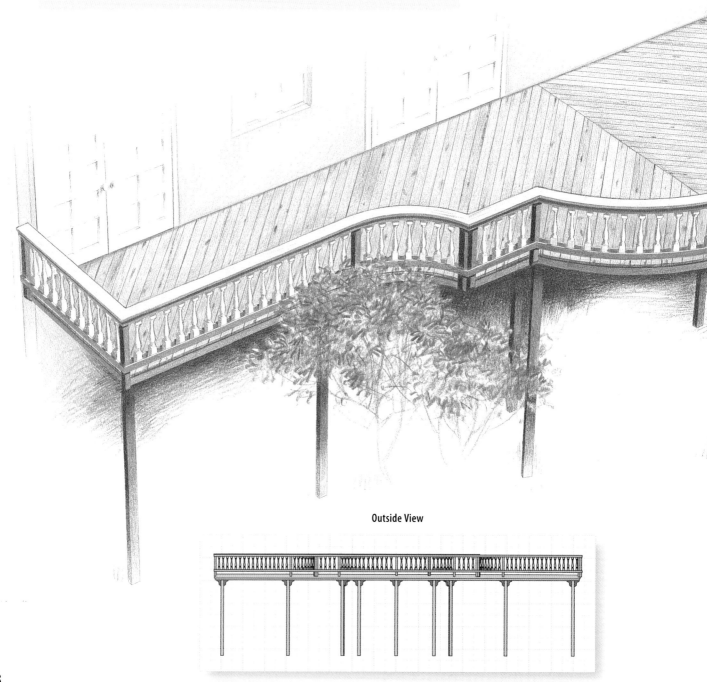

Outside View

Note: Sway bracing and earthquake bracing are not shown. Verify any similar design with a structural engineer.

DESIGN CONSIDERATIONS

Scientists claim that they can quantify beauty in human features: the more symmetrically aligned the eyes, nose, and mouth, the more beautiful (or handsome) the face appears to us. In a deck, however, symmetrical features often mean boring features. But if you start with interesting contours and want to maintain a formal aspect, symmetry may be the best way to go.

The master bedroom, dining and family rooms, and a second bedroom all look out onto the deck. However, the homeowners don't need to look downward to glimpse the treetops and adjacent bay, so Marsh didn't lower the deck as he typically would have.

What the owners now see is a railing with dignity. It features turned balusters that have been painted a classic white, and the railing cap has a round-over detail that you'd expect to see on fine furniture.

Symmetrical Design. The deck has a 16-foot semicircular bulge in its center that feels almost as if it were a ship's prow as you stand looking outward. It provides ample space for a large table and chairs. On both sides, the deck has rectangular sections that each measure about 8 feet wide—large enough for barbecuing, lounging, or dining at a small table.

To further enhance the sense of symmetry, Marsh arranged the diagonal decking boards to meet in the exact center without a divider board. This apparently simple touch requires a lot of meticulous work, but it gives the decking a finished feel like that of an interior floor.

PROMENADE WITH CIRCULAR VIEWING AREA

Note: Sway bracing and earthquake bracing are not shown. Verify any similar design with a structural engineer.

DESIGN CONSIDERATIONS

The house has clean, spare lines and floor-to-ceiling glass walls that allow the homeowners to gaze out over the treetops to the bay below. They wanted a deck that would wrap around the house to provide a view from two sides, something the existing deck didn't offer. The existing conventional wooden railing also blocked the limited view it did provide.

The homeowners didn't need a large space, nor were they interested in the usual cooking and dining areas. They did, however, want to link their home more effectively to the outdoors, so Marsh designed a promenade of sorts—wide enough for strolling and placing potted plants with a larger area in the middle for engaging in conversation.

An Eye to the View. With a deck that measures only 8 feet wide in most places, it wouldn't make sense to step the structure downward to improve the view. Each step would eat up at least a foot of usable width.

Instead, Marsh designed a railing that, safe and sturdy though it is, barely seems to exist as you look through it. Made of steel and anodized dark green to blend with the leaves just beyond it, the structure has a contemporary Euro look, but its color and curving contour give it an organic feel. As a complement to this, the glass walls create an unusual relationship between the deck and the house. From certain angles, the decking appears to be an extension of the interior floor rather than a separate space.

Marsh's clients in this case owned a newer home that was set on a severely inclined slope. This factor limited the overall size of the deck, but with the house's modern styling, Marsh felt free to choose almost any shape. The solution he came up with has a pleasantly straightforward look and a distinctive metal railing that doesn't obstruct the view.

Outside View

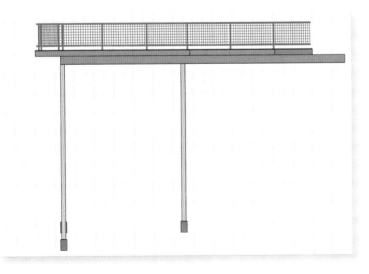

Rick Parish of Decks Appeal, located near Dallas in Plano, Texas, is one of the few deck builders in the country to have his own showroom. There, you'll see deck samples that show some of his signature design elements, as well as outdoor furniture pieces made to blend well with the decks. By spending all of his time meeting with customers and designing decks, Parish keeps three or more construction crews busy. He starts by listening to the homeowners to get a sense of how they intend to use their deck and how they envision its general contours.

DECKS APPEAL

Plano, Texas

www.decksappeal.com

TECHNIQUES, TIPS, AND TRICKS

Many of Parish's designs are less complicated than they look. He often achieves an appearance of furniture-like detailing by adding simple pieces. However, such detail work requires precise cuts in order to look good. For this purpose, you should consider a quality power miter saw (chop saw) a necessity rather than a luxury.

- Much of the distinctive look of Parish's decks comes from his materials. After carefully selecting dark-colored Con Heart boards that have no loose knots, he chooses the best pieces for the most visible elements of the deck.

- His post design adds elegance without requiring a lot of work. By attaching 2x2s that run up the center of each face of a standard 4x4, he creates a classically fluted column. He also installs banding at the top of each post made of 2x2s and ripped 2x4s, although this detail requires careful cutting and fastening.

- In his designs, Parish avoids butt joints in the decking, which tend to mar its unbroken appearance. This sometimes means dividing a large deck into smaller sections. He's rarely found a good reason to make a deck surface that measures more than 20 feet (the longest standard decking length) in both directions. Though butt-jointed decking can look fine if you prefer a rustic look, avoid it if you want a more finished appearance.

- Not only does Parish recommend regular staining to reduce the punishing effects of sunlight, he also urges customers to avoid damaging their decks with furniture and pots. For instance, by using simple trivets made from 2x2s to hold flowerpots off the deck, they can prevent water stains and scratches, and eventually more serious damage.

- If a deck has gone gray due to neglect, Parish cautions against using a high-pressure washer. These machines, which are sold in home centers and touted as cure-alls for wood surface problems, may actually do more harm than good. On softwoods such as redwood, they can remove the soft part of the grain, leaving a rough surface that can be made smooth again only through heavy sanding. Instead, he recommends a two-step solution: first, spray or sponge on a 50-50 mixture of household bleach and water, which will make the gray disappear almost immediately. Rinse and then brush the deck with a mixture of oxalic acid (wood bleach) and water. This will leave you with a deck that is nearly white. Apply stain, and the wood will look like new.

- Parish designs overhead structures, or pergolas, carefully to provide the desired amount of shade. He runs the top slats, usually 2x2s, in a north-to-south direction so that the sun can shine directly between them only at noon. In the Dallas area, he's found that 2x2s laid 3 inches on center (spaced 1½ inches apart) provide full shade for an hour or two (in the morning on an east-facing deck and in the evening on a west-facing deck). For the rest of the day, the overhead structure will provide filtered shade of varying degree. This much planning may sound complicated, but it will increase the utility of your deck and save work in the long run.

- Parish uses a lot of curves, not only on his decks and railings but sometimes on overhead structures as well. To the homeowner, curves can look daunting, like something better left to a professional. They also cost more in materials; you often need to start with a 2x12 and then waste nearly half of the board. But if you have a professional-grade saber saw and the patience to do things right, you can add impressive-looking curves to your project.

- Parish uses a router fitted with a roundover bit to create the finished look of his decks, usually following up with a sander. If you take some time beforehand to practice your routing on scrap material, you'll find that you can get the near-furniture-quality results you see in his work. Unless you have a lot of experience with a belt sander, however, use this tool with great caution and only with fine-grit sandpaper. It removes wood very quickly and can leave gouges and other blemishes that can't be repaired.

The shade structures, opposite, designed by Parish provide filtered shade for most of the day.

FREESTANDING DECK
WITH SPA AND FIREPIT

Ground View

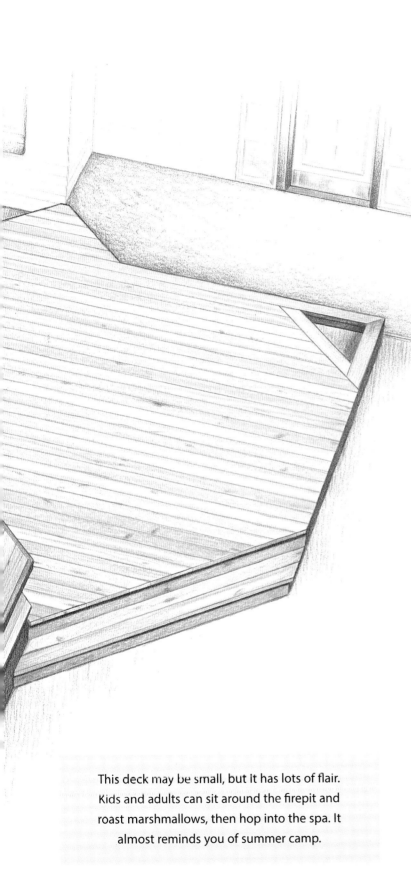

This deck may be small, but it has lots of flair. Kids and adults can sit around the firepit and roast marshmallows, then hop into the spa. It almost reminds you of summer camp.

DESIGN CONSIDERATIONS

With decks that sit low above the ground like this one, you don't have to worry about space for parties. When guests show up for the occasional large get-together, they can simply spill over onto the lawn if need be. For the rest of time, this design provides plenty of room for cozy get-togethers—family lounging, barbecuing, and soaking, as well as gathering around the fire.

Parish surrounded the spa with just enough decking so that guests could sit and dangle their legs. (The spa cover, which gets stowed next to the house, doesn't require deck space.) The unit sits three levels up from grade, or about 21 inches. Parish finds that this height makes spa installation easier.

A railing runs around one-half of the spa, more for privacy rather than safety. A "railing" that leads up to the spa actually serves as a towel rack, with two horizontal rails made of rounded 2x2s.

About 5 feet from the spa, a brick firepit rises about 8 inches above the decking. The pit is not intended for cooking—a conventional grill works better—but it makes an ideal place to gather after supper. With a crackling fire, relaxed conversation naturally takes place. A bench curves halfway around the pit, facing toward the spa.

The first level measures about 12 feet square, allowing enough room for a dining table and cooking area. In one corner, a triangular opening makes a distinctive spot for planting flowers or a small shrub. In fact, angles tend to dominate throughout, giving the deck a pleasantly jumbled look. The assortment of odd angles showcases the spa and firepit, both of which are octagonal.

CIRCULAR EATING AREA

Here's a bit of whimsy: a round platform, just the right size for a table with chairs, that can be set on top of a deck or patio. The railing is just for looks, while the benches provide a comfortable conversation area.

Ground View

DESIGN CONSIDERATIONS

This little deck offers just enough space for a circular patio table with chairs, plus room for a server to walk around the chairs while people are eating. Whenever you plan an eating area such as this one, with clearly defined borders, first test the dimensions by setting your furniture in place to find out how much room you'll really need.

Although not a safety requirement here, the railing gives the little deck a sense of enclosure. Leaning on it as they look toward the pool, adults can easily keep an eye on the kids—while the railing is there to remind the children that this is adult space.

Parish positioned the benches to the rear of the deck and behind the railing, creating a semi-secluded conversation area. The benches' curved shape makes for good groupings. People are forced to look neither at nor away from each other.

TWO LOW LEVELS WITH ANGLES AND AN OVERHEAD

Ground View

Despite their flat yard and the low threshold into their home, these homeowners asked for a deck with at least two levels. To accommodate them, Parish came up with an unusual solution: a deck that rises above the house's floor level, rather than descending from it. Interesting angles, a bench/planter, and an elegant overhead structure make this a soothing place to relax.

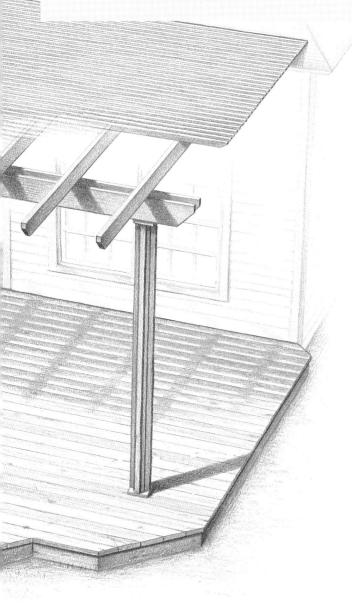

DESIGN CONSIDERATIONS

The homeowners wanted to expand the area occupied by an existing rectangular concrete patio—and provide some shade at the same time. For structural reasons, Parish's design follows the shape of the patio, but has dressed up the deck with interesting features that effectively disguise its basic rectangular outline.

Although it has plenty of angles, the deck's perimeter makes use of theme and variation to avoid a jumbled or confused look. For example, the forward section of the upper level, which angles away from the house at 45 degrees, parallels several other lines in the deck. By restating the theme in different ways, Parish avoids a ho-hum symmetrical effect but still ties the whole design together.

The main level offers plenty of room for a table with chairs and a grill, while the upper level provides a pleasant area for conversation, lounging, or just enjoying the foliage. The bench joins two planters that rise slightly above the seat level. With some fairly tall plants, this provides a naturally secluded place to sit and read. The benches form a semicircle of sorts, a shape that promotes conversation during a party.

The overhead structure is supported by "fluted" posts made of 4x4s and 2x2s. Though it requires only a bit of extra work and expense, this detail makes a big difference. An unadorned 4x4 post set in the middle of a deck would look drab and dreary; this variation adds grace and interest. The 2x2 roof pieces run north to south to provide maximum shade. In a region that gets a lot of sun, the orientation and spacing of these top pieces requires serious planning. (See "Techniques, Tips, and Tricks," page 302, for more information on this and on making "fluted" posts.)

GLOSSARY

Actual Dimension: The exact measurement of a piece of lumber after it has been milled, generally ½ inch less each way than the advertised size. For example, a typical 2x4's actual dimension is 1½ x 3½ inches.

Architectural Scale Ruler: A three-sided ruler that enables you to convert large dimensions to a small scale in a drawing, including ⅛-, ¼-, and ½-inch scale.

Balusters: The vertical pieces, generally made of 2x2s, that fill in spaces between rail posts and provide a fence-like structure.

Beam: The term for any large framing member of four-by or doubled two-by material.

Breadboard Edge: A long strip of wood, typically 1x2 or larger, fastened along the edge of a deck to cover the end grain of decking boards.

Bridging: Usually short, solid blocks of lumber made of joist material that are cut to fit snugly between the joists to prevent twisting.

Building Codes: National and local rules regulating building practices. Generally, codes encompass structural, electrical, plumbing, and mechanical remodeling and new construction. Code compliance is checked by on-site inspections.

Building Permit: An authorization to build or renovate according to plans approved by the local building department. Generally, any job that includes a footing or foundation or that involves any structural work or alterations requires a permit.

Cantilever: The outer part of a deck floor frame that extends beyond the main beam, floating without additional support.

Carriage: A cut stringer with a sawtooth shape on its top edge that runs at midspan on wide stairs.

Countersink: A shallow hole drilled to house the head of a lag screw or bolt. The hole diameter is generally the size of the washer used with the fastener.

Curing: The slow, ongoing chemical action that hardens concrete.

Dado: A channel cut across the grain of a piece of wood to house the end of another component in a joint.

Dipping: A treatment in which wood is immersed in a bath of preservative for several minutes, then allowed to air-dry.

Fascia: A facing board (generally one-by material) that covers the exposed ends or sides of deck framing.

Footing: A masonry base, usually concrete, that supports a post, beam, or steps.

Frost Line: The maximum depth at which soil freezes, as specified by local building departments, which require footings below the line to prevent heaving.

Grade: Ground level. At-grade means at or on the natural ground level.

Header Joist: The outermost joist, also called a belt, set at right angles to and across the ends of the on-center joists that support the decking.

Joist: Horizontal structural member, usually two-by lumber, commonly set 16 inches on center to support deck boards.

Joist Hanger: A U-shaped metal connector that joins a joist, generally at right angles to another board, such as a ledger. Similar hardware is available for other structural joints.

Kickback: The lurching, backward action of a power saw when the blade binds in a cut.

Lattice: A cross-pattern structure generally used for skirting that is made of wood, metal, or plastic.

Ledger: A horizontal board attached to the side of a house (bolted into the framing) that supports one end of the deck joists.

Nominal Dimension: The identifying size of stock lumber, such as 2x4 and 2x6, even though the boards are a half inch smaller each way.

On Center: A point of reference for measuring framing that is installed in a modular layout. The spacing, typically 16 inches, is figured from the center of one framing member to the center of the next; abbreviated o.c.

Penny: The colloquial measure of nail length, generally abbreviated with the letter d, as in 10d (ten penny). (2d, 1 in.; 3d, 1¼ in.; 4d, 1½ in.; 5d, 1¾ in.; 6d, 2 in.; 7d, 2¼ in.; 8d, 2½ in.; 9d, 2¾ in.; 10d, 3 in.; 12d, 3¼ in.; 16d, 3½ in.; 20d, 4 in.; 30d, 4½ in.; 50d, 5½ in.; 60d, 6 in.)

Pier: A masonry support, similar to a footing, generally made of concrete poured into a form that extends from below the frost line to a few inches aboveground.

Plan Drawing: A drawing that shows an overhead view of the deck and specifies the locations and sizes of components.

Plumb: Vertically straight in relation to a horizontally level surface.

Plunge Cut: A cut with a circular saw that starts in from the edge of a board

Post: A vertical component, usually a 4x4, that can support beams, joists, and railings.

Post Anchor: A metal fastener that secures a post to a concrete pier and inhibits decay by holding the post a bit above the concrete.

Posthole Digger: A clamshell-shaped tool used to dig holes for posts.

Power Auger: A tool (generally rented) powered by a gasoline engine that excavates post holes with a large auger screw.

Rabbet: A ledge-shaped recess cut along one edge of a board.

Rail: A horizontal component placed between or on a row of posts.

Rip Cut: A cut made with the grain on a piece of wood.

Riser: A vertical board (set on edge) that closes off the open space between treads.

Site Plan: A drawing that shows your project at a scale small enough to include the house, yard, and nearby property lines. To obtain a permit, a site plan is typically required, along with drawings that show construction details.

Skirting: Material that covers or screens the space between the edge of the deck and the ground, generally made of narrow slats, such as 1x2s, or lattice.

Span: The distance on a horizontal component, such as a joist, between supports. Span limits for all types and sizes of lumber are controlled by building codes.

Stringer: A wide, angled board that supports stair treads and risers. Cut or housed stringers run on the outside edges of stairs.

Synthetic Decking: Any engineered decking material made from plastics and/or recycled wood products.

Toenailing: Joining two boards together by nailing at an angle through the edge of one board into the face of another.

Top Cap: A horizontal piece of lumber laid flat across the tops of posts or top rails.

Tread: A horizontal stair board (generally several spaced boards in deck construction), laid flat on stringers.

Treated Lumber: Wood that has had preservative forced into it under pressure to make it decay resistant. In the past, arsenic was used to treat wood. Today, alkaline copper compounds are the primary treatment chemicals.

Metric Equivalents

Length

1 inch	25.4mm
1 foot	0.3048m
1 yard	0.9144m
1 mile	1.61km

Area

1 square inch	645mm^2
1 square foot	0.0929m^2
1 square yard	0.8361m^2
1 acre	4046.86m^2
1 square mile	2.59km^2

Volume

1 cubic inch	16.3870cm^3
1 cubic foot	0.03m^3
1 cubic yard	0.77m^3

Common Lumber Equivalents

Sizes: Metric cross sections are so close to their U.S. sizes, as noted below, that for most purposes they may be considered equivalents.

Dimensional lumber	1 x 2	19 x 38mm
	1 x 4	19 x 89mm
	2 x 2	38 x 38mm
	2 x 4	38 x 89mm
	2 x 6	38 x 140mm
	2 x 8	38 x 184mm
	2 x 10	38 x 235mm
	2 x 12	38 x 286mm
Sheet sizes	4 x 8 ft.	1200 x 2400mm
	4 x 10 ft.	1200 x 3000mm
Sheet thicknesses	¼ in.	6mm
	⅜ in.	9mm
	½ in.	12mm
	¾ in.	19mm
Stud/joist spacing	16 in. o.c.	400mm o.c.
	24 in. o.c.	600mm o.c.

Capacity

1 fluid ounce	29.57mL
1 pint	473.18mL
1 quart	0.95L
1 gallon	3.79L

Weight

1 ounce	28.35g
1 pound	0.45kg

Temperature

Fahrenheit = Celsius x 1.8 + 32

Celsius = Fahrenheit - 32 x 5⁄9

Nail Size and Length

Penny Size	Nail Length
2d	1"
3d	1¼"
4d	1½"
5d	1¾"
6d	2"
7d	2¼"
8d	2½"
9d	2¾"
10d	3"
12d	3¼"
16d	3½"

INDEX

Note: Page numbers in *italics* indicate deck designs by featured designers.

Index

Index

Index

PHOTO CREDITS

Illustrations by: Vincent Alessi, Clarke Barre, Ron Carboni, Craig Franklin, Michael Gellatly, Kathleen Rushton and Paul M. Schumm

All photography by John Parsekian/CH, unless noted otherwise.

Front cover: Todd Caverly, design: Peter Bethanis & Associates
Back cover: *top* Brian Vanden Brink, architect: Stephen Blatt; background Artazum/Shutterstock
page 1: Lertsakwimon/Shutterstock **page 2:** John Parsekian, design/builder: Bob Kieter **page 3:** Irina Mos/Shutterstock **page 4:** Brian Vanden Brink **page 5:** David Schiff page 6: **page 7:** Steve Budman **pages 13–15:** Charlie Byers **page 17:** Mark Lohman **page 18:** Charlie Byers **page 19:** top Charlie Byers **page 27:** Todd Caverly, design: Peter Bethanis & Associates **page 29:** Brian Vanden Brink **page 30:** all courtesy of California Redwood Association **page 36:** David Schiff **pages 37–39:** Charlie Byers **page 42:** top Brad Simmons; center Tria Giovan; bottom Brian Vanden Brink, architect: Pete Bethanis **pages 16–17:** top right Brian Vanden Brink; bottom left Michael S. Thompson **page 46:** Brian Vanden Brink, design: Weatherend Estate Furniture **page 47:** top Tria Giovan; bottom carolynbates.com **page 48:** carolynbates.com **page 49:** Tria Giovan **page 53:** Brian Vanden Brink, architect: Stephen Blatt **pages 56–57:** left Mark Lohman; center Michael S. Thompson; top right Brad Simmons; bottom right John Glover **page 58:** Randall Perry **page 59:** top Ron Sutherland/Garden Picture Library; bottom Jessie Walker **page 60:** Jessie Walker **page 61:** top Brad Simmons; bottom courtesy of California Redwood Association **page 62:** Tria Giovan **page 63:** top Ron Sutherland/Garden Picture Library; bottom Brad Simmons **page 67:** Tony Giammarino/Giammarino & Dworkin **page 69:** Jessie Walker **page 71:** David Schiff **page 72:** Maria O'Hara/Garden Picture Library **page 75:** Brad Simmons **page 85:** Tony Giammarino/Giammarino & Dworkin, design: Arthur Ritter **page 86:** Derek Fell **page 92:** top right Jessie Walker **page 101:** Tony Giammarino/Giammarino & Dworkin, design: Cheryl Palmore **page 111:** left top and bottom David Schiff **page 116:** courtesy of Arch Wood Protection **page 124:** Jessie Walker **page 130:** Tony Giammarino/Giammarino & Dworkin, design: Arthur Ritter **page 139:** Mark Samu, architect: Andy Letkovsky **page 141:** Mark Samu **page 143:** Tony Giammarino/Giammarino & Dworkin, design: Vicki O'Neal page 146: carolynbates.com **page 155:** David Schiff **page 156:** David Schiff **page 161:** David Schiff **page 167:** David Schiff **page 175:** top Shutterstock/ John Rehg; bottom Shutterstock/Christina Richards **pages 176–177:** Charlie Byers **page 181:** Flat Rock Photography **page 183:** Brian Vanden Brink **page 182:** David Schiff **page 185:** David Schiff **page 191:** Brian Vanden Brink **pages 189–201:** all David Schiff **pages 216–217:** top middle Steve Budman; top right Steve Cory; bottom right Flat Rock Photography; bottom middle Dan Sellars, courtesy of California Redwood Association; bottom left Jay Graham **pages 242–245:** all Steve Budman **pages 264–283:** all Flat Rock Photography **pages 284–287:** all Jay Graham **page 300:** top & center Rick Parish; Dan Sellers, courtesy of California Redwood Association **page 301:** Dan Sellers, courtesy of California Redwood Association **page 303:** Greg Hursley, courtesy of California Redwood Association

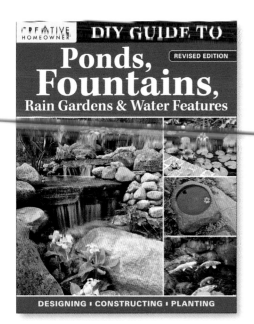
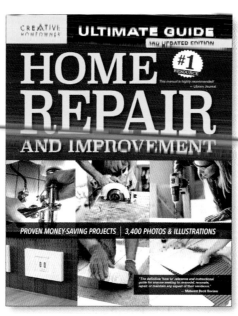
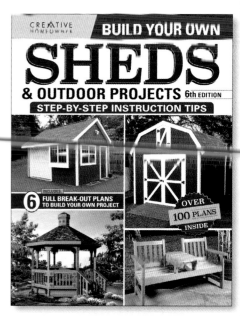
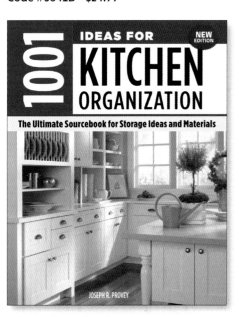
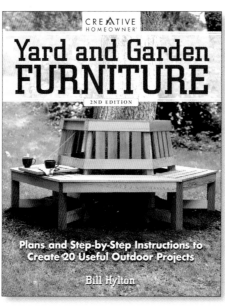
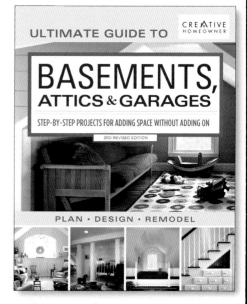